IN THE SHADO
SHACKLETON'S CROSS

Beverley McLeod

ISBN 978-1-84986-031-4

Cover photographs by Nigel Bonner

Published in 2014 by

OTCEditions

An imprint of

ORION TRADING COMPANY UK LTD

Registered under the Companies House Act

Number 4968193

www.otceditions.co.uk

DEDICATION:

For Mum and Gerald

With my love xx

ABOUT THE AUTHOR

Beverley was born in Stanley, Falkland Islands in 1951.

Between 1957 and 1961, she lived on the Antarctic island of South Georgia.

In 1963 she won a scholarship and was sponsored by the Falkland Island Government to attend a girl's boarding school in Dorset, England, to complete her education.

After a career in teaching, Beverley lives in Bristol, England.

CHAPTER 1

THE *DARWIN*

The grey-hulled ship, about the size of an inter-island ferry, slipped through the sheltered waters of Port William. To starboard, a low hill rippling with tussac in the wind, supported the long neck of the Pembroke Lighthouse. Although the winter light was fading, the beacon was still unlit and the Master of the *Darwin* had to rely on his navigational skills to head her safely out into the ocean.

At the very instant when the *Darwin* pushed her nose beyond the security of Port William, her bow jerked upwards and her stern sank low as the full force of the South Atlantic Ocean hit her. Up on deck, the twelve passengers swayed and threw out uncertain hands to grab the white railings for support. It was now cold in the wind and necks had to be craned over the side to steal a last glimpse of land. Drunkenly, eleven passengers moved in a body towards the companionway and the warmth of the passenger lounge below. The twelve-year old birthday and Scholarship girl turned in the opposite direction and took the outside companionway down to the lower deck. She skirted the hold, keeping well out of the way of the deck hands who were coiling ropes, checking crates and securing the hold covers in preparation for the wild weather which was certain to come. She negotiated her way to the stern, which was deserted. Leaning over, she watched as the propeller rose and fell in the sea. It slashed at the waters with its shiny blades, churning it into a blue and aquamarine lace tablecloth which stretched out behind the ship in undulating motion towards the disappearing shore.

In the fading light, like Atlantis, the low treeless hills of East Falkland slipped slowly and inexorably below the surface of the sea. Standing on tiptoes, eyes swimming with tears welling in torrents and streaming down her blotchy cheeks sinking wetly into the front of her new brown coat, she strained for a last view of her homeland. Behind her in Stanley, her mother, father and little brother would be walking back to Drury Street, heads bent forwards against the prevailing wind, silent in their individual contemplation of her departure. And here she was, shivering, bereft, her light body struggling to withstand a combination of biting wind and the crushing weight of loss and good fortune.

The Falkland Islands were gone! Her mind tried to encompass the magnitude of two whole calendar years which had to be lived through before she could return to her family again. In her right hand, her handkerchief sodden and snotty was unable to absorb any more tears. Another blow of her nose and it resembled a soaked leaf of slimy gelatin. Glancing down at it, she held the handkerchief gently between her finger and thumb and, as if it were a funeral wreath, bequeathed it to the sea in memoriam of the home which no longer was.

She was enough of a drama queen to acknowledge the momentary thought that, if this was the closing scene of a film and she the heroine, she would turn quickly on her heel. With a resolute toss of her head, she would walk boldly forward into the unknown, determined to make a success of whatever trials life might have in store. But this was unscripted reality. She crept unseeingly, hugging the starboard rail of the ship, past the deckhands once more, holding her face directly into the spray-laden wind. When she stepped into the shelter of the passage, no one she met must know that she had been crying like a baby. A toss of her short, damp curls, a tinkling laugh and an adroit comment about the rough weather would be more than enough to fool any adult she chanced to meet.

CHAPTER 2

THE BISCOE TO SOUTH GEORGIA, MAY 1957

As we jostled our way through the double green doors of the Infant's school and flew down the steep concrete steps into the playground, we habitually glanced over the red corrugated-iron rooftops to the harbour. The *Fennia*, a rusting three masted hulk, danced and pulled at her anchor, her nose pointing to our right and her body parallel to the shore. "The wind's blowing from Canopus today!" we shouted, our embryonic sensibilities acknowledging that the *Fennia* was Stanley's weather vane, but not able to comprehend the intricacies of the points of the compass. To the adults, there was

"A ruddy great storm brewing from the east, Chay!" and it blew our light cotton dresses up around our necks to reveal uniformly white cotton petticoats and knickers, all bought from our one big shop, the West Store.

This was my last week at school and I stood in the playground surrounded by boys. They were the bees to my honeypot, the marmite to my toast! They were envious that I was actually going to be sailing on the Biscoe and in the playground they gathered around me, talking animatedly about what a fantastic state-of-the-art ship the *Biscoe* was, how she could cut through the ice with her reinforced hull and how she could fight the roughest seas. I basked in the hitherto unknown glory of boy-worship. The other girls watched me closely while pretending that they weren't at all interested, but I could see them out of the corner of my eye as they skipped and chased each other round and round our group, straining to hear every word that was spoken. Being with the boys gave me a sense of superiority over even the bigger girls and I revelled in it!

The dream for many Falkland Island boys was to work on either the *Biscoe* or on the *Darwin.* This would be their passport to the big world outside, to a good pay packet and to adventure. I was getting it all at the age of five and their envy was channeled into generous excitement at my good fortune. Their exaggerated stories, learned at the knees of older men who were prone to exaggeration, were related back to us all in the playground as the Gospel truth! The thrill of my new-found status dimmed somewhat as the *Biscoe* grew daily into a super-ship, ready to take on icebergs, enormous blue whales and mountainous seas which would bring her to the brink of disaster, when only the bravery of the few Falkland Island boys onboard would snatch her from the jaws of the deep. As my last day at school drew nearer, my adventurous trip south lost some of its lustre, despite the adulation.

Doctor Slessor had eventually agreed that Mum could take three-month old Gerald to South Georgia as he felt that the baby was now strong enough to cope with the voyage and 'the May *Biscoe*' was the last ship to sail to the Antarctic that year. Everything we would need for the next six months had to be taken with us and Dad had sent money up to Stanley for Mum to spend as she chose. She had shopped with determination and not a little pressure, as anything she forgot would have to be done without for the next six months. We had wooden boxes packed to capacity with household goods, clothes, tinned and dried foods of every description, Gerald's pram and most importantly, my toys.

Grandad walked us down to the *Biscoe*, carrying only our two small cases because the rest of our luggage had been loaded onboard the previous day. The *Biscoe l*ay at the public jetty. She was small, only two hundred and twenty feet long, but to me she looked huge as she lay in the calm seas of the harbour, nudging gently into the jetty as she rode the light swell. The *Royal Research Ship John Biscoe*, with her grey hull and white superstructure, had been commissioned by the Falkland Islands Dependency Survey or FIDS, (the precursor to British Antarctic Survey), as a passenger and cargo vessel to support the Antarctic bases. She carried the FIDS scientists, explorers and other personnel to South Georgia and to the British bases on the Antarctic continent itself. She had only been in the Falklands for two seasons and last year, had been hit by an iceberg off the South Orkney Islands and was nearly lost with all hands. To be going to sea in such a famous ship, which had already survived storybook Antarctic adventures, is what had made me the toast of my peers.

Grandad carried Gerald onboard and Mum held my hand in a vice-like grip as we clattered across the wobbly gangway which shook and rattled against its chains. Once onboard we were taken down below to our cabin. There were two bunks with drawers beneath the lower one. Beneath the porthole was a small fold-down table. The only other furnishing was a daybed attached to the bulkhead opposite our bunks.

"You'll sleep in the top bunk, Bev and I will sleep in the bottom one with Gerald", Mum said. It just got better and better! Hugging my favourite doll, I scrambled up the tiny ladder at the foot of the bunks to my own special place where no one else would go. It had curtains which I could draw and even its own light with a hanging cord for switching it on and off, turning my bunk into a private den.

Up on deck I was too excited to stand still. I ran about looking across the harbour to the storage tank and single house at the Camber on our port side and picking out all the houses of everyone I knew in Stanley from the starboard side. The hum of the generators in the background reminded me constantly that we were about to go to sea. Without moving an inch from the jetty, this was already an adventure.

Eventually it was time for Grandad to leave us and go ashore. Mum was tearful but I was too excited to worry about leaving family and Stanley behind. I was an explorer like Shackleton and Scott, and I was going south on the *Biscoe* to accomplish great things and to do great deeds. I was going to come back and tell the other children in school about my adventures and they would be amazed by my bravery and the sights I had seen. They would crowd around me in the playground, but this time it would be me who was telling the tales. In my head I was already the heroine of my own story.

The main engines burst into life and a huge puff of smoke belched forth from the funnel. The crew in their navy blue uniforms caught the lines, as the Stanley jetty-gang let them loose from the moorings. The propeller started with a whirr and we felt a deep vibration throughout the ship as she moved forward and away from the jetty. We waved until Grandad was out of sight and the *Biscoe* nosed out through the Narrows into Port William. We watched as the Cape Pembroke lighthouse slowly disappeared from view and then went below as the wind was blowing coldly and the sea out here was decidedly choppy. As we walked down into the bowels of the *Biscoe*, the aromas of cooked food wafted upward from the galley below. These mixed uncomfortably with the odour of hot oil and excessive heat which escaped from the engine room every time the door was opened for an engineer to go in or leave.

It wasn't long before the seas grew angrier and the *Biscoe* was being thrown about between huge waves. From my top bunk, I listened as the waves laughed at us, demonstrating their strength and power, tossing us between their crests as if we weighed no more than a football. I pulled the curtains back on my bunk and gazed through the porthole, now covered completely by green seawater as we rolled heavily to starboard; now split by a diagonal line between the grey sky and the green sea as the *Biscoe* was thrown roughly to port. Mum soon succumbed to sea-sickness and I lay in my little house above, fingers in my ears to block out the sound of her retching and the 'twing' and 'plop' as her vomit landed in the metal bucket on the floor beside her bunk. Lying on my back, I counted and recounted the number of rivets which held together the steel frames supporting the upper deck above my head. I followed the conduits which carried the electrical cables across the ceiling. I played with my doll and told her endless fairy stories. I slept soundly and dreamlessly through each rocky night, moving easily in my bunk to the same rhythm as the *Biscoe,* as I did throughout the day.

For three full days we were yawing and rolling, stressing and straining to push our way southeastwards against the groaning might of the South Atlantic. The ocean showed us no mercy and poor Mum begged God to please let her die. She managed to feed and change Gerald while continuing to throw up into her bucket. As she ate nothing, I was unable to understand where all the vomit was coming from. She sipped a lot of water but that didn't seem to me to be an adequate answer to the conundrum. Our cabin boy, Tony, was Mum's second cousin. He brought food into the cabin for us and emptied the sick bucket several times a day, but it wasn't often enough to prevent the stench of vomit from permeating every corner of the cabin. I was sure I could still smell it, even when my head was fully underneath the blankets. I only left my bunk to walk along the companionway to the toilet and to the bathroom to wash. As I climbed down from my den or back up into it, I studiously avoided looking into Mum's bucket. If she retched while I was near her, I rushed out the door and only came back in when she told me she wasn't going to be sick again for a while.

Then suddenly, all was calm. I lifted my head from my pillow and listened. There was nothing to hear except the hum of the engines and the whirr of the propeller. Beyond the gentle shuddering of the metal plates of the ship trying to release themselves from the confines of their rivets, all was quiet and still. Mum gingerly climbed out of her bunk, I scrambled down from mine, and with Gerald held securely in Mum's arms, we ventured up onto the deck. Fresh air! Tangy with salt, cold and moist, real fresh air! We drank it in in huge gulps and our weak legs staggered uneasily for a few steps across the slippery planks of the deck. That evening we ate in the dining room with the officers and other passengers. At the end of our meal the Captain stood up and announced that it was calm enough for a film to be shown up in the officers' mess.

Mum adored the silver screen, her dream was to have been a dancer like Betty Grable or Ginger Rogers, so she determined to find her sea-legs and let them carry her, however uncertainly, up to the officers' mess on the deck above. All the chairs had been unscrewed from their permanent positions around small tables and placed in neat rows. A screen had been erected at the front of the room. As the only lady onboard, Mum was given the best seat in the middle of the front row.

Down below in our cabin I lay on the lower bunk with Gerald sleeping beside me. We were being cared for by Tony who sat on the daybed. Even though he was only seventeen, Tony had been south several times before. He told me stories about skiing in the deep snow and about the penguins and seals which were even now living outside the door of our new house at King Edward Point, just waiting for us to get there.

From its origin in the depths of the Antarctic Ocean, a mountain of icy water had been moving silently north, growing ever higher as it built up speed and strength. Without warning, the *Biscoe* hit this vertiginous rogue wave bow-on and it brought her to a sudden and shuddering halt. As the vessel was lifted upwards by the towering wave and suspended in mid-air, in the officers' mess, Mum and her companions were hurled forwards, bodies and chairs flying crazily across the room, landing in a heap with her at the bottom of it.

Down below in our cabin, the g force threw me roughly and precipitately down to the opposite end of the bunk. Gerald's little body executed a perfect parabolic curve as it flew from the bunk across the cabin. Tony, pitched forwards from the daybed himself, threw his arms wide and twisted his body in the air to grab the baby and pull him in towards his chest like a rugby ball. Tony's back smashed into the cabin door and he slid, winded, down the door and across the cabin floor until he was lying prone, safely clutching the baby to his breast. We lay stock still as the *Biscoe* shuddered and shook with its propeller fully out of the water. After what seemed like long minutes, she started to fall. Sharply and deeply she fell into the abyss of the wave-trough. The force with which she hit the water transferred itself through the superstructure of the ship into our bodies like a heavyweight's punch in the solar plexus. Green water covered our porthole as she sank deeper into the ocean under the force of her own weight. We stayed frozen in our uncomfortable positions, barely daring to breathe. I knew from the pregnant silence around me that this wasn't something that the Captain or the crew could put right. Our lives were in the hands of the *Biscoe* herself.

We waited, motionless, straining our ears for every telltale noise. I was paralysed with fear. How deeply into the sea was she sinking? Were we sinking too deeply for her to recover? With a mighty jerk, the *Biscoe* bounced back up to the surface like a cork and water fell away from our porthole. Finding her propeller back in its rightful medium, and with a sigh of relief, she made a tentative and uncertain movement forwards. Uncomfortable and jerky as her motion was, we knew that she hadn't let us down and we were safe. In our cabin Tony and I stirred gingerly. Gerald woke but, seeing nothing untoward, went straight back to sleep. Tony scrambled to his feet and tucked Gerald tightly under the covers at the back of the bunk and put me in the front this time.

"You can be his guardian angel, Bev. My God, but that was a close one!" He sat down on the bench again, pale and shaking.

After some minutes we heard heavy footfalls and Mum's screaming voice from the companionway outside.

11

"Bev! Gerald! What's happened to my babies?" She flew through the door like a virago and threw herself onto the bunk. Tony laughed.

"They're fine Pearl! You should see your face. You look as if you're ready to beat me to death. I bet they haven't even got a bruise!" But the hugs Gerald and I got from mum! There was so much love in the squishing and kisses that covered my face and head that I have never forgotten that moment.

The seas stayed calm and on the morning of the fourth day at sea we reached the island of South Georgia. Mum and I were so excited about seeing Dad that we were ready hours before we were due to tie up at the jetty. Gerald looked handsome in his blue hand-knitted romper suit with matching mittens and bootees. Mum had wrapped him in so many blankets against the cold that I wondered how Dad would ever find him.

While Mum waited in the officers' Mess, I joined the FIDS up on deck. South Georgia rose sheer and majestic out of a blue-green sea. Snow covered mountains and blue glaciers glittered and sparkled in bright sunlight. "Look Bev, see the tallest mountain in the middle of the island? That's Mount Paget. It's nine thousand six hundred feet high and you'll never have seen a mountain like that before, I bet!" Mount Paget stood tall and proud, its peak towering above a circle of lesser mountains, their heads bowed low in respect for its grandeur.

As we skirted the north coast of the island, distant huddles of smoking chimneys, rusty buildings and small ships in rounded bays were pointed out to me as whaling stations.

"See Bev, there's Leith Harbour, then Stromness and over there, Husvik. I expect your Dad will take you there one day. If you're lucky you may get to go on a whale catcher!" I was already brimming over with excitement. What a place of wonders South Georgia was turning out to be and we hadn't even landed yet!

As the *Biscoe* nosed her way into Cumberland Bay, we were surrounded by snowy beaches on all sides. I ran around the deck determined not to miss anything. Then I saw it! The palace of the Snow Queen. Dominating Cumberland Bay and hidden in drifts of pure white snow, the towers and turrets of the Ice Palace shone like mirrored glass. Windows were suffused with an inward light, just as Hans Christian Andersen said that they would be! Inside, in a vast empty hall, I knew that the Snow Queen, intelligent and lovely, was sitting on her white ice-throne in the middle of a frozen lake, fully aware that we were approaching her kingdom. Between the Ice Palace and the *Biscoe*, small icebergs and growlers floated lazily in the calm sea. They looked innocent and unthreatening, but I knew better! They were the Snow Queen's guards, watching every move we made and ready to fly and attack us if she gave the order.

"That's the Nordenskjöld Glacier, Bev, nearly two miles across and two hundred feet high, one of the largest glaciers on the island." I smiled secretly to myself, the FIDS believed it was the Nordenskjöld Glacier simply because they were grown-ups and couldn't see that it was the Ice Palace, but I could!

"Bev! Bev! What are you doing there? You're on the wrong side of the ship. Quickly, come round to the other side or you won't see Daddy." Hearing Mum call me, I tore my eyes away from the Ice Palace, and ran round to the port deck. Mum was standing there clutching a bundle of assorted blankets tightly to her bosom. I assumed that Gerald was somewhere inside. One of the FIDS motioned for me to come and stand beside him. As I stood with my hands on the rails he pointed to a huge mountain, very close to us and rising sheer out of the sea.

"That's Mount Duse, Bev. It's over one thousand six hundred feet high. You'll be skiing down that in no time at all!" The sheer sides of Mount Duse fell straight into the ocean. I was never allowed to contradict an adult but, ski down that? Never! He must be out of his mind, even if he was a scientist with a good English education.

As we sailed closer to the shore, I could see a few seals swimming in the clear waters, their noses screwing up in disdain as they looked over their shoulders at us and at the noisy ship which was invading their territory.

"Bev! That's Hope Point with Shackleton's Cross on it. Now you've reached King Edward Point!" We were very close inshore, sailing past a rocky bluff with a small white cross perched on the top of it. We skirted along the short length of a shingle promontory, so close that we could almost see into the windows of the low white houses with their red or green roofs and dark green fascias, as they rested comfortably amongst a thin layer of snow and partly-exposed tussac bogs. Three tall Radio Masts sprouted symmetric aerials. The *Biscoe* blew her siren and figures scuttled out of the houses, waving and calling out as they ran along the beach beside us.

"So you got here then. About bloody time too!"

"Shut up you grouchy old bugger! Get a bottle opened!"

"Haven't got any bloody bottles left! That's the bloody trouble!"

14

We rounded the narrow point at the end of the stubby promontory and came alongside a small jetty crowded with a knot of wellington-booted, thick-jumpered men. I looked for Dad but couldn't see him. I felt panic rise in my chest. Why hadn't he come to meet us? I couldn't believe that he wouldn't be here waiting for us. Two strong arms slid around my waist and lifted me up from behind. As the *Biscoe* slid in towards the jetty, my assailant said, "Here Peter, would you like a present?" I was swung lightly over the side, across the deep, watery gap between the ship and the jetty, into the arms of a tubby, bearded stranger.

"Hello, Beverley Blue!" said the stranger as he hugged me and planted several scratchy kisses on my cheeks. This was my Daddy of course, but not as I had expected to find him! He had put on weight in the six months that we had been apart and he had grown a bushy beard. I could hardly see his face beneath those long, black whiskers and I searched to look into his green eyes to find the laughter which always lurked there. There was no laughter in his shaded eyes and my face tingled from the scratchiness of his bristly kisses. I threw my arms around his neck to give him the enormous hug I'd been saving for him, stretching my neck so that I could kiss him on the top of his cheek as that was the only piece of hairless pink skin within my reach. His bristles irritated my chin and left me wanting to have a good scratch. Dad passed me to my Uncle Henry who was standing beside him and Uncle Henry gave me a nice, non-hairy kiss and a hug. I held on to Uncle Henry's hand as the gangway was fixed between the *Biscoe* and the jetty and Mum and Gerald were carefully helped ashore. Mum and Dad shared a self-conscious kiss before the large crowd of onlookers then Dad unwrapped Gerald and showed him around to the assembled company like a birthday present. Carrying Gerald, and with his arm around Mum's shoulders, Dad led us up a well-trodden snow path past the power station and tall oil tank on our left to the lower of the first two houses.

The Wireless House was the oldest building on King Edward Point and stood on a brick base, elevated above the ground, both to raise it above the snowline and to keep out the rats which had been introduced to South Georgia from visiting ships. The walls of the white, single-storey building were constructed from tongue and groove planks of wood topped by a red corrugated iron roof, Falkland Island style. Dad led us up three open rustic wooden steps, made from rough pieces of wood nailed together, to the back door which opened into a small square entrance area with a pantry door leading off it to the right and another door straight ahead of us which led into

16

the kitchen. Inside was a table with four chairs, all of which had been made for us by the carpenters around the bay in the whaling station at Grytviken. A sink and worktop were set beneath a window which looked up to Discovery House. An electric cooker on the far side of the room caused Mum to squeal with pleasure.

"Oh Peter! An electric cooker! No more peat or cleaning a Stanley range!"

"It gets better!" said Dad as he led us through into a long passage with a shorter arm to the left. On our right was a toilet and beside it, a separate door opened into a bathroom.

"All the rooms have got radiators," said Dad, "the houses here have got full central heating and it's all powered free by electricity from the power station we passed as we came in."

We followed him down the long passage.

"This is Gerald's bedroom on the right and the carpenters from Grytviken are bringing a cot around for him later. This is our room opposite his and Beverley is next door to us. Through those doors at the end of the passage there is the Generator Room, the Billiard Room and the Wireless Room, but you can see them another time." Dad turned round and ushered us back along the passage into its side arm. He opened the single door on the left and we trooped into the sitting room. It was a lovely room with a sofa in front of a three-bar electric fire with glowing imitation coals beneath, two easy chairs and a drop-leaf table nestling against the far wall beneath a window. But my interest was captured by a second window and an open glass door in the wall. I walked through into a small conservatory and looked out in a north-easterly direction onto the sweep of King Edward Cove and Mount Duse towering above us.

From the conservatory I could see that the cove swept round in an arc, first to the right then to the left, hugged by a shingle beach. Tussac bogs stood taller than me, forcing their spiky leaves upwards through the inches of snow which covered the undulating triangle of land between our house and the foot of Mount Duse. The lower slopes of the mountain sheltered a dam, below which the slopes were much gentler than those we had sailed past on the Biscoe. Perhaps I would be able to ski down Mount Duse after all! I strained my neck to look out to the left and could just see past the power house to a collection of smoking buildings nestling on the far side of the cove. Dad came and put his arms around my shoulders and gave me a hug. "That's Grytviken, Beverley, the biggest whaling station on South Georgia. When you've learnt to ski, I'll take you around there. In the spring, when the snow melts, we can walk around and I'll show you how they process the whales on The Plan."

"Will I learn to ski soon, Daddy?"

"Strand, the blacksmith from Grytviken, will come round soon and he will measure you up then make some skis for you. Did Mummy buy you some ski boots?"

"She bought me boy's lace-up ankle boots which are hard and ugly and horrible but she said they were what I had to have. Please don't make me wear them, Daddy!" I hated those boy's boots with a passion. Perhaps Dad would tell Mum that I didn't have to wear them. He laughed and placed his hand on my shoulder, giving it a gentle squeeze.

"They are exactly what you need to have and nobody will notice what they look like here!"

For a few hours while the *Biscoe* unloaded her cargo, Uncle Henry was on The Point with us. He walked the twenty yards down to our house from Discovery House with a grey cat draped around the back of his neck, like a comforter.

"This is Blaze, Bev, named after my favourite pin-up! You might like to play with him sometimes. He likes being carried around like this so that he keeps warm and doesn't get snow on his paws." He passed Blaze down to me and I stroked his soft fur, holding him close to me as he purred softly and contentedly in my arms.

"I would love to have a cat, Uncle Henry!"

"Then you can keep him here at home with you Bev, he's yours!" I was thrilled to have a cat of my own and I hugged Uncle Henry to thank him for giving Blaze to me. I learned, years later, that Blaze belonged to John Quigley who was the manager of the power station and that Uncle Henrys' generosity was somewhat misplaced. However, John was too much of a gentleman to allow a small detail like rightful ownership get in the way of my pleasure and Blaze became mine.

Later that afternoon the *Biscoe* left King Edward Point to sail further south to the Antarctic Bases. Uncle Henry boarded her for his return trip to Stanley. His intention was to travel to England and from there to New Zealand to join Grandad McLeod and the rest of the McLeod clan who had emigrated from the Falklands several years ago. Dad and I walked down to the *Biscoe* with him to see him off. Uncle Henry was not a great drinker but he had had quite a few farewell bevvies in Discovery House and wasn't walking steadily. He swayed as he held my hand and together we traversed an uncertain path down to the jetty, both of us laughing as we sashayed

19

along. Once he had been guided up the gangplank and the ship's moorings were released, the *Biscoe* turned round easily in the deep waters of the harbour and I ran along the shingle beach beside her, waving to Uncle Henry until he was lost from sight as the Biscoe sailed beyond Hope Point. I watched until her black hull became a small blur in the distance, then walked back home.

Just before dusk Dad perched me on a chair in front of the sitting room window and told me to look out for some men skiing around the cove from Pesca.

"Where's Pesca?"

"Pesca is what we call Grytviken down here. Actually, the whaling station was started by a famous Norwegian called Captain Larsen but the company which provided the money to set it up was an Argentinian company called Compania Argentina de Pesca Sociedad which means 'fishing company', so that's why we call it Pesca. Anyway, Pesca is easier to say than Grytviken! Tell me when the men get here."

A short time later two men came into sight, skiing round the cove from Pesca. One was harnessed to a large sled on top of which was fastened a heavy wooden cot. The second man skied along behind, steadying the cot as the sled crested little rises and slid down into dips. After a while the men changed places and before long they were skiing up to our house.

"Dad! The men are here!" Dad opened the kitchen door and welcomed our visitors.

"Knut! Blom! Good to see you! I thought the carpenters were bringing the cot round?"

"No, Peter, we thought we would bring it ourselves."

"Thank you, I'm very grateful. Come in and meet my family." Shyly I shook hands with the two gentle Norwegians. Blom Petersen was short and slightly built with very fair, receding hair and icy blue eyes. Knut Haraldsen was younger, taller, with strong features, a pencil moustache and with an obviously foreshortened right arm. I made sure that I looked anywhere but at his arm although I was conscious of it the whole time. His arm was normal down to the elbow, but the lower arm was very short, although the wrist and hand at the end of it seemed to be of a normal size. When Dad introduced him to Mum, Knut took her hand in his right hand and kissed it. I had never seen anyone do such a thing before, I thought it only happened in stories, and he used his little arm to take her hand with! I was enchanted. Then I was quickly taken aback because when Dad introduced me to him, Knut turned to me and took my right hand in his right hand too as he bowed over it.

"It is good to meet you Beverley," he said, a huge smile lighting up his green eyes and stretching his moustache into an almost disappearing line, "we will be good friends, I think." With difficulty the three men lifted the cot through the door and carried it into Gerald's bedroom. It was a large and very solid structure, one side slid down to give easy access and silently slid upwards again until a barely perceptible click told you that the safety catch had slipped into place. Mum was thrilled with this gift and immediately filled the cot with the mattress and bedding she had brought with us from Stanley. We all stood and watched as she tucked Gerald into the bed and pulled up the side, leaving him asleep in perfect safety.

"How about a noggin?" Dad said, "I got some new supplies in today on the *Biscoe* and we need to wet the baby's head!" After a long and exciting day I was tired and Mum tucked me into bed with a big hug and a kiss. Dad had

21

gone up to Discovery House to invite his friends to join him, Blom and Knut for a drink so he couldn't come in to say goodnight. Much later I awoke and heard laughter and the loud voices of many men emanating from the sitting room. Clearly the baby's head was getting very wet.

CHAPTER 3

OUR FIRST WEEKS ON SOUTH GEORGIA

The next morning I awoke to a grey sky. The light was diffuse and the snow looked flat and uninviting. Dad slept late, his snores sliding under the door of their bedroom into the passage. Mum was so happy to be back with Dad and to be in her own house that her face wore a permanent smile.

"We'll soon get the house how we like it, Bev, and your Dad could do with some home cooking. Isn't your bedroom nice and big? I wonder if we can get any pink paint down here for the walls, I never thought to bring any down with me. I could do with some blue for Gerald's room too." Mum had cleared up after the previous night by the time Dad appeared. He put his arms around her and gave her a kiss. Mum's face shone pinkly with pleasure. After Dad had eaten his toast and some of the bacon which Mum had brought south for him from Stanley, he told me to put my coat on and he would take me for a walk around The Point. My mood lifted and my heart sang! My Daddy and I were going out together on our own, just like we used to do in Stanley! I treasured our time together, particularly when no one else was there and I had him all to myself and that hadn't happened for six long months. Eyes shining with happiness, I slipped my hand into his, trying to swing his arm and skipping to keep up with his long strides. From our kitchen door, we walked up the slight rise to the L-shaped Discovery House, very similar in style to ours.

"This is where the single men like Uncle Henry live, Beverley. You never go in there unless you are expressly invited."

"Yes, Daddy." Hand in hand we walked on to a second large house with the shingle beach falling away to the sea on our right. I tried to swing Dad's arm again as we always did when we had walked together in Stanley, but his arm remained resolutely stiff. A lone seal swam inshore, following in our wake and watching our every move.

"This is the Magistrate's house, Beverley. The Magistrate is Mr Matthews and he is the Queen's representative on South Georgia. It's his job to keep order on the whole island. Actually, he also checks that the Norwegians and the Argentinians pay their proper dues to the Queen for using South Georgia for their Whaling Stations and for harvesting her whales and seals. He is a very important man. Remember that."

"Yes, Daddy." This wasn't the walk with my Daddy that I had expected, this was becoming an education! I didn't want an education, I wanted to tell him about the things I had been doing at school and how everyone was envious of me because I was here and they were still back in Stanley. I wanted to tell him that I was good at reading and sums so that he could say how pleased he was with me. I wanted him to swing me around and tickle me like he used to do before he left us, but none of these things happened. I was puzzled and stopped skipping.

Just beyond the Magistrate's House stood a tall flagpole with a Union Jack fluttering gently in the breeze. Dad told me that Basil raised the flag each morning and took it down each evening to reinforce the fact that King Edward Point and therefore South Georgia, was a British Territory.

"Every ship that comes into The Point or to Pesca sails past the Union flag. They are also required to fly the British Flag Of Courtesy when they enter the harbour. Remember, Beverley, that our presence here is primarily to retain these islands for The Crown."

"Which crown, Daddy? Is it the one the Queen wears on stamps?"

"By 'The Crown' I mean that these islands belong to Queen Elizabeth and Britain. I explained that to you a few moments ago when I told you about the role of the Magistrate in particular. Have you forgotten?"

"No Daddy, not at all. I just didn't know what you meant by 'The Crown', that's all." Now that Dad had reinforced it though, I certainly wouldn't forget again.

I watched the seal out of the corner of my left eye, and he was still swimming along behind us.

"Look Daddy! That seal has been following us!" Dad threw a brief glance towards the beach.

"It is an adolescent sea elephant, you can tell that from the shortness of its trunk. Actually, you must learn about the animals which inhabit South Georgia while you are here. It will be a good education for you." I looked at the seal more carefully and counted two ripples in its trunk when it flared its nostrils and sniffed at us. I wasn't sure what 'adolescent' meant, but it was obvious that a sea elephant with two ripples was one. I noted that fact too for future reference.

We swung left around the Magistrate's house onto the main path, which ran the length of The Point between all of the houses. To our right was the unoccupied Customs House and to our left, a modern bungalow. Then in front of us, surrounded by a high wire mesh fence, was a large area of concrete patterned by some faded white lines.

"What's that for, Daddy?"

"That is a tennis court. Tennis is an English game, but no one ever plays it here now. You can play there in safety."

"Thank you, Daddy."

We walked on past the small jail with bars at its windows. I averted my eyes as we walked quickly past as only bad people went to jail and the building might be occupied. If a bad man was in there he might see me and want to come and get me sometime. I shrank, making myself as small as possible beside Dad, using his bulk to hide me from any prisoner. If I didn't see him then he was unlikely to see me, so I would be safe. It wasn't until we passed Betty and Basil Biggs' house that I was brave enough to look up again. Basil was the policeman and general handyman, and Betty and Mum had been friends from childhood. Mum was looking forward to seeing Betty again today and to bringing her up to date with all the Stanley gossip.

With my hand still grasped tightly in his, Dad led me past the last small, green-roofed bungalow which nestled beneath a small rise. We climbed up the little hill on to a plateau which stretched back towards the foot of Mount Duse and beyond. To our right was the higher rocky bluff, on which stood a stone cairn, topped with a white, wooden cross. This was the cross which I had seen the previous day from the deck of the *Biscoe.*
"This is where I'll teach you to ski, Beverley. It's a nice, gentle slope and you can ski safely on to the flat snow below. But come up here to the cross and look down." We trudged through the snow to the edge of the high bluff which gently slid away behind the cross then sheered down dramatically to sharp black rocks below with deep sea swirling around them. A forest of brown tree kelp circled, rose and fell in the swell. Across Cumberland Bay, Mount Paget and the Allardyce Mountain range formed a spectacular backdrop.
"You can come up to Shackleton's Cross whenever you want to but you must never go beyond it to the edge. If you fell down there you would die, there's no doubt about it." My hand tightened within Dad's grasp as cold fingers of fear tiptoed lightly down my spine. I could see that he wasn't lying.
"What is Shackleton's Cross, Daddy and why is it built so near the edge?"
"You know that Sir Ernest Shackleton was a great explorer who lost his ship, the *Endurance*, in the Antarctic ice and had to sail across the ocean to South

27

Georgia in an open boat?" I nodded sagely, not wanting to disappoint him by showing my five year old ignorance.

" Well, when Shackleton landed on the south side of the island, he had to traverse the mountains in winter conditions to get to the whaling station at Stromness to get help to rescue his men. They were stranded on Elephant Island, eight hundred miles south of here near the Antarctic peninsular. He rescued his crew and didn't lose a single man, which shows you how great a leader he was. Actually, Shackleton didn't die here until several years later in 1922. He had come back to South Georgia to explore the islands further, but he suffered a heart attack and died almost as soon as he arrived here. He was such a great man that his men and the crew of his ship, the *Quest*, built this cairn of rocks and planted the cross on top of it so that everyone would know where Sir Ernest Shackleton had died and would remember him."

'SIR ERNEST SHACKLETON
EXPLORER
DIED HERE
JANUARY 5TH 1922
ERECTED
BY HIS COMPANIONS'

"Poor Shackleton!" I said. I thought to myself how dreadful it was that poor Sir Shackleton had had a heart attack and died somewhere so dangerous. He could easily have fallen over the edge.

Once he had pointed out the dangers near Shackleton's Cross, Dad told me to look out across the bay to the mountains in the far distance on the other side.

on South Georgia, which you can see clearly from here. Now, what are those mountains called?"

"The Allardyce Mountains, Daddy, and one of the FIDS pointed Mount Paget out to me when we were coming in on the *Biscoe.* It is very tall."

"Good. Now I am going to teach you a Golden Rule which you are never to forget. Are you concentrating on what I'm about to say?" Dad bent down so that his face was more in line with mine and he looked directly at me. It was hard to hold his eyes with my gaze and I tried not to blink too much.

"Yes, Daddy, I'm concentrating very hard."

"Then listen carefully. In South Georgia the weather can change at any time, much faster than it does at home in the Falklands. The only clue you get that the weather is changing is when you see a weather system rolling down the mountains, or in across the bay towards you. Snow and gales can arise at any time, without warning. Whenever you are out playing on your own, you must look up at the mountains and across Cumberland Bay every few minutes. It has to become a habit with you. If you see clouds rolling in or if a wind begins to blow, you are to come straight home. Now, repeat this Golden Rule."

"I must always look out across the bay and up the mountains every few minutes. If I see that the weather is changing, I have got to come home straight away."

"Promise me that you will obey this instruction to the letter" He pointed his finger at me.

" Actually, if I ever have to get the men from The Point to help me to search for you because you have got lost in bad weather, you will feel the full force of my anger."

29

I promised. There wasn't an option for doing anything else and anyway, I wanted him to stop looking at me so hard so that I could blink back the tears that were threatening to fall. Dad's anger was to be feared and avoided at all costs so I was never going to be caught out in bad weather, that was a given.

As we began to descend from Hope Point, I ran down the slope, trying to pull Dad along with me. This was a game that we played in Stanley whenever we crossed the Green outside Granny McLeod's house in Drury Street. We scrambled and slid down the bank, trying to keep our balance together, laughing and slipping in unison. I wanted us to do the same in the snow here!

"Fe farn!" exploded from Dad's mouth and his arm pulled me roughly back. I stopped in the snow and looked at Dad's hard, set features. The laughter in my throat choked me and the sparkle in my eyes fell to the ground and froze in the snow. Where the snow was soft and had blown into small drifts at the base of the incline, I sank through and it came over the top of my wellington boots. It seemed sensible not to complain or draw Dad's attention to my discomfort.

We walked back towards the house and Dad gave me my last instruction. I was never to paddle, as the sea shelved deeply and suddenly and, even had I been able to swim, the cold would kill me within three minutes. I was upset and annoyed that my Daddy should speak to me like this. I was nearly six and I wasn't stupid. I felt that he was treating me like a baby. I'd been so happy to go out with my Daddy on my own to see around The Point, but it had turned into a day of instruction and dos and don'ts. I was disappointed that our time together hadn't been fun as our days in Stanley had been. I didn't understand why he had changed towards me. The snow in my wellies melted and trickled coldly downwards to soak my feet and compound my misery. I was pleased when we got back home and he let me go off to my bedroom to play with my dolls on my own.

That afternoon Betty came round for coffee. Instant coffee, sugar and tins of evaporated and condensed milk stood ready on the kitchen table. Mum had been busy baking ever since she arrived as a string of visitors had been to the house to welcome us. Mr Matthews, the Magistrate, had come in for a formal introduction. He was a gentle man, slightly balding with a small beard and a ready smile. As he was 'Her Majesty the Queens' representative' on South Georgia who had to keep order, I felt very shy in his company and only ever spoke to him once he had spoken to me first. But it was Betty who Mum had been looking forward to seeing and they spent long hours together, meeting on most days for coffee and cakes, never running out of conversation and always laughing freely. Betty fascinated me. She had long, blonde hair which she often wore in plaits wound round her head. She looked as if she had just walked out of an illustration in my Hans Christian Anderson book. I knew that she was a Falkland Islander like us, but she seemed different. She spoke with a low voice which I never once heard her raise. Her diction was excellent, very similar to Dad's and with no trace of the Falkland Island twang. A bit younger than Mum, Betty had three children, all of whom were at school in Stanley. Peter was the youngest, only a few days younger than me. Mum and Betty had been in hospital together after giving birth to us and in one of their giggly moments, they had performed a little ceremony in which they betrothed Peter and me to each other. Not that Peter and I learned about it until we were much older.

Scrupulous about cleanliness, Mum scrubbed the house from top to bottom, even though Dad had done a reasonable job getting it nice for our arrival.

"I can't live in a dirty house, Bev, you know that," and I went off to play in my bedroom out of the way. When she got into cleaning mode I was liable to get cleaned up along with everything else. She moved through the house like a whirlwind, Clifton tongue gripped between her teeth as she concentrated on removing every recalcitrant stain or mark. Nothing was safe from her X-ray vision or from her swirling cloth. Lampshades hanging from the ceiling swung in crazy motion around their electric wire as she reached up and hit them repeatedly with a duster in case any fluff had dared to float upwards and come to rest above our heads; radiators shook with fear as she kneeled in front of them, inserting her cloth into their private recesses around the back.

Windows were thrown open and their sills washed even though they would remain closed throughout the winter.

"If I know it's dusty, Bev, I can't rest."

It wasn't long before Mum and I discovered that what made the days and nights pass more quickly in South Georgia, was parties. As soon as we were settled and the house was shining like a new pin, Dad invited everyone to a party to meet his family. Mum got straight into baking, her favourite occupation. She had to improvise because she could only use the ingredients she found in the house together with the foodstuffs she had brought down with her, but she had been doing this all her life in the Falklands anyway, so it wasn't a problem.

That night we realised that Dad hadn't been lying. When he said he'd invited everyone to the party, it seemed that he had. The nine people who would be based on King Edward point with us for the winter, arrived first. They had just been given their drinks when Dad's friends from Pesca arrived. The Norwegians took off their ski boots and left them dripping on the lino in the tiny bit of passage inside our back door, beside the pantry. It soon resembled a ski boot shop. Wearing crisp white shirts, ties, tailored trousers and ski socks, they came in to join the party. Knut bent over Mum's hand and kissed it before he did the same to me. I loved it, but blushed in a maidenly way. Einar Strand was introduced to me next and I was taken aback. I knew from Dad that Strand was a local legend because he had been working at Pesca for more than twenty years and he was the blacksmith who was going to make me a pair of skis. I imagined that a blacksmith would be a big, strong giant of a man. Instead, I was shaking hands with a short, slight, bespectacled, elderly man in a pin-striped suit who was clearly a bit hard of

33

hearing. I repeated my name twice before he looked quizzingly at Knut, who said loudly,

"Beeverley," and Strand nodded in comprehension and repeated,

"Beeverley? Ah Beeverley! Yes. Good! Very good!"

Einar Strand had been introduced to me by Dad as Strand, but when I spoke to him, I called him Mister Strand. Dad overheard me and took me aside.

"Beverley, you say 'Strand', not 'Mister Strand'. Adult men in Norway are never addressed as 'Mister', but only by their surname."

"Daddy, wouldn't it be rude if I just call Mr Strand by his surname?"

"It may seem rude to us, but it is the polite thing to do in Norwegian society, so we must make our friends feel comfortable in our house by using their names as they want us to."

The younger Norwegians were introduced to Mum and me by a single name too, but their nomenclature was a shortened version of their surname. So, Odd Rasmussen was known as 'Ras' and Carl Thorsen was known to us as 'Thor'. Thor was an engineer, working in the meat plant. His father had worked at Pesca too and the family were one example of several who had strong ties with the whaling station over generations. Last came Blom, shy, quiet and never coming forward until asked. I doubt if there has ever lived a more gentle man on the planet.

Before we went through into the sitting room to join the rest of the party, Blom asked Mum for some string and a pair of scissors so that he could measure us for our skis.

"Beeverley, please stand up tall and put your hand as far up above your head as you can." I did as I was asked and Blom measured the distance between the tips of my outstretched fingers and the floor in string, cutting the length

34

and rolling it into a ball. Next, he measured the distance between my flexed arm and the floor to give him an idea about how long my ski sticks should be. "Now if you please, Pearl," and the process was repeated for Mum. "If you will please bring me your ski boots, I will take them in my bag to Pesca and the carpenter will make skis of the right size for you both. Strand will make the metal plates in his workshop and we will bring the skis round to you very soon."

"Thank you, Blom, that's very kind of you both," said Mum, as she went to find my heavy boy's ankle boots and her men's work boots, which Dad had insisted she buy for us in Stanley. The thrill of getting my own skis wasn't quite enough to wipe out the distaste I still had for those hard leather boots. I liked girlie things and boy's boots didn't fit in with my image of myself in any way at all. I decided that I would ski in my wellington boots, which were at least girls' wellingtons.

Dad was in charge of drinks at the party and my roles were to be 'seen but not heard' first and a good waitress second. Mum had laid out all the food in the kitchen, but Dad instructed me to hand food around to our guests during the course of the evening. In between handing round the Falkland Island sausage rolls, cheese straws and ham sandwiches, Blom took time to sit on the sofa with me. He talked softly to me about his wife and his two daughters back home in Sandefjord, in Norway. His daughters were similar in age to me and as he talked longingly about them, his pale blue eyes glistening with sentimental tears, I could see how much he minded being away from them in South Georgia. I began to understand how hard it must be for men to be so far away from home for six or seven months of the year, or, in Blom's case, for eighteen months as he was staying south for two

35

summer seasons and the winter in between. I felt sorry for Blom as his smile never quite managed to mask the sadness and loneliness which was always present in those palest of blue eyes.

When the party really got going, Knut caught my attention. I watched him out of the corner of my eye as he circled the room poking people in the ribs surreptitiously, making sure that he was out of the way when they turned round so he wasn't seen. He walked away, laughing mightily to himself, then joined another group where he played the same trick. I circled the room with him but at a distance, watching how cleverly he did it and how much fun he was getting from his sleight of hand. Eventually, someone caught on and turned on Knut with his fist raised. Knut smiled and held up his hands in mock submission, his foreshortened right arm to the fore. His opponent got the message and dropped his fist, no one was going to hit a man with a deformity! Knut sat in the chair chuckling happily to himself as the others grumbled loudly about ' bloody Bonski'!

" Knut, are they calling you Bonski?"

"Yes Beeverley, they are. It is my… how do you say it? My other name."

"Like a nickname?"

"Yes, that is it. You can call me Uncle Bonski if that is your wish. Yes, my nickname! It means I like to have a drink! It makes me laugh!" He shook with pleasure as he chuckled loudly at his own joke.   I sat beside him on the arm of his chair while he made fun of everyone in the room and everything he said made him laugh long and loud.

Dad pushed the furniture in the sitting room back against the wall and put 'Rock Around The Clock' on the record player to get the party going. Mum, Betty and I jived with most of the men in turn, while Dad and the other

36

non-combatants watched from the passage, or from their perches on the unwanted furniture. Mum was in her element. A rhythmic dancer and light on her feet, she jived and moved sinuously in perfect rhythm. The rest of us hopped and swayed in her wake, having fun, but unable to match her effortless grace.

"I will show you something!" said Uncle Bonski loudly, as he commandeered the middle of the room and shooed us all out of the way. With a full glass of beer in his right hand, Uncle Bonski sat down on the floor and stretched his legs out in front of him. With his arms outstretched at right angles to his body, he bent his right leg and placed his foot flat on the carpet. With a pronounced forward movement, he transferred all of his weight onto his right leg and pushed himself upright, holding his left leg parallel to the floor and without spilling a single drop of beer!

"How did you do that without using your hands?" was the question we all asked.

"I do it easy. I show you again," and Uncle Bonski repeated his party piece. "It is only to be done with a full glass of beer or whisky!" he laughed, as he downed the contents of his glass in one long gulp and offered it to Dad for a refill.

By the time Mum shooed me off to bed, many of the men were 'three sheets into the wind', to use one of my father's phrases. Dad himself was staggering and fell into the armchair where he stayed, offering his glass to me or to anyone else who passed by within his orbit for a refill of scotch.

The following morning I found Dad asleep on the sitting room sofa, comfortable in a cocoon of blankets which Mum had obviously wrapped around him. This was my first day of being left alone to fend for myself. I dressed in a cotton dress and wellies as always, but today I was also wearing my new red coat which Mum had bought especially for South Georgia. Before I left the house she carefully rolled up the sleeves at the cuffs as she had sensibly bought a coat which was two sizes too big for me and the arms hung down several inches below my hands. With my coat flapping around my calves, I left the house feeling very proud and smart. I followed the path through the snow past the power house and the tall oil storage tank towards the harbour.

I walked around the edge of the jetty, looking down at a myriad of fish swimming in the deep, crystal clear sea below me. In Stanley you might see one or two fish, but here there were dozens and dozens. I lay down on my stomach and hung my head over the side of the jetty. The fish came in broadly two shapes, a normal fish shape, similar to the trout and mullet which Grandad caught in Stanley Harbour, and another with a longer body. This second species had a large head, its triangular face ending in an ugly long snout beneath two high set eyes. From its high back, its body tapered down to a narrow tail which looked a bit like a feather. It was light brown in colour, with darker brown spots covering the entire length of its body in a random pattern. These were the most extraordinary fish I had ever seen, there was nothing in my knowledge base to compare them with. I watched as the two species darted about beneath me in perfect harmony with each other, playing in the light then darting under the jetty to hide in the shadows.

It was too cold to stay still for very long on a snowy jetty, so I stood up and walked along the beach, just below the snow line. Beside the jetty there were two boathouses, standing beside one another. Both had windows which I could just peer in through if I stood on tiptoes. The first boathouse protected a sleek, varnished, clinker built motorboat. She had a cabin built into the front part of her hull with a deep area behind it where the men could stand to sail her. This was the Resolution, our motorboat for The Point. In the second boathouse there was an old, battered, long rowing boat, her oars lying neatly side by side across her seats. She had once been white, but there was very little paint left on her now. She had certainly seen better days.

As I walked around the actual point of the promontory which King Edward Point had been named after, the beach shelved steeply into the sea. Further along the length of the promontory towards Hope Point, the beach shelved less steeply until, near Hope Point itself, it was quite gentle. It was too cold and snowy to sit down anywhere so I decided to walk on past the small building above me to Discovery House. As I walked, the door of the little building opened and a very Scottish voice said,

"Hello, Beverley, what are ye up to today, then?"

"Hello, Mr Borland. I'm not up to anything really, just going for a walk around The Point."

"Well first you can call me Danny like everyone else and second, you can come in and have a look at the Meteorological Station here if you want to."

"Yes please, Danny," and I followed him into a room crammed with meteorological equipment and a few mementos of Glasgow Rangers Football Club.

"I won't bore you with telling you about what each piece of equipment does, but there is something which you might like to help me with. See these white and red balloons? Twice every day, I release one of these balloons up into the sky and I watch it very carefully until it rises so high that it goes out of sight. If ye want to, ye can come and help me launch the balloons."

"That would be lovely, thank you Danny."

"Well, we'll launch one now. Hold the balloon while I blow it up with this gas." I held on to a very large red balloon and watched carefully as it began to inflate. For some minutes nothing seemed to happen. The flat balloon took on a little more of a three-dimensional shape but there was very little to see. After some time, the balloon began to round-out like a flat, circular cushion. Then, as it took in more gas, the balloon came to life in Danny's hands. As it filled to capacity, the balloon eclipsed me in size and tried to break away from my grasp.

"Hold on, Bev, or ye'll take off with it!" I held on tightly as the balloon rose gently and decisively into the air.

"That'll do!" said Danny as he closed the neck of the balloon with a twist, "we'll take it outside and launch it now." Manoeuvring the balloon out through the door was more than I could cope with on my own. As we stepped outside the light wind caught the balloon and it bucked in my hands for a few seconds. Danny grabbed my elbow.

"Hold on, Bev, it's the balloon that's supposed to go up, not you! Now, hold it straight and then let go when I give ye the word. One, two, three, let go!" As I released my grasp on the balloon, it floated up into the grey sky, blown out across the harbour by the wind.

"Come back later this afternoon and I'll give ye a red balloon for yeself, Bev, I bet ye'd like that wouldn't ye?"

"Oh, yes please, Danny, I'd like a balloon very much! I'll come back this afternoon! Goodbye!" I immediately accepted Danny's suggestion that I should come back later this afternoon as a dismissal. I was sorry that he'd told me to go because there were so many things in his weather station that I would have liked to look at and he was fun to be with. Still, I was going to be given a big, red balloon of my own later so I had something special to look forward to.

While I sat at the kitchen table waiting for my dinner, Mum and I chatted about her morning in the house. I told Mum about my morning too and we shared laughter and stories and relaxed together, enjoying the warmth of one another's company. When we heard the door from the Generator Room open and Dad walked along the passage, I folded my hands neatly in my lap, sat up straight and waited silently for him to come in. He washed his hands in the bathroom sink, then joined me at the table while Mum served our food. Dad liked to find me sitting upright with my hands out of sight. I knew to speak only when I had been spoken to.

"So, what adventures have you had this morning, Beverley?"

"I went down onto the jetty and looked at the fish. I've never seen so many fish, Daddy, and especially not such ugly ones!"

"Now that I have begun my food, you may begin yours, Beverley."

"Thank you, Daddy," and I picked up my knife and fork and began to eat.

"As for your ugly fish, they are called crocodile fish and they're found in southern waters, quite abundantly around South Georgia. Actually, when the snow melts and the weather gets warmer, I'll take you and your Mum down to the jetty to do some fishing. The Antarctic cod will make a nice change for us to eat, but we'll throw back any crocodile fish we catch."

"Can't you eat them then, Daddy?"

"Can't you eat what, Beverley? Be specific when you begin a new sentence."

"I'm sorry, Daddy. I meant to ask you if crocodile fish were fish that humans can't eat."

"Actually, I'm not sure that they're inedible, however there are so many cod in the seas here that we've never had to try a crocodile fish. They look so unappetising that no one would want to eat them!"

"Danny let me help him to launch a balloon and he said that he would give me a balloon this afternoon if I go back to see him again."

"You may do so this once, but I won't have you annoying Danny or anyone else for that matter. Everyone here has an important job to do and they don't want you interfering with it. Make sure that this is the last balloon you ask Danny for."

"I didn't ask him for a balloon, Daddy, he offered me one."

"Who offered you a balloon? You're not listening to me. When I say that a sentence should be specific that means that it should make sense on its own. 'He' and 'it' are not acceptable in a sentence which has no subject. You are old enough to remember that and to put it into practice. I will not have my daughter speaking anything other than the Queens' English. Repeat the sentence back to me correctly."

"I'm sorry, Daddy, I meant to say that Danny had been kind enough to offer to give me a balloon without me having to ask him for one."

"Do you mean that you would have asked him for a balloon if he hadn't offered to give you one?"

"No, Daddy, I would never be rude enough to ask Danny for anything."

"Nor anyone else I hope. You may accept this balloon from Danny and be sure to thank him properly for his generosity. Now, I'm going to go back to work. You may leave the table when your mother gives you her permission."

"Thank you, Daddy." After Dad left the room, Mum stretched her hand across the table and gave my hand a warm squeeze.

"You haven't done anything wrong sweetheart, so don't think you have. Your Dad just wants you to be polite and speak properly, that's all. You go back later and get your balloon from Danny, he'll be pleased to see a lovely girl like you!" I slipped down from my chair and ran around the table to Mum for a hug and to feel her warm kisses on the top of my head. Since we had come to South Georgia, Dad often left me feeling as if I needed them.

If there is one thing you can rely on in South Georgia, it's the unreliability of the weather. Before our meal was over, the wind rose. By the time Mum had washed the dishes, the wind was howling and snow was drifting in swirls against the windows and walls of the house. By late afternoon I was watching the clock and the weather through the window, the afternoon was drawing on and the wind wasn't abating at all. I was desperate to go up to see Danny and get my balloon, but Mum refused to allow me to go outside in such a gale. When it started to get dark, I couldn't bear it anymore, so I tried to plead with Mum again.

"Please let me go up to see Danny, Mum. You can watch me all the way there and all the way back through the kitchen window. No harm can come to me."

"Open the door and walk outside, Bev." I opened the door and the snow-laden wind howled in, lifting the doormat up off the floor and throwing it into the kitchen. I took a single step outside and was pushed backwards by the strength of the wind. Mum pushed past me and heaved against the door to close it.

43

"There you are, Bev, you can't stand up against the wind on your own, so you can't go up to see Danny today. He'll still have a balloon for you tomorrow." Tears welled up in my eyes, I hated being thwarted and I longed for a red balloon above everything else. Mum saw my tears and softened, as she always did when she knew that I was upset.

"I know what we'll do. As it's only about twenty yards up to Danny's weather station, we'll leave Gerald in his cot and go up together. If we hold on tight to each other, the wind won't be able to blow two of us over. It'll be our special game!" Tears forgotten and with my face wreathed in sudden smiles, I grabbed my coat and put on my wellies. Mum did the same. She carried Gerald to his cot and put up the side securely. I gave him his favourite little cuddly panda and a kiss goodbye.

"He'll be fine for ten minutes," Mum said, "No harm will come to him here. Now, hold my hand very tight and we'll brave the wind together!"

With our arms wrapped around each other, Mum and I fought our way down the three steps onto the snowy path. The wind threw horizontal snow into our faces and against our legs. With heads bent forwards against the gale, we turned to our left and began the short climb up to Discovery House and the weather station beside it. Mum wrapped her right arm more forcibly around my shoulders and held me tightly against her. With two of us so closely intertwined, the wind seemed less frightening and we made good progress up the path.

"This is fun, Mummy!" but my voice was lost in the howl of the wind as it whipped in across the wide expanse of Cumberland Bay. It took an enormous effort to remain standing in the teeth of the wind and each step was

44

a milestone, but without mishap, we arrived at Danny's door and banged against it, before falling inside as Danny threw it open.

"I didn't expect to see ye this afternoon, Bev, this isn't the weather to be out of doors in, I can tell ye! Ye needed your Mum to be with ye, that's for sure!" Mum and I were tousled and breathless, the wind had thrown its might at us but, together, we had beaten it. This was a real adventure! Mum and Danny chatted about the weather and people on The Point, but all the while my eyes were fixed on my red balloon which was growing ever larger on the end of Danny's pump. When it seemed as if the walls of my balloon could expand no more and one more push of air from the pump would burst it, Danny expertly twisted my balloon off the pump and tied a knot in the free end.

"Here ye are, Bev, it'll go down over time but it won't burst easily because the balloon is made from a special material which is very strong. Now, Pearl, will ye be able to get it home or shall I carry it for you? The wind'll catch it and make it hard for you to carry." I looked at Mum with pleading eyes, I wanted to hold my balloon and take it home myself.

"Thank you, Danny, but we'll be fine together, won't we Bev!" I flashed her my biggest smile of gratitude and flushed with pleasure as Danny put the balloon into my hand. It was an enormous sphere, as tall as I was but very much rounder, and a beautiful deep pinky-red. It bounced satisfyingly against my wrist and hit me lightly on the face.

"Right, Bev, let's get back to Gerald. You hold the balloon and I'll hold on to you. Thanks again, Danny. Goodbye!"

"Yes, thank you very much, Danny, I love my balloon."

"You're welcome, Bev, anytime!" I hoped he meant that I was welcome to come and get a new balloon at any time, but I wasn't sure. Grown-ups were often ambiguous and sometimes they forgot completely what they had promised you.

Carrying a huge meteorological balloon in a gale isn't an easy task. With such a huge volume of air in my hand, the wind was forceful enough to lift the balloon and me off the ground together. Because Mum had one arm around my shoulders and another holding the balloon with me in my hand, our combined weight was too much for the wind so, in its anger at being thwarted, it strained to steal my balloon and carry it off up into the air. My wrist hurt and my arm felt as if it was being wrenched off as the wind fought to take it away from me. The rapacious wind buffeted my balloon this way and that, hitting it into my face, onto my head, onto Mum's head and then pulling it away towards the harbour. The twenty yard walk was exhausting, painful and completely exhilarating. Together, Mum and I fought to balance ourselves from being blown over forwards by the wind lashing at our backs as we were forced to run down the shallow incline towards our house. We kept our heads down, laughed through our gritted teeth and held on to the balloon and each other. When we got to the back door, Mum threw it open and pushed the balloon inside with me after it. She had to use her full weight against the door to close it in the teeth of the wind, then we collapsed onto the kitchen floor, two white ghosts hugging each other and laughing together in a shared celebration. The red balloon sat on the floor behind us, not quite still, as the draught from the wind outside crept in under the back door and gave it a permanent twitch.

When Dad came in from the Wireless Room after completing the last transmissions of the day, he pointedly looked at the balloon and then his dark glance swept over me. The balloon and I shivered beneath his icy stare, then he looked away and we both melted and breathed again.

My red balloon was too big to play with indoors so I sat on it, sinking into its softness as if it were a spherical beanbag. As it was so huge, I had to run and launch myself onto its airy softness. When I landed heavily on top of it, the balloon rolled over under my weight and threw me off onto the floor. The balloon nearly always won and I nearly always lost, but together we spent happy hours rolling around the sitting room and along the passage or sitting together in perfect harmony. Over the next three days the balloon and I kept each other company, while huge snowflakes fell in endless droves outside the window and the tussac bogs began to disappear beneath a sparkling white carpet.

CHAPTER 4
WINTER BEGINS

From the end of May and into June, the winds died down and snow continued to fall. I sat in the conservatory wearing my coat and wrapped in a blanket, following the paths of huge fluffy flakes as they drifted lazily down to cover the tussac bogs in layer after layer of sparkling white. I held a saucer out through the open window to catch the biggest snowflakes, pulling them inside and scrutinizing them closely under Dad's magnifying glass before they melted, to see whether or not they were the Snow Queen's guards, shaped like 'great, ugly porcupines' or 'snakes rolled into knots with their heads stretching out', or even 'little fat bears with bristling hair'. I repeated the Lord's Prayer over some snowflakes, hoping, like Gerda, that my breath would take shape and become 'little bright angels', carrying spears and wearing helmets. Even though my saucer froze and the snowflakes held their shape for some time, they never changed into a guard, nor my breath into an angel. My neck tingled with fear and anticipation as I studied each new snowflake. What if it was a guard? What would I do? If I threw him down or let him melt, what would the Snow Queen do to me then? What if there was an angel? If I let her melt, would both the Snow Queen and God be angry with me?

Day after day I searched the snowflakes for signs that the Snow Queen, sitting on her throne in the Ice Palace on the other side of Cumberland Bay, was sending her messengers to communicate with me. I recognised great beauty in the sixfold symmetry of the snowflakes but their intricate patterns failed to quell the keen sense of disappointment I felt at the end of each day as I reluctantly closed the conservatory window and walked to my warm bedroom alone. I had to admit to myself that the Snow Queen was ignoring The Point and me completely.

Soon the snow was lying four or five feet deep and the contours of each individual tussac bog disappeared as the landscape was transformed into a flat world of pure white talcum powder. The beach was encircled by a cliff of snow which held its position and would not be washed away by anything except for the most determined lapping of the gentle waves at high tide. Walking outside was impossible as the snow was so soft. I stepped off the top back door step into a snowdrift. As my feet sank deeply into it, like quicksand, snow filled my wellingtons and rode up beneath my dress. In panic, I screamed

"Mum! Mum! Help me!" Like a virago, Mum shot out through the door and grabbed my flailing arms, pulling me roughly out of the cold and suffocating hole I found myself buried in. There was a loud 'sluuurp' as my feet slipped out of my wellington boots leaving them empty and forlorn, buried in the snow.

Dad went outside every morning and afternoon on his skis, taking his spade with him. He dug out the entrance to the henhouse which stood outside the Billiard Room and checked that the chickens were being kept warm by the electric fire hanging on the inside wall of their wooden shed. He fed the hens with a porridge of hot corn and food scraps which Mum cooked up in a metal bucket on top of the cooker. Terrified of hens, this was the worst part of the day for him! When he opened the door, all the hens flew

49

down from their perches and ran clucking towards him as he carried in their food. In panic, he threw the contents of the food bucket sloppily into the feeding trough on the floor of the henhouse, slammed the door shut, locked it and skied back to the house as fast as he could.

"When you get your skis, Pearl, you can feed the bloody hens! I give that job to you with pleasure!"

I was still stuck firmly inside the house and I was running out of things to do. My balloon had lost lots of its air and was no longer even round; looking for guards and angels was no fun because they never came and my dolls relied on me to do everything for them which became tedious after a while. Hans Christian Anderson was my standby, but I knew the stories so well that I hardly even needed to read them anymore. I remembered that I had been given a small package of school books when I left the Infant's school in Stanley so I opened the package and took out the books. There were four reading books which I read quickly and put away. There were two small exercise books for practising my writing, ruled in order to make the sizing of letters easier and more uniform, and an arithmetic book. The arithmetic book was fun! On each page there were addition and subtraction sums, with ruled lines at the bottom of each one to write the answer in. I didn't even have to copy them out! I sat at the dropped-leaf table in the sitting room and worked my way through the book. They were similar to the ones I had been doing in my last weeks at school. At dinner time I took my work in to show Dad.

"Daddy, this is my school work from Stanley and I've done all of the sums."

"What word would it be better to use than 'done'?"

"Sorry, Daddy, I have completed all of the sums."

"That's better, Beverley. Just because you are in South Georgia, it doesn't mean that you can stop speaking the Queen's English properly, as you know."

"No, Daddy."

"Now, let me look at your work." As he ate his Norwegian meatballs in tomato sauce, Dad scanned my sums.

"These seem far too easy to me, Beverley, I'll give you some harder ones to do."

"Thank you, Daddy!" This was exciting! Daddy was going to be my new teacher and I would have him all to myself at last.

"Was that all of the work you were given to bring down with you?"

"No, Daddy. I have four reading books but I've read them all. There are two writing books and I haven't done any writing yet."

"Are those the only books you've brought down with you to read?"

"I've got my Hans Christian Andersen book. Shall I show it to you?"

"Please do." My anthology of stories was written for children much older than me and Dad was impressed, I could see. I read him the first page of 'The Snow Queen'.

"That was well-read, Beverley. What do you do if you come across a word which you can't pronounce or don't know the meaning of?"

"I ask Mum for help."

"Good. You must continue to read through the Hans Christian Andersen book, asking your mother for help. You can read a page to me from time to time and I'll question you about the story. It's not enough to be able to read well, it's what you have understood from your reading that counts. I'll set you some more arithmetic to do too. Do you know your multiplication tables?"

"I don't think I do, Daddy."

"What is most important is that you learn your multiplication tables fluently. Your mother will write them out for you after dinner and I expect you to recite a new table to me every week, until you've learned them all. I also expect you to copy from your fairy tale book in order to practice your handwriting. Show your work to me every Friday."

"Yes, Daddy." This was better than wonderful! My Daddy was going to see my work every Friday. I wanted him to be proud of me. It was already Tuesday, so I needed to get to work! Straight after Dad had gone back to the Wireless Room and Gerald had been put down for his nap, Mum and I sat down together and we went through the two times table. She explained that you were doubling the numbers each time and I thought it was very clever. I was determined to learn my two times table by Friday.

Through the doors which marked the end of our living quarters, was a huge room which housed an old generator. From the left hand corner of the room, a narrow passage led to two small rooms on the right, a large Billiard Room in an extension to the left, and straight on into Dad's Wireless Room. While the weather was still too bad for me to go outside, and before I received my skis from Strand, I spent hour after hour watching Dad at work. I sat on a chair at the end of the workbench, being seen and not heard. I was fascinated by the speed with which Dad used a Morse key to send messages from sub Antarctic South Georgia around the world and translated their Morse replies back, typing them directly as telegrams.

The equipment in the Wireless Room had to be operated and maintained by Dad and Jack, the other operator. They donned their headphones, turned the knobs on the grey faces of the tall transmitters and receivers to make contact with other stations, signalling to each other through gestures whenever there was a problem transmitting or receiving messages, so that they maintained speed and accuracy. Dad was clearly in charge and no problem was ever too difficult for him to solve. He thrived on pressure and I sat in rapt attention, admiring his skill, expertise and intelligence. Because it was winter, Dad had Jack as his assistant, but during the busy whaling season, a second assistant was going to be sent down from Stanley or 'borrowed' from a whaling station if no one suitable could be found.

Opposite the entrance to the Wireless Room was a long desk, where the typewriter stood in front of the grey Auto Alarm, a radio receiver, tuned permanently to 500kHz, the International Maritime Distress Morse frequency. When he was on duty, Dad kept a continuous watch on it. In Dad's bedroom and in the bedroom which the wireless operators used in Discovery House, there was an alarm bell which rang if a distress call came in when the operators were off duty. When he came on duty at eight thirty in the morning, Dad's first task was to turn off the overnight alarm watch. It was a finicky piece of electronics which required different day and night settings and readjusting it was difficult. The readjustment was accompanied by a long and colourful stream of language which I instinctively knew wasn't acceptable for me to copy as it definitely wasn't the Queen's English.

After dealing with the Auto Alarm at eight thirty every morning, Dad and Jack opened up the King Edward Point 'ZBH' call-sign and contacted the whaling stations at Leith Harbour and Husvik, exchanging 'traffic' for local delivery or for onward transmission to Stanley, or to anywhere else in the world. Salvesen's at Leith Harbour usually had much more traffic than Husvik, especially during the whaling season. All the traffic was copied onto signal pads and sorted prior to preparing it for onward transmission to Stanley. After completing these formalities, Dad closed the circuit down with a cheerful "hl" for hilsen, the Norwegian for regards.

The daily schedule which Dad worked involved a morning, afternoon and evening contact with Stanley. Watching the 'scheds' with 'VPC' were much more fun than watching those with the whaling stations because for his contact with Stanley, Dad used a complex Duplex Circuit so that he and Jack could receive and transmit messages simultaneously, saving a lot of time.

Although much of our food for the winter had been brought down with us from Stanley and was stored in the cellar and attic, Mum was able to get other supplies from Pesca. She could wire orders back to Stanley but our next chance of getting supplies from there would not be until the *Darwin* came down for her first ever mid-winter visit. To order food from Pesca, Mum gave Basil a list of the stores she needed each Thursday, together with a large cotton bag. Basil either went over to Pesca in the *Resolution*, or skied around the three-quarter mile harbour track to take our orders. On Fridays, again in the Resolution or towing a sled behind him, Basil returned to The Point with our stores. Pigs were kept in the piggery at Pesca and he brought back the cotton bag stuffed full of huge cuts of pork and sometimes, a piece of frozen mutton left over from the flock which had been brought down from the Falklands but which had failed to survive the previous winter and the poor grazing. Sometimes, Pesca presented us with frozen reindeer or whale meat which had been culled or caught during the previous summer season.

On Saturdays, Basil repeated his trek to Pesca. This time he brought back freshly baked bread from the Bakery which, like the meat, was given free to us, paid for by the Falkland Island Government. He also brought food from the Pesca cold store, which, unbeknown to Mum, was supplied in catering proportions. Mum had ordered black pepper and it came in a one pound tin. Cocoa, custard powder, jam, butter, fruit and many other comestibles arrived in five or seven pound tins. Cheese came in large blocks and looked and tasted like pale yellow rubber. Mum used it mainly for making cheese straws.

"Well, Bev, it's not as good a flavour as I'd like it to be, but beggars can't be choosers so we'll just have to put up with it!"

There was some fresh produce too. We could buy a kilo of apples for one shilling and eleven pence, a kilo of carrots or a dark cabbage for sixpence each.

Milk was a particular problem as there were no cows on the island so we drank either the powdered milk or tinned evaporated milk which Mum had brought down with us from Stanley. On our first Saturday after Basil had delivered our stores, Mum opened her first tin of evaporated milk which had been shipped down from Argentina. She read the printed instructions twice just to make sure that she had read it correctly, then said

"Peter, listen to this!

'This milk conserved without sugar is pasteurised and sterilised owing that it conserves all the qualities and conditions of pure milk. In all uses it may be used as fresh milk, for drinking, ice creams elaboration, cakes or other common use. It is used pure or adding water till 40% according to the wish in every case. When you open this bottling the period of conversation is equal as fresh milk.' Well, I suppose I couldn't ask for clearer instructions!"

As we didn't have a refrigerator, unlike the three new bungalows which had been fitted with one, Mum kept our food fresh by storing it in the pantry. This walk-in cupboard at the corner of the house had no central heating and Mum insisted that we keep the door between the kitchen and the vestibule, where the pantry and outside door were, closed. Ice formed on the window of the pantry and stayed there for the whole winter. If she needed to freeze something, Mum wrapped it in a tea cloth and popped it in the snow outside the back door. Mixing together evaporated milk, sugar, cocoa and custard powder, she made a thick custard which she placed in a bowl, covered it with an upturned plate, and pushed it deep into the snow just before I went to bed. The next morning I dug out the treasure and ate the best chocolate ice cream you could ever taste.

Uncle Bonski held several positions at Pesca, but his main role was as the Manager's clerk. Once or twice a day, he came round to the Point, either in the Pesca workboat or by skiing around the harbour. He brought traffic for Dad to transmit from Pesca and returned with replies from the Wireless Station. Uncle Bonski liked to time his arrival each morning for 'smoko' at around ten o'clock. He called in to the Wireless Room then followed Dad through into the kitchen and bowed to Mum, kissing her hand and asking, "Pearl, can I have coffee with you today please, if you are kind?" We sat companionably around the kitchen table, the adults exchanging gossip or any news which they had gleaned from the world outside. Mum always had freshly baked cakes or biscuits neatly arranged on plates, but with a few extra ones hidden beneath a tea towel on the draining board to sustain Uncle Bonski on his journey back to Pesca.

One morning when we were having smoko with Uncle Bonski in the kitchen, he opened his knapsack and brought out the two pairs of ski boots which Mum had given to him and Strand, so that our ski bindings could be made to fit. He smiled at me and said

"Beeverley, tonight Strand and me, we will bring skis for you. And for Pearl too, of course," he added, bowing his head in Mum's direction.

"Thank you Uncle Bonski, I'm so excited about learning to ski!" and I really was. I was looking forward to getting out of the house as I had been shut in for several weeks by the snow. I longed for the evening to come.

The snow was lying too deeply against the conservatory windows for me to see over it, but from the higher sitting room window, I could stand on a chair and look across to the path that wound its way round the harbour from Pesca. In the deepening twilight, I saw two figures, one tall, the other short, skiing towards The Point. As they came closer, I could see that each man had a pair of skis and sticks strapped to his back. When they arrived at the back door, Uncle Bonski took the skis from Strand's back and passed them to me. My own skis! At last!

My skis and Mum's were laid side by side on the kitchen floor. Strand took my boy's ankle boots and bent down beside mine.

"See Beeverley, I have made the metal plate to fit your boots. The lip?" looking up at Dad, who nodded, "Yes, the lip of the metal plate is made to be over the sole of the boot where I have filed it to make a dip. It will hold the boot good for you. Good. Very good, yes?" he asked and we all smiled and nodded our heads in agreement.

"They are excellent, Strand, thank you very much." said Dad. "Go and put on your ski boots, Beverley, and we will see how well the skis fit you then." I went to my bedroom and put my feet into those horrible boy's ankle boots and walked back to the kitchen, dreading what everyone would say when they saw how ugly they looked. Nobody made any comment, which came as a welcome surprise. It seemed as if the grown-ups saw nothing untoward in my clodhoppers, so I relaxed a little and stood beside my skis.

"Slip your foot into the metal plate, Beverley. Carefully! That's it! You have to ensure that the toe of the boot slips in underneath those rims there at the side. Good! Now, bend down and fit the leather strap behind your heel where the ridge is and tighten it as much as you can." I struggled with the new leather strap, which I had to fit into through a buckle lying against the outside of my left ankle. Dad said,

"No Pearl! Don't help her! She can't ski if she can't cope with the bindings on her own. When she falls over, her ski can come off and she can't come running to you for help to put it on again." I persevered with the strap and eventually managed to thread it through the buckle and fit the metal pin through a hole in the leather.

"Well done, Beverley! Now, you must fit the other one." Fitting the ski on my right foot was much easier, as the buckle was on my right hand side and soon I was standing proudly on the kitchen floor, two wooden skis firmly attached to my boy's ankle boots and with my two thin, spindly legs and cotton dress hovering happily above them all. Uncle Bonski put two ski sticks into my hands.

"Push your hands through the leather loop, Beeverley, then hold on to the stick. Most good, you look like a Norwegian girl now. But in the snow you must wear trousers! Ha! Ha!"

"And you can't wear those socks either," Mum observed as she fitted on her own boots and slipped them into her skis. We both took a few steps across the kitchen floor, everyone laughing as we shuffled forwards for a few feet like deep sea divers, shuffling on dry land in their leaden boots.

Two days later I pulled back my bedroom curtains on a calm morning and only a light smattering of snow was falling. I gulped down my breakfast, threw on my outdoor clothes and stood outside the back door to fit on each ski. With my hands holding the sticks, I moved forward hesitatingly. The snow was soft and sticky and my progress was slow, but I skied the twenty yards to the powerhouse and, making a huge arc, skied back to the house. I had been stifled and incarcerated by the heavy snowfall and the lack of skis. Now, suddenly, I was free! I could explore The Point on my own and have Antarctic adventures. The wind, blowing a few snowflakes gently into my face, was exhilarating. I was released from captivity and I felt 'sing out loud' happy.

"Hello Beeve! I am happy to see you on your skis. How do you go?" Uncle Bonski appeared around the end of the house, having skied round from Pesca with that morning's traffic.

"I'm doing well I think, thank you, Uncle Bonski. Look at my tracks, I've skied to the powerhouse and back."

"You have done some good tracks I see. Ha! Ha!" and Uncle Bonski skied on round to the Generator Room entrance to go into the Wireless Room. I felt unusually cold so I took off my skis and went inside. My feet were frozen, even though I had only been outside for about half an hour. I lay down on the sitting room floor and pushed my feet up against the radiator. When Dad and Uncle Bonski came in for smoko, I joined them and Mum in the kitchen. Mum was telling Dad that my knee socks, which she had bought in Stanley, were far too thin to keep me warm when I was skiing.

"She'll just have to wear a pair of your socks, Peter, even if she'll be swimming in them."

"Pearl, if I can say," interjected Uncle Bonski, "I will bring for Beeverley this evening from Blom in the Slop Chest, the most small ski socks it is possible to have here. She must have warm feet to be in the snow all day and Norwegian socks are best in the world!"

"Thank you, Bonski, that will be just the thing for Bev," said Mum, "Will you have another piece of Victoria sponge with your coffee?"

"I will have. Thank you! Ha! Ha!"

When Uncle Bonski had left to return to Pesca, Dad told me to put my skis back on and he took me up to Shackleton's Cross for a lesson. On the way across the flat snow, he showed me how to glide and get into a comfortable rhythm, so that my skis moved over the snow with the minimum of effort.

"This is what the Norwegian's call 'langlaufing', Beverley. It's a form of cross-country skiing. They get into a rhythm and it enables them to traverse miles and miles of snow-covered terrain in a single day. You can langlauf all over The Point perfectly safely on your own. When you are a competent skier, we will langlauf around to Pesca together to visit Bonski." For me, langlaufing wasn't using minimum effort and I failed to find an easy rhythm which allowed me to keep up with Dad. My skis moved jerkily instead of smoothly and the points sometimes got stuck under the surface of the powdery snow. When this happened, I had to stop and pull my ski backwards out of the snow before I could continue forwards again.

"Don't give up, Beverley, you'll get the hang of it in no time at all." I hoped that I would get the hang of it soon, my legs were already tired and we hadn't yet reached Hope Point.

The gentle hill up to the small plateau from the bungalow below Shackleton's Cross on Hope Point was inviting and pristine. No one had disturbed the snow and it beckoned, smooth and welcoming. Dad told me to wait at the bottom and watch him.

"You can get up the slope quickly by keeping your skis parallel and walking sideways up the slope. Like this!" Dad stamped his way up the slope, leaving parallel tracks in the snow for me to slip my skis into. This was easy and I speedily followed him to the top of the rise.

"Now, there are two ways to ski down this slope. Because it is a gentle and low slope, you can ski down it doing nothing more than keeping your skis parallel and looking straight ahead. Watch me, then follow me down!" Dad skied down the slope in seconds and stood watching me from the bottom.

"Now, Beverley! Get your skis parallel and facing down the slope, then just push yourself forward with your sticks, keep your knees bent and let yourself go!" I did as I was bid and I flew down the slope, the wind whistling past my face and the shore rushing towards me.

"That was fantastic, Daddy! Can we do it again, please?"

"Not in the same way. I am going to show you how to control your speed when you're coming down a steeper slope. The style I'm going to show you is called a 'snowplough'. When you have mastered the snowplough properly, then you can join the adults on Mount Duse. Until then, you must only ski here." We stood in front of Shackleton's Cross together.

"Push your heels outwards until they are the same distance apart as your shoulders and point your toes inwards at the same time." Together we stood in the classic snowplough position, safely stationary on the relatively flat top of Hope Point, but looking straight down the slope to the flat piece of land below.

"Now, when I push myself forward," Dad said, "I can control how fast or how slowly I go down the slope. If I want to slow down or even stop, I point my toes inwards more and push down on my skis and that controls my speed. Watch!" Dad snowploughed down the rise, stopping himself halfway down so that he could turn and look back up at me. I watched carefully until he was at the bottom and it was my turn. With some apprehension, I pushed myself over the top of the rise and, to my surprise I went very slowly down the slope too. My confidence rose and I stopped beside Dad and looked up at him, a smile of pure pleasure lighting up my face.

"Well done, Beverley! What you can do once Bonski brings you round some proper ski socks is come up here every day and practise your snow ploughs until you're ready to demonstrate to me how competent you are. When you are really proficient, then you can come and join us on the mountain. Now, let's go back home before your mother gets cross with me for letting your feet get cold."

I stayed indoors and waited impatiently for Uncle Bonski to arrive back from Pesca with his next packet of traffic and my new ski socks. He didn't disappoint me and at teatime, he handed me four grey and white woollen socks.

"Thank you, Uncle Bonski, I'll try them on straightaway!" The small-sized men's socks were still numerous sizes too big for me and when I pulled them up, they covered my knees. Behind me, two bulbous protrusions emanated from my calves, caused by the heels of the socks, and gave me a look of singular disfigurement. When I slipped my feet into my ski boots though, the transformation was surprising. Mum had sensibly bought boots for me in Stanley which were a whole size too big, so that I could grow into them. With Uncle Bonski's man-sized ski socks on my feet, the boots fitted much more snugly and made skiing easier. I neither thought nor cared about how I looked anymore.

I spent most of my days at Hope Point, singing my multiplication tables to myself as I climbed up the slope towards Shackleton's Cross and laughing with exhilaration as I sped downwards. I langlaufed around The Point, making it my own and I only went home for smoko, dinner and afternoon tea.

One afternoon after I had returned from skiing and Mum was feeding Gerald in the kitchen, there was a knock on the door. Mum shouted, "Come in!" but there was no response.

"Go and open the door, Bev." I pulled the door open and came face to face with an enormous Viking. I threw my head back and my upward gaze followed the contours of a full, bushy red beard, to look into deep blue eyes which in turn, were looking interestedly down into my own. The tall beard bent down towards me and the moustache twitched as it parted in a smile, revealing a missing front tooth.

"Hello. I am Eskedal. You like Kino?"

"Please come in!" Mum rose to meet the Viking and offered him her hand, "Would you like some coffee and cake?"

"I would like, yes please. I not speak English good. I come say - you like Kino?"

"I'm not sure if I like 'Kino' because I'm not sure what 'Kino' is! Can you tell me more about it, please?" Mum asked.

"Kino is film house. Bang, bang!" and Eskedal configured his two hands into guns and shot at us from the hip. "Dance," as he twirled on the kitchen mat in front of us, "Marilyn Monroe!" He threw us a kiss and finished in triumph.

"Oh, the cinema," Mum replied, " I love the cinema! Yes, I do like the Kino!" As we ate cake and drank coffee together, we explored the full extent of Torgeir Eskedal's English. He showed a lot of interest in the illustrations in my Hans Christian Andersen book and with many smiles and nods of the head, we made conversation and became firm friends.

"Kino tomorrow. I come six o'clock." Our date was made.

The following evening at six o'clock exactly, Eskedal knocked at our backdoor and Mum and I, wearing our best trousers and coats, walked with him down the new path to the jetty which the men on The Point had dug out. With great care, he handed Mum into the Pesca launch then lifted me in. I sat beside him and Eskedal, his fiery beard waving ever more wildly in the wind as we pulled further out into the harbour, let me help him steer the launch. When we arrived in Pesca, we drew up at the jetty near to the floating dock. Eskedal walked with us past the guano store and along a cleared path to the Kino.

"This path is so wide!" I exclaimed, gesturing with my arms at the width of the snow path,

"Tractor. Four tractor in Pesca. Good for path!" Eskedal replied, his smile appearing then disappearing beneath his undulating beard.

As we walked towards the yellow, two-storey wooden Kino, my eyes were drawn beyond it towards a beautiful little white wooden church nestling in the lee of the mountainside, its green steeple roof peeping out from beneath a bobble hat of white snow.

The Kino was built to seat three hundred people. Downstairs it was heated by a very efficient stove, creating a nice warm fug which enveloped us as soon as we stepped inside out of the cold.

"You go up, please," said Eskedal, gesturing towards some stairs to the left of the entrance, "I wait with you in guano shed." Before we could thank him, Eskedal was gone. I followed Mum up the stairs and to our surprise, we walked into a gallery with a projector, in front of which were rows of wooden benches, lined with bearded men, all wearing patterned, high-necked, woollen jumpers. As the 'over-winterers' turned as one to look at us, we felt very self-conscious and wondered whether we should be there at all. A man near to us stood up, asked if we wanted to see the film and when Mum smiled and said,

"Yes, please," he guided us to the front of the gallery where a balcony divided the upper floor from the main part of the Kino below. With gestures and fast Norwegian, our new friend instructed two men who occupied the best seats in the middle of the gallery, to vacate their seats and offer them to us. Gratefully, Mum and I sat down. I looked over the balcony rail down to the floor below which was packed full of bearded whalers sitting huddled together on long benches. A screen hung from the ceiling and rested on a low stage. To either side of the screen stood a three-foot high wooden carving of a king penguin, their bright yellow neckerchiefs adding a splash of colour to the uniform grey of the whalers' jumpers. Word was obviously spreading that females had come into the Kino and myriad pairs of eyes turned to look up at us. We felt even more exposed and were grateful when the lights went down and the film began.

This was the first adult film I had seen. When the title came up, Mum whispered

"'The Student Prince', this is my favourite film! I saw it in the town hall in Stanley. I love the singing of Mario Lanza!" In glorious technicolour and cinemascope, I stared intently at the screen as the hapless Prince was sent off to Heidelburg University to learn how to loosen up a bit. A low hum of chatter reverberated around us and when the reels were changed, there was an exodus for the door as the smokers went outside for a cigarette. When Prince

Karl met Kathie in the Biergarten, shouts and whistles exploded from the audience and heavy-booted feet stamped on the floor, causing the walls of the Kino to shake. Mario Lanza's pitch-perfect tenor was accompanied by a choir of raucous voices, following the tune several notes behind him. I soon forgot the film and leaned forward over the balcony rail to watch the men below me in the auditorium. When the Prince and Kathie made their tender farewell to each other, moans and expressive poking hand gestures suggested what the Norwegians thought he should be doing instead. When the Prince returned to the Palace to assume his royal duties and marry the Princess chosen for him, the audience left him in no doubt about what their opinion was. Even though the comments were all in Norwegian, I had a pretty good idea what the men's sentiments were even if I didn't understand fully what they were suggesting he should do in detail.

I had a wonderful time at the Kino. The film was exciting, the Prince handsome and the singing of Mario Lanza, magical. Watching the men on the floor below me only added to the fun and I couldn't wait for our next film! As he had promised, Eskedal was waiting for us beside the guano shed and he delivered us safely back across the harbour to our door. Dad was in the sitting room with a whisky, reading a yellow-covered back copy of past editions of the Daily Express newspaper which he had ordered from England. "Come in and have a whisky, Eskedal," but Eskedal asked for coffee and we sat around the kitchen table eating chocolate cake, as Mum animatedly described the plot of the film to Dad. Not a cinema goer himself, Dad showed little interest and said that he would babysit for Gerald whenever Mum and I wanted to see a film.

"We have two Kino every week, Pearl. I come when new picture to be seen every time," offered Eskedal, and our dates with him were made for the whole of the winter.

I was soon able to ski on the slopes of Mount Duse with the adults. They had created a piste from the base of the dam and, although Mum and I confined ourselves to the lower part of the slope at first, we were able to ski with the others quite confidently. Mum had been kitted out like me in Norwegian ski socks brought down for the younger and smaller mess boys to wear, a red knitted jumper decorated with large white stars and a matching red woolly hat. She left Gerald in Dad's care each afternoon and together, we skied for an hour, racing one another down the slope and laughing when we fell. When Mum went back to the house, I stayed on the mountain and became increasingly brave as my skills improved, climbing further and further up the mountainside towards the top of the piste at the base of the dam.

One morning after he had dropped the traffic into Dad, Uncle Bonski watched me ski down the mountainside then came to join me on the slope, instead of skiing past me with a cheery wave as he usually did.
"Norwegian girls do not ski with the snowplough, Beeve. I will show you how to ski downhill like a proper Norwegian girl. Watch me!" Uncle Bonski rapidly herringboned up the mountainside to the dam, digging his skis deeply into the snow to increase his traction. He turned to face downhill towards me and shouted,
"I come now! You see!" He skied straight down the mountain, his skis parallel, swivelling his hips to avoid the bumps in the snow.
"That was wonderful, Uncle Bonski, and so fast!"

69

"Each day, Beeve, I will ski with you and we will ski downhill with our skis together and go very fast. You will surprise your parents, I think!"

"But won't you get into trouble if you get back late to Pesca every day?"

"I will say to them that the transmitter has broke again and Peter cannot mend it. They will believe me. Ha! Ha!" Uncle Bonski's teaching style was somewhat haphazard. I had to follow him down the slope, keeping my skis parallel and moving my hips in time with his. Watching his hip movements and looking at the piste at the same time was testing and to begin with, I couldn't control either my speed or direction. I frequently hurtled off the slope at an angle, with my skis coming to a sudden halt and my momentum hurtling me face first into the soft snow.

"That is no good, Beeve, but you will be good soon, I know! Ha! Ha!" Uncle Bonski shouted, gliding effortlessly across the snow to help to dig me out of the snow pit which I was sinking deeper and deeper into as I struggled to get myself upright again and back onto my skis. After about half an hour, my lesson came to an abrupt halt as Uncle Bonski said,

"I must ski back now very fast so the boss will be happy. Goodbye, Beeve, we will ski again tomorrow!" With a cheerful wave, he set off along the track to Pesca. I watched him go, my eyes shining with admiration. His long and smooth langlaufing style and his parallel downhill speed were all I wanted to emulate. I had found my first hero on South Georgia.

This became the pattern of my days throughout our first winter. When the weather was clear and sometimes, when a little weak sun peeped over the top of the mountains above Pesca, I climbed up the mountainside, my skis moving to the rhythm of my chanted tables:

"Nine sevens are SIXTY THREE and ten sevens are SEVENTY, eleven sevens are SEVENTY SEVEN and twelve sevens are EIGHTY FOUR!" I sang at the top of my voice, trying to stretch the tables out so that I reached the base of the dam exactly on twelve 'somethings' which gave the exercise a nice, rounded feel to it and fitted in with my sense of neatness. At the base of the dam, I turned carefully to face down the slope, using my ski sticks and a snowplough to hold my position so that I could look out across The Point. Instinctively now, I searched the sky with a quick glance for signs that the weather was changing. Then I took my time and feasted my eyes on the white, smoothed out shapes of the houses and the undulations of the mossy mounds which hugged the base of the mountain below. I looked out across the ice as it clung to the shoreline and which extended further out into the harbour with each passing day. I looked across the harbour to Pesca, quiet and pristine, nestling in the lee of the mountains whose peaks shone in the sunlight and whose steep slopes were hidden in grey shade. The cross on top of the tiny spire of the church was just visible beneath a delicate snow-hat. Directly ahead of me, across Cumberland Bay, the mountains and glaciers glistened and sparkled and the Snow Queen rested in solitary splendour in her Ice Palace. Once I had surveyed my kingdom and had drunk in its peace and tranquility, I lifted my ski sticks up into the air and sped downhill, parallel skiing as fast as I could, my growing hair flying out horizontally behind me beneath my home-knitted bobble hat, as I hurtled towards the harbour and houses below. This was pure freedom and pure exhilaration. The world was full of beauty and absolute stillness. And it belonged only to me!

There came a morning when we were sitting at the kitchen table eating our breakfast and Dad was throwing multiplication questions at me.

"Three nines?"

"Seven fives?"

I was answering quickly and accurately enough to make him smile, and the thought entered my head that I should tell Dad the conundrum which Jack had caught me out with the day before. I knew how clever Dad was so I thought that he would be able to answer it straight away and that it would make him laugh! I wanted him to notice me even more and to think that I was clever too. I wanted all of this so badly that I blurted out

"Daddy, what goes over the water and under the water but never, ever, touches the water?"

Dad lifted his head and looked at me directly, the smile dying on his thin lips as they disappeared into his beard. Mum froze in the act of spooning porridge into Gerald's mouth. Even Gerald was caught in arrested motion, his mouth in a holding 'O', waiting for food which didn't arrive. As one second slipped into two, then three, my courage drained out through the soles of my feet and my body slumped deep into my wooden chair. With studied quiet, Dad said,

"I am sure I don't know, Beverley. You tell me." I swallowed and wished that I was anywhere other than where I was at that moment. I had misjudged Dad's mood and now I had to suffer the consequences. I delivered the punchline with as much panache as I could muster.

"It is an egg in a duck's tummy!"

"May I ask how you came to know this... er... conundrum?"

Now I was lost! I was going to get Jack into trouble too.

"Jack told it to me yesterday and I didn't get the answer. I thought that you might know it."

"Happily it is not something that I was aware of until now. Please be good enough to use your common sense and not repeat such things even if they are told to you. You haven't mentioned this to anyone else have you?"

"No, Daddy, not at all!"

"I am pleased to hear that, Beverley. We will keep it that way shall we?"

"Yes, Daddy." The breakfast table tableau sprang back into life. Mum took a deep breath and filled the 'O' of Gerald's mouth with porridge. Dad took a sip of his coffee and I bit a crumb from my toast, knowing that I could never swallow again. Once Dad left the table for the Wireless Room, I slipped on my coat and escaped into the conservatory to lick my wounds in solitude.

Wrapped in my coat in the conservatory, the wind outside howling in tune with my dry sobs, the thought came to me, striking in its clarity, that there was something about Dad's behavior that I needed to become more aware of and attuned to. The carefree days of fun and laughter which we had shared in Stanley had not been repeated on The Point. We walked hand in hand sometimes, now that the snow had formed a hard crust, but we never swung our arms and laughed together. Dad laughed and smiled with his friends and told them jokes. He exchanged loud and contentious words with them when they were discussing politics, especially when they had had a few too many drinks. But with me, my Daddy always wore his solemn, closed face beneath his bushy beard, even when I reached up on tiptoe to kiss him on his cheek at bedtime. His eyes never sparkled when he looked at me. I thought about this for most of the morning and finally decided that it must be because I was nearly six. If I was always 'seen and not heard', used excellent manners and spoke the 'Queen's English', then my Daddy would love me and be proud of me. Resolutely, I shook my head, stood up and walked into the kitchen for dinner where Mum was waiting to give me a big bear hug. When Dad came in from the Wireless Room to eat with us, I was sitting quietly at the table, hands neatly folded in my lap, an innocent expression on my face and a knowing gleam in my eyes. I knew how to behave and I was determined to show Dad that I could always be good. I promised myself that I would never tell a joke or a conundrum again.

Although his behavior towards me had changed, Dad seemed to treat Mum in the same way as he always had. He hugged Mum, called her 'sweet' sometimes, and on occasion, he gave her a peck on the cheek when he left the kitchen to walk down the passage to the Wireless Room to work. On one or two mornings I noticed a bruise or two on Mum's arms and once she had a swollen ear which she called her 'big cauliflower ear!' When I asked her how she had hurt herself, she said,
"You know your old Mum, clumsy as always," and I didn't think any more about it.

In the afternoons, Gerald had a nap and Mum and Dad often went to bed and had a nap too. I was far too energetic for that, so I langlaufed from the base of the mountain across the mossy mounds, covered in the deepest, softest snow, as far as Hope Point or even beyond, keeping close to the base of the mountain as I left the houses behind me. On my way back, I said hello to Shackleton as I skirted around his cross and skied down the nursery slope back to the house. My days were solitary in the main, but I loved the freedom and the silence of my compact, white world. On many days there was a little weak sunshine for a few hours, but as the winter progressed, the sun dipped for ever longer periods of time below the mountains until finally on the sixth of June, it slipped along the jetty and disappeared completely into the sea, and our world succumbed to monochrome grey. There was nothing to break the peaceful pattern except when the prevailing winds, blowing along Drake's Passage from around Cape Horn, kept me firmly indoors. Gales almost reaching one hundred knots were frequent. We were Falkland Islanders, used to high winds, but on those days when a gale struck, we stayed indoors, unable to block out its howls and laments and living under artificial light because the wind lifted whole banks of snow and hurled them against the windows, blocking out the natural daylight, such as it was.

On occasion, the weather was even more wild. Frequently, katabatic winds, resulting from cold air flowing down the valleys between the mountains, caused violent snow squalls. Whirlwinds, which we called williwaws, tore between the houses and blew themselves across the beach and onto the harbour. Their tracks were easy for me to follow from my vantage point at the sitting room window. Safe in the warm, hugging the huge radiator, I watched as the winds whipped the surface water into whorls and concentric circles, drawing vortexes into the air and hurling them towards Pesca. Then they wheeled, turned and tore back around the coastline towards the house, hurling snow at the windows with such speed and force that they became covered in a thick, dense white exterior curtain which changed my indoor world into a deep, dark one in seconds. An eerie twilight enveloped us as the williwaw swooped and howled around the outer corners and walls of the house like a Banshee in pain.

I was awakened one dark night by raised voices penetrating through the wall from my parent's bedroom. I lay in bed, straining my ears, trying to pick out the words that were being flung around in anger, but they were too muffled for me to be able to discern their meaning. Suddenly there was a mighty thump followed by a short, but high-pitched scream that obviously came from Mum. Then silence. I lay shock still, hardly breathing, knowing that something wasn't right but unsure as to what it was or what I should do about it. Usually, if anything upset me during the night, a violent dream about big, black bulls chasing me through Stanley perhaps, I would jump out of bed and run into my parent's room and scramble into their bed beside Mum where I would be comforted and safe. But tonight was different, somehow. I wasn't sure how or why it was different, but I had a strong sense of unease and was afraid to go into their bedroom. I was afraid of what I might find in there; afraid that Dad would be made even more angry by my intrusion when it was excrutiatingly obvious to me that he was already in high temper. I strained to hear any sound of movement, but failed to hear anything. For what seemed like hours I stood with my head against the bedroom door, my despair weakening my legs until I sank down in a heap and crawled to the mat where I lay inert, every sense heightened, until I heard their bed creak and someone quietly leave the next door bedroom. I waited until it was quiet again then pushed open my bedroom door just enough for me to squeeze through, and tiptoed along the passage. The kitchen light was on and as I peeped around the door, I saw Mum leaning over the sink, wetting a tea towel under the tap and using it to dab at her eye. Had it been Dad there, I would have tiptoed back to my room straight away, but as it was Mum, I walked into the kitchen and whispered,

"Mum, are you alright? What's wrong with your eye?" To my surprise and disconcertion, when Mum turned towards me there was blood streaming from a cut above her left eye, and enormous tears were pouring down her cheeks in a silent torrent. I ran to her and put my arms around her waist. Mum sank onto the nearest chair and I held her in my arms as she wept silently, her shoulders shaking with each racking sob. Near to my face was the tea towel and I watched in terrified fascination as its red bloodstain grew ever larger as Mum pressed it against her forehead. For long minutes we held each other until, eventually, Mum's sobs became little hiccoughs and then stopped altogether. She held the tea towel under the tap, wrung it out, and held it against her wound again, although by now the bleeding had nearly stopped. "Mum, did Daddy hit you?" I asked.

"Yes he did sweetheart, but it's nothing for you to worry yourself about. He just got a bit drunk that's all. He didn't mean to hurt your old Mum, you know. Now, let's both get back to bed. We both need our beauty sleep don't we?" and she gave me a weak smile. Hand in hand we crept silently along the corridor. Mum tucked me into bed and gave me a big goodnight kiss. I clung to her, my heart full of love for her, but bursting with fear and angry emotions against my father, emotions which I couldn't name. Mum left me and I heard her go into Gerald's room to check on him, then she crept into her own room and the house fell into an uneasy silence. I stayed awake for a long time, my ears still straining for any untoward noise, but the house remained calm and I eventually fell into a deep, uneasy sleep.

The following morning I sat quietly in my chair at the kitchen table, my hands neatly folded in my lap, waiting for Mum to serve our breakfast. Gerald gurgled happily but Mum and I didn't speak. Mum's left eye was swollen and an irregular cut stood out red and angry, the decoration on a balloon of purple bruising. When Dad came into the kitchen, smart as always in his freshly laundered white shirt and tartan tie, grey flannel trousers and highly polished shoes, all courtesy of Mum's hard work, he sat at the head of the table and ate his food silently. I kept my eyes lowered, not wanting to risk upsetting him in any way. After a tense breakfast, Dad put his arms around Mum, kissed her on the cheek and whispered something in her ear. Then he left to do the morning sched in the Wireless Room and Mum and I were free to relax.

"Mum, why did Daddy hit you last night?"

"When your Dad gets drunk, he gets angry and hits out at whoever is nearest to him, and that is usually me. It's nothing for you to worry about, sweetheart, your Mum is fine. Still, I want you to go up to Betty's and tell her that Mum is tired and she won't be coming up for smoko today. I don't want her seeing my eye like this if I can help it."

I walked up to Betty's house beside the jail and gave her Mum's message. Betty looked straight into my eyes and said,

"Tell your Mum that I'm coming down to her for smoko tomorrow no matter if she's tired or not." From the forthright way in which Betty delivered her words I was left in no doubt that she had an inkling that my message from Mum was a smokescreen. As I turned away, I thought I saw a sympathetic smile sweeten Betty's face, but she turned too quickly on her heel and walked back into her house, shaking her head and making her blonde pigtails dance.

As winter took hold, the harbour froze over quite quickly. Eskedal took his launch out every day to keep a passage open between Pesca and The Point and he usually popped into our house for a cup of coffee and some of

Mum's cake. On most days, the old whaling boats the *Sabra* or the *Bouvet* came round from Leith Harbour to keep a passage open between the whaling stations and to break the monotony of the days for the over-winterers. They often brought us a gift of some meat or bread and our kitchen regularly accommodated a large group of bearded men speaking a patois of broken English and Norwegian as they ate their way through mountains of Mum's cakes, or jam tarts with whipped cream which was their favourite.

"Pearl, we bring you tins of Morfat cream and jam and you make more?"

"Oh yes, if you bring the ingredients, I'll make more!" Mum replied. Our pantry wasn't large enough to store the sacks of flour, huge tins of jam, butter and cream which she was given and soon the cellar beneath was filled too. She baked every morning, expecting visitors, and we didn't often spend a day alone.

Now that Mum and I could ski competently, Dad tied Gerald to his back in a sling, and we skied round the harbour to Pesca as a family. As we reached Pesca, we skied up and over the raised wooden walkway which protected a rope of gigantic proportions. The rope was anchored into the mountain by vast metal bolts and stretched down to the water's edge where it was used as a mooring anchor for the large transport, tanker and cargo ships which would bring in supplies for Pesca from Argentina and the United Kingdom in the summer. The mooring anchor was secure enough to hold the ships during the regular gales. To our left, anchored against the Harpon Quay, were the snow-covered Pesca sealers and support boats, *Albatross,* *Petrel* and *Dias*. The *Dias* I knew about. She had been requisitioned by the Royal Navy during the First World War. As an armed trawler, she bravely hunted and sank several German U-boats before coming to Pesca. More exciting even than the *Dias* was the little huddle of houses directly before us. The first was the old bunkhouse then Dad pointed out a smaller house behind it, an old harpoon gun standing proudly in front of it, its contours softened by its snow shroud.

"That is the Manager's House, Beverley, where the Manager and senior staff live. Mr Butler is an Englishman and he has been the Manager at Pesca since 1955. In the last two years he has completely overhauled Pesca. You are now standing in the most modern whaling station in the world. Every part of the whale is used and thirty fin whales can be processed here every day. When the whalers are here in the summer and Pesca is working to its full capacity, it will be nothing like it is now."

To the right of the Manager's House was the small Bakery. Dad knocked on the door and we followed him in to the small wooden building.

Warmth and the smell of yeast tantalized our senses. Delicious aromas emanated from its every pore. Bread and pastries, the like of which I had never seen before, were offered to us on huge wooden trays. The baker spoke no English and we spoke no Norwegian, but we communicated with smiles and gestures. With a sticky bun in one hand and an even stickier pastry in the other, I offered my thanks politely as we left the store. We stood in the snow, savouring each delectable mouthful.

We carried our skis a few yards past the Manager's House and stood them up against the wall of a large, two-storey building on the right. This was the Slop Chest, the store where the men could purchase everything that they needed while they were at Pesca. Uncle Blom ran the Slop Chest and its opening hours were very irregular, especially during the winter.

"Come in! Come in! I will show you all!" Uncle Blom smiled. He led us through two floors of an Aladdin's cave. I couldn't open my eyes wide enough to take in all of the goods displayed there! Everything was stored in quantity. Mens' thick woollen jumpers with star or snowflake patterns, lay in cardboard boxes piled high. Heavy shoes and boots formed a mountain against the lower wall. Trousers, underwear, overcoats and leather gloves covered deep shelves. Another area displayed razors and toiletries, towels and writing paper. A whole wall was a treasure trove of good things to eat. Chicklets and Beech Nut chewing gum, liquorice hats, toffees, bars and boxes of chocolate of many varieties; and chunky rolls of marzipan coated in dark chocolate, glistened in shiny red wrappers. These were just some of the delights on offer. Uncle Blom presented Mum with a large box of chocolates with a gentlemanly bow.

"You would like some sweets, Beeve?" he asked me.

81

"Yes please, if I may."

"What would you like? You can have whatever you please." There was so much! How could I choose! I pointed to the liquorice hats.

"May I have some of those, please?"

"You can! You can!" and Uncle passed me a whole carton of sweets. I saw Dad look at me disapprovingly. I took my cue.

"Thank you very much, Uncle Blom, but I only meant to ask for a small packet of sweets, not a whole box."

"In my Slop Chest we have only boxes. Now you must have one more. I think you would like chewing gum, yes?"

"Thank you, I do like chewing gum but…" He handed me a carton of Chicklets. I had trouble holding both cartons in my hands they were so heavy.

"Thank you very much, Uncle Blom, you are very kind."

"You are spoiling her, Blom, and we don't want that!" Dad said, but he said it with a smile as he packed our gifts into his haversack, so I knew it was alright.

We put our skis on again and followed Dad in single file through Pesca, around the back of the guano store and the rear of The Plan, the hub of the whaling operation, to the Smithy where Strand was king. Dad knocked on the door and Strand, soot clinging to his chin and apron, opened the door to us.

"Come in! Come in! Very welcome!" he beamed. Taking Gerald from Dad, Strand led us into the Smithy. The heat hit me with immense force after the cold of the winter day outside. Flames from the fire emitted yellow and orange beams of light, making the grubby equipment glow like gold. Strand found Mum a chair to sit on and he handed Gerald to her.

"I will make coffee", Strand said, "you will see me!" He grabbed a huge pair of tongs and lifted a large stone into the fire. As soon as the stone glowed red, Strand removed it from the flames and set it down on the top of his anvil. As if by magic, he produced a coffee pot and stood it upon the red-hot stone. Within minutes, the coffee pot issued steam from its spout and the coffee was ready for drinking. Strand filled tin mugs with the steaming liquid and added generous dollops of sugar from a battered serving spoon. Even I, who didn't like coffee very much, drank down the sweet nectar with relish, feeling its warmth spread through my frozen limbs, giving them new life.

When we arrived back on The Point, I opened my wardrobe door and placed the two boxes of sweets on top of the other boxes which I had been given. Through the generosity of our Norwegian friends, I had already been given more sweets than any child could ever ask for or eat, and the over-abundance diminished my appetite for them. I closed the wardrobe door and walked away.

CHAPTER 5

A FAMILY IN WINTER

As the long winter progressed, there was very little for anyone on The Point to do. Traffic in the wireless room was light as there were no whaling ships for Dad to contact and few ships braved the wintry Southern Ocean. Maintenance work couldn't be done to the buildings as they were encased beneath their deep, snowy blanket. John worked hard in the power station to keep us supplied with enough electricity for light and permanent heating and Danny carried out his weather checks each day, but for everyone else, the days were very long and leisurely, and recreation came in the form of a beer, gin or whisky bottle. When the weather was too poor for me to ski, I stayed indoors and played with Gerald, or copied pages and pages from my book of Hans Christian Anderson stories. The men read books, drank their way conscientiously through their many cases of beer and spirits, and discussed and argued, sometimes in a friendly way, sometimes not.

As there were no other children for me to play with, the adults accepted me into their lives and I became obsessed with being able to do grown-up things so that I fitted in as well as I could. I listened to their stories and only spoke when I was spoken to. I copied the way the adults walked, talked and conversed with each other. I tried to hold adult conversations, asking each person about what they had done that day and trying to link what they were saying in with whatever else I had gleaned from others. It mattered on every level that I should be able to talk, read and write fluently so that I could join in more with the things that the adults did. I read the telegrams that I delivered around The Point for Dad, even though I knew that they were private to the person receiving them. They were my entry into the adult world and even though the content meant nothing to me, I strained to read every word that Dad had typed.

In the all-enveloping near darkness of our world, when even the white snow failed in its attempts to source enough light to reflect into our houses and our eyes, the radio was our savior. We could pick up Stanley Radio so Mum and Betty were able to keep up to date with Falkland Island news and gossip. Every evening Dad sat down in the sitting room to listen to the BBC World News, followed by a fifteen-minute episode of 'The Archers', a soap opera about a farming community in rural England. 'The Archers' were about as far removed from South Georgia as it is possible to be, but every day the adults chatted about what crops were being planted or harvested in Ambridge and if anyone did anything wrong or out of step, we asked, "I wonder what Dan Archer would think of that?" Several times a week the men and Mum and Betty and I got together in one of the houses for a social evening, swapping stories and having long discussions which occasionally ended in full-blown, heated arguments.

The least contentious topic of conversation which often came up early in the evening when the general feeling was mellow and relaxed, was the retelling of everyone's personal involvement in the royal visit to South Georgia. Last January the *Royal Yacht Britannia* had sailed into King Edward Cove carrying Prince Phillip, who was making a world tour. As the

Duke came ashore at The Point, the Pesca whale catchers, which had all lined up together, fired a twenty-one-gun salute from their cannons in his honour. "Couldn't see the catchers for smoke, Chay!" was Basil's comment. After everyone on The Point had been introduced to the Prince at a reception at the Magistrate's House, the *Britannia*'s launch took him across the harbour to Pesca where he watched several fin whales being flensed on The Plan before he visited Shackleton's grave in the cemetery. Mum and I were still in Stanley at that time, but together with the other children, I stood outside the Jubilee Villas waving my little union jack with gusto as Prince Phillip stepped ashore from the *Britannia*'s launch onto the public jetty to be greeted by the Governor, resplendent in his full dress uniform, the feathers on his plumed helmet dancing a spirited jig over his head in the wind. I was a little disappointed in Prince Phillip although no one took my feelings seriously when I voiced them. I thought that, as he was the Queen's husband, a Prince would be dressed much more grandly than the Governor was. To my dismay, Prince Phillip wore his naval uniform. He did look very smart and he sported a nice lot of gold braid, but the Governor in his uniform with the dashing red stripe up the leg and with masses of gold braid topped off with a tall helmet and feathers flying, outshone Prince Phillip completely.

One of the most lively topics which raged on and on, concerned the incident the previous year when a group of Argentine national activists came to South Georgia as crew on the Ryan ship, the *Harpon*, expressly to assert their country's claim over the island. They refused to fly the British flag of courtesy when they entered the harbour and also refused to supply a clean bill of health. The Magistrate was put in a quandary and Basil, Uncle Henry and the other men on The Point took up their rifles in readiness for a showdown with the Argentinians in Pesca. By some kind fate, the Royal Navy ice-patrol ship, *HMS Protector,* was within sailing range so the Magistrate gratefully called her in to assist him to restore order and the men on The Point stood down. *The Protecto*r, providentially again, was carrying a detachment of Royal Marines on board, and they were set ashore in Pesca and defused the situation very quickly. The Argentine activists were fined heavily and banned from ever returning to the islands. Dad was outraged by the incident (especially after a few drinks) and said that his .303 rifle was always at the ready,

" in case the buggers ever come back!"

Basil who had lived on The Point the longest, kept us entertained with lighter stories too and helped us to forget the numbing boredom of life lived under permanent electric light in a silent world where the tons of snow which enfolded each house like a giant's feather duvet, muffled even the loudest sound. One evening, lounging loosely in the armchair at a 'social' in our house, his pencil moustache and narrow upper lip forming an arc around his hand-rolled cigarette, Basil looked across at Dad and said,

"I'll tell you about your brother, Chay! Did you know that I had to lock the bugger up for shooting up the Met office? No? Well he did! It went like this…

Last year while the Marines were deployed in Pesca to keep the Argies under control, we weren't allowed to go round to the Kino or the Slop Chest or anything. Henry and a new bod called Ian who assisted Lofty in the Met office, were fed up with being stuck on The Point, like the rest of us were to be fair, so they hit the Old Glory rum one night, determined to get completely and utterly blasted! Henry is like yourself, Peter, a bloody good shot, which is why we had him in The Point Rifle Shooting Team and gave him a .303 too for practising with. By the early hours Henry and Ian were totally pissed, as well as being pissed off, and they decided that no bloody Marines were going to stop them visiting Pesca if they wanted to! Henry dug out his .303 rifle from under his bed and decided to go to war! He took a box of shells from the ammo store in the jail and they staggered over towards the jetty. At about two o'clock in the morning this was. Henry was so drunk by then that he couldn't hold the rifle steady so he rested it across Ian's shoulders and the crazy bugger held the muzzle only a few inches from Ian's head. Ian didn't care a damn but he was bloody lucky he wasn't killed!

Anyway, Henry shot off about thirty rounds across the cove towards Pesca but luckily he wasn't in range so he didn't worry the Marines and they never let on to us that they even heard the shots! Anyway, Henry got bored when the Marines didn't fire back so he changed his target to the navigation light, which was closer. You know the one, the one beside the Met office. Henry was so smashed that he didn't even manage to hit the navigation light once, but quite a few bullets screamed into the walls of the Met office and some hit the gadgets on the roof. The noise woke us all up and Spivey, who was the Magistrate then, and me took the crazy buggers off to the jail and locked them up. They were so completely drunk they could hardly walk and they were laughing like jackasses, both of them! Bugger me then, when Lofty crawled out of the Met office, white as a bloody sheet! He thought the Henry and Ian were out to get him and he said his last prayers! You had to laugh, him crouching down behind the desk while bullets flew past his head, too scared to say a word and thinking his days were numbered! Why he was in the Met office at that time of night I'll never know!

The next morning Spivey was ready to send them back to Stanley to stand trial on the charge of wanton destruction of Government property but as he had given Henry the rifle in the first place, I don't know how the charge would've stuck! Funny bit was though, Spivey and me, we'd locked them in the cell where the rifles and ammo was stored by mistake and Henry spent the next morning poking a rifle through the bars of the jail and threatening to shoot anyone's head off who came near! Silly bugger, but it gave everyone a laugh!

Anyway, Spivey kept them in jail though I never locked the door, then, as luck would have it, the *Magga Dan* arrived three days later with Vivien Fuchs onboard, on his way to Halley Bay to start his Trans-Antarctic Expedition. Fuchs agreed to try Henry and Ian and we set up a courtroom in the Magistrate's House all right and proper. He stood Henry and Ian to attention in front of the Union Jack and I had to read out the charge, all dressed in my best uniform, bib and tucker let me tell you! To cut a long story short, we made it seem more as if Henry had only been aiming at the beacon and not at the Marines and that only a few shots had hit the Met office. We didn't mention Lofty! They both pleaded guilty and Fuchs gave them a good telling off and fined them twenty quid each! Then the buggers were able to return to work and do some extra shifts to pay back for the time they'd had with their feet up in my jail eating Betty's best dinners and chocolate cake which she kept feeding them with!"

"Henry never told me about that!" Dad said.

"Ah well, just goes to show, Chay!" Basil replied, shaking his head, "Didn't want his big brother to know he was a jailbird! Ha! Ha! Ha!"

Although I watched Dad closely as he laughed and chatted happily with the adults on The Point and from Pesca, I could hardly remember my smiling Stanley Daddy anymore. Inside the Wireless House, my South Georgia Daddy was morose and moody, quick to use his hands and his tongue to hurt us. He was angry and grim and had to be watched surreptitiously for every nuance of mood change. He had to be humoured, placated and served all the time.

One evening after what he described as a particularly quiet and boring lunchtime sched in the Wireless Room, Dad drank his first double whisky as soon as he came into the kitchen. By the time Mum put Gerald to bed he was singing the chorus of the 'Eriskay Lovelilt' to himself and smiling,

"Bheir me o, horo van o
Bheir me o, horo van ee
Bheir me o, horo ho,
Sad am I, without thee."

As the evening progressed and Dad continued to drink, the peaty whisky darkened his features and his thoughts. He swore frequently,
"Fe farn!"
"Fe bloody farn!" banging his fist repeatedly against the arm of the sofa as impotent anger boiled up inside him and coursed through his brain, igniting the very tissue.
"Woman! Bring me another drink and hurry up about it!" Mum refilled Dad's glass. "Leave the bottle here beside me." I was playing with my dolls on the carpet at Dad's feet and I stood up and made beds for them in the other

armchairs so that I physically moved myself away from him and out of reach of those huge fists which were clenching and unclenching in a fearsome manner.

"Beverley, sit still! Stop moving about and annoying me! Fe bloody farn! A man can't follow his own train of thought."

"I'm sorry, Daddy, I'll sit still on this chair while my dolls have a nap." My ploy worked! I was out of his reach without making him too angry about it. The evening wore inexorably on and Dad swallowed his whisky in gulps. I sat completely still, not daring to make a noise and upset him again. Mum stayed in the kitchen out of harms way. Once dad had drunk himself into a stupor, his chin fell forwards and rested on his chest. The glass too, hung drunkenly forward in his right hand. I thought he was snoring softly. He hadn't told me to go to bed and I wasn't sure whether to leave the room or not. What would make him most angry, me staying up late or me going to bed without his permission? I was about to sneak out of the room when Dad's head shot up and whisky splashed from the glass.

"Pearl! Bring me a bowl." Now thoughts of right and wrong, what would make him angry or not, were abandoned. He was going to be sick! I couldn't bear it! Whatever the consequences, I abandoned my dolls, stuck my fingers in my ears, ducked down behind the sofa then fled from the room. I passed Mum in the passage as she ran into the sitting room clutching the washing up bowl. Though all sound was muffled by the covering hands over my ears and my bedroom door was firmly shut, I still heard the toilet flush as Mum emptied the contents of the bowl into it. Later still, I heard her help Dad along the passage and put him to bed where he snored loudly, making a noise like the ones that we had made in the playground in Stanley when we had played at being pigs in farmyards. I sat up in bed and tried to make sense of what was happening in our house. I could vaguely remember other times when Dad had hit Mum, but I had been too young to really understand the enormity of it. Mum didn't want other people to know so she was obviously ashamed about it, and I felt ashamed too without understanding why. But Mum never once criticized Dad to me and he always seemed to be genuinely sorry about it the next morning. I came to understand that husbands getting drunk and hitting their wives was obviously how marriage worked. I was able to accept that from my experience of my parents' marriage and I didn't question it. What I did question though, was Mum having to hold a bowl for Dad to vomit into then clean it all up afterwards. If that was what marriage meant then I promised myself there and then that I would never, ever get married. When I grew up I would get a good job and earn lots of money and look after myself. A spewing husband would be more than my soul could bear.

There were three great events for us to look forward to that winter, the Grytviken Indrettsforening, a hotly contested ski race at Pesca which took place every mid-winter in June, followed later by Winter Sports at both Pesca and Leith Harbour. Eskedal brought the motor launch across the harbour to pick us up on a crisp and clear morning. He still hadn't shaved since leaving Norway nearly a year before and his luxuriant red beard now reached right down to his waist. When he stood at the tiller, the wind caught and twisted it into a flaming corkscrew, which flew upwards and hid his cobalt blue eyes. When we had sailed out into the middle of the harbour, he let go of the tiller and said,

"There, Beeverley, you are the manager of the boat now!" I felt very important and grown-up as I took the tiller and basked in the warmth of his toothy smile.

When we arrived at Pesca a few minutes later, we walked up from the quay, past the guano store, the abattoir and the fuel oil tanks to the soccer field where the starting point of the race was. Uncle Bonski was waiting for us with all the other over-winterers. About twenty men were busily waxing the bottoms of their skis before fixing them to their feet and sliding them swiftly forwards and backwards in the snow to test their speed. The choice of wax was a great secret and each man did his utmost to hide from the other competitors which wax he had chosen to use. Snow conditions, whether wet, dry or powdery affected their choice, as did the terrain of the course itself which required sticky wax for the uphill climb to Gull Lake, but not for the downhill sections where friction needed to be at a minimum to allow the contestant to benefit most from increased speed. The men lined up, with the 'Racer Boys' at the front. These were the expert skiers who raced in Norway and were confident that they would complete the course in forty-five minutes. The older men and less experienced skiers from The Point lined up behind the Racer Boys, and at the Manager's command, they started off in a south-westerly direction towards the mountains. We watched as the skiers climbed the hill towards Gull Lake and then they disappeared from sight.

"We will not follow the others on our skis and watch them," said Uncle Bonski, "We will go to my room for something to drink and see them when they return." We trudged back along the path towards the New Barracks where Uncle Bonski had his room. Inside the building we followed him along a central passage with rooms leading off either side. Uncle Bonski's room had a small window, a single bed and a single chair. He disappeared into other rooms which were without their occupants and unceremoniously acquired two more chairs. We sat comfortably and Dad drew a half bottle of whisky from deep in his pockets and Uncle Bonski poured them each a liberal measure.

"Skol!," he said, raising his glass first to Mum and then to Dad. Uncle Bonski sat on his bed and noticed that my eyes were scanning the pictures of semi-naked women which papered the walls.

"Ah, I see you look at my women, Beeve. Do you like? Very beautiful eh?"

"They are all very beautiful, Uncle Bonski. Are they all friends of yours?"

"No, Beeve! But I wish! Here, look at this woman. This is my special woman, she is called Anita Ekberg and she is the most beautiful. She comes from Sweden and is, how do you say it, Peter, for Beeverley's ears?"

"She is a woman who is much admired for her physical beauty, Beverley. She is a pin-up for lots of men."

"She is a pin-up, yes! I pin her up too! Ha! Ha!" Uncle Bonski laughed loudly at his own joke and kissed each hand extravagantly in turn, blowing kisses towards Anita, whose voluptuous red lips smiled down at him from above his pillow, her smile failing completely to draw his eyes away from her magnificent bust-line for even one second.

Uncle Bonski led us from the New Barracks and we walked along the well-trodden snow path from the main building around the harbour towards the hydro-electric power house, and the wireless station.

"Look, Beeve, you can just see the first skiers coming back." Sure enough, in the distance I could pick out two or three matchstick men moving determinedly in our direction, following the shoreline.

94

"They skied up to the, how do you say it, Peter, the flat land?"

"The plateau."

"Yes, they ski up to the plateau where there is Gull Lake. They climb to nearly three hundred meters then they go around the south shore of Gull Lake towards the beach at Hestesletten. Then they turn back to Susa Point, about sixteen kilometres for all."

"That's about ten miles," Dad explained, "I'll take you to Gull Lake for a picnic in the summer. We'll walk to the beach at Hestesletten too, it is one of the main breeding beaches for elephant seals and king penguins."

"And now we see the skiers on the last foot!" Uncle Bonski shouted, "Shout for them Beeve!"

"On the last leg," Dad said, correcting Uncle Bonski's use of colloquial English.

"On the last leg? I think the last foot is better! Ha! Ha! Now Beeve, we will shout for them to ski back very fast!" We joined the crowd as they ran alongside the skiers who were clearly tired and were straining over the last metres to reach the finishing line back at the soccer field. We shouted encouragement and waved our arms in the air. After a few minutes, I thought I heard among the Norwegian words, the word 'fart'. I knew what a fart was and I thought the Pesca men were being very rude to encourage the skiers on by telling them to fart. Obviously Mum heard it too because she whispered to Dad,

"Why are they using that word?"

"In Norwegian it means 'go faster'," Dad said. That explained it then, but we all shouted encouragement with polite English phrases like,

"Keep going!"

"Don't give up!" and,

"Come on! Come on!" rather than join in with the Norwegians who were shouting

"Fart! Fart!" Loudly and in unison. When the first man arrived back at Pesca, Uncle Bonski lost interest in the race and we trooped back to his room.

"So, no Falkland Islander won the British Ski Race this year, hey Peter? You did not want to be like your brother?"

"No. Skiing isn't really for me, Bonski. But if Henry had been here, he'd have walloped the lot of them again!"

"Why would Uncle Henry have walloped them, Daddy?"

"Last year your Uncle Henry entered the ski race. Nobody gave him a cat in hell's chance but he won the prize for the best British entrant, beating all the Englishmen and the one Australian from The Point and they were furious! They didn't want a Kelper beating them! We'll never let them forget it! Ha! Ha!"

After we had eaten lunch with the Pesca men in the Mess, we gathered below the ski jump or 'skihopp'. This was built high in the mountainside near to the church and groups of men were stamping down the snow on the jump itself and in the landing area below to pack it very firmly. Eighteen men entered the competition. They herringboned high up into the mountainside to the jump and I held my breath as, one by one, they crouched down on their skis and hurtled towards the end. They threw themselves forwards into the sky, bodies straight and their hands pinned to their sides. They flew through the air for up to forty-five metres then landed, either in a heap of flying skis and tangled legs, or like a graceful bird, touching down without disturbing the snow, legs bent in a graceful curtsey and arms held out to the side. Most of the ski jumpers were the young men who worked in the galleys and barracks, caring for the older over-winterers who were more experienced whalers, but some were serious competitors who competed in high-level competitions in Scandinavia. The boys were handsome and lithe, and I fell in love with them all.

Leith Harbour held the Inter-Station Winter Sports soon after and Mum and I were invited to go with Dad and everyone else from The Point. We were to be picked up by the *Sabra* at six o'clock in the morning. Still sleepy, I stood on the jetty holding Dad's hand as the little, old, puffing *Sabra* stopped briefly against our jetty without tying up after she had collected the Pesca men from across the harbour. It was a windy, dank day with low cloud swirling around us as we waited on the jetty. The *Sabra* danced in the choppy sea and we had to be carefully helped aboard as her sides were dipping up and down and simultaneously tilting towards then away from the jetty. As we sailed out of the relatively sheltered cove into Cumberland Bay, the *Sabra* began to roll heavily and the sea broke over her bow, sending cold seawater swirling along her narrow deck. Sea spray stung our eyes and chilled our exposed faces.

"You will please use my cabin, Pearl," *Sabra's* Captain invited and we followed him as he carried Gerald down below into a small cabin fitted with a bunk, a folding table and a sink. The *Sabra* was an old steamship and the heat from her engines and the smell of burning fuel hung heavily in the air of the cabin and churned my stomach. Mum, who unaccountably was fine, told me to stop thinking about it and concentrate on the fact that we would be at Leith Harbour within the hour.

"Mummy, please let me go up on deck. I'm feeling sick and I can't bear it if I'm sick. Please let me go up and get some fresh air."

"You will stay where you are, Beverley. It's much too dangerous for you to go up on deck in this weather and I can't leave Gerald alone to go up with you. You'll be fine. We'll be there before you know it." But I wasn't fine. Fight it as I might, the contents of my stomach refused to lie low and they pushed their way burningly up my oesophagus and exploded in a multicoloured gush into the cabin sink. I kept my eyes screwed shut so that I didn't have to see the vomit and I turned my head away as soon as I could to remove my nostrils from the source of the acrid smell. Mum held me and comforted me.

"Never mind, darling, you'll feel better now!" But I didn't and I was sick again before we pulled alongside the jetty at Leith. I vowed never to go to the winter sports again if I had to travel on the *Sabra*. I christened her the disgusting ship.

Leith Harbour was much like Pesca in layout. Built as a working whaling station its processing areas were similar with rusty tin sheds protruding in a seemingly haphazard pattern out through the snow. When we arrived at the station we walked down a wide path which Dad said was called Pig Street, to the Manager's Villa for breakfast. The food was hot, smelled delicious and was plentiful. I sat with my face turned away from the table, trying to think of anything but food. My stomach was still churning and I was determined not to let any morsels pass my lips until I got back to The Point. That way, if there was no food in my stomach, I couldn't possibly be sick on the homeward journey.

After the cross-country race was concluded, we ate with the men in the Villa again and I persuaded Mum not to make me eat anything, protesting that I was still feeling unwell whereas, in reality, I had been feeling fine for ages. Mum, always keen to learn about anything culinary, noticed an ingenious implement for cutting cheese. Uncle Bonski was sitting next to her and, when he offered her the cheese board, she took the implement and commented,

"I've never seen a cheese knife like this before. How does it work?"

"If I can show you please?" Uncle Bonski said and, holding the handle, pulled the leaf-shaped blade flat across the top of a hunk of cheese. A thin sliver of cheese appeared through an inverted slit and sat neatly on top of the blade. Uncle Bonski tipped it onto Mum's plate.

"I see how it works now," Mum said, "there is a nick cut into the blade which slices the cheese thinly. It's excellent. I've never seen a cheese slice like that before!"

"We have them in Norway all the time. I will ask one for you if you like?"

"I would like that very much. Thank you Bonski!" Mum's day was made!

That night we had a smoother trip back from Leith Harbour. When we got home, Mum put Gerald and me to bed and the men congregated in Discovery House for an impromptu party. Mum stayed to care for Gerald and me, and we had been fast asleep for several hours when we were both awakened by Dad stumbling noisily along the passage and swearing loudly. "Fe bloody farn! Where are you, woman? Can't a man expect to come home and at least be looked after by his bloody wife?" Mum got out of bed and I heard her open their bedroom door.

"I've been asleep, Peter. It's two in the morning, you can't expect me to wait up all that time for you."

"Yes I bloody well can! I'm working every bloody day to keep you and all you have to do is look after the house and feed me, so why is it too much to ask you to stay up and wait for me to come home? Pray tell me, I can't wait to hear your excuses!"

"I'm not making any excuses, Peter. Now, let me help you to get into bed."

"Don't be so bloody rough, woman!" and I heard Mum cry out in pain. I jumped out of bed and crept into the passage. I knelt outside their bedroom door, straining to hear every sound, shaking with fear but too frightened for Mum to be able to get back into my own bed again.

"Fe bloody farn! Nobody knows what I have to put up with. Isn't Pearl lovely, they all say. They wouldn't think you were so bloody lovely if they knew what I had to put up with from you."

"Just keep still, Peter. There, now you can get into bed."

"Don't you tell me what to do in my own bloody house!" Crack! I heard the sound of Dad's fist hitting Mum. I sensed that she had fallen backwards onto the floor from the dull thud that her body made as it hit the carpet. I wanted to run into their bedroom and see if Mum was alright, but I was too afraid of making Dad's temper worse, he could do anything when he was in this mood. I knelt in the passage, my body rigid with fear, my eye trained on the small gap in the door but unable to see anything. For long minutes I waited. Mum was silent and so was Dad. What was happening? Silence was worse than noise. At least when they were talking I knew that Mum was alright. What did the silence mean? Was she too hurt to speak? Had he killed her? I waited and waited. I got cramp in my legs but was too frightened of making a noise to move them. I was getting cold but was too afraid to creep back to my bedroom and fetch something warm. Eventually, I heard Dad snore. A gentle nasal snort as he inhaled, was followed by a full-throated grunt as he exhaled alcohol-laden air through his slack, open mouth. If Dad was asleep then I could creep into their room. As I gently pushed the door open, I could see Mum lying prostrate on the floor. I crept across to her and cradled her head in my arms. She opened her eyes but her look was dazed and it took several minutes for her to focus clearly on my face.

"Help me to get up," she whispered. Using all my strength, I helped her to her feet and we stumbled crazily from the room. We staggered uncertainly towards the kitchen and Mum sank down gratefully into a chair.

101

"Bev, get me some water please." I filled a glass from the tap and helped her to hold it in her shaking hand. She took small sips of water and appeared to find strength from it.

"I think he must have knocked me out that time. I'm going to have another shiner over my left eye tomorrow. I wish he wouldn't drink so much. When he does, he doesn't know his own strength."

"I hate it when he hits you, Mum. He shouldn't do it! You're smaller than him and it isn't fair. I thought he might have killed you tonight because I couldn't hear you making any noise."

"Life isn't fair, sweetheart, but your Dad is a good man really. You never need to worry that he will kill me, your Mum is made of strong stuff. Now come on, let's both get back to our beds. I've got a splitting headache and I need some rest before your brother wakes up." We hugged and kissed goodnight in the passage and went into our separate bedrooms. Relaxed now that I knew that Mum was safe, I curled up beneath the blankets and was soon asleep.

I developed a habit of sleeping very, very lightly. Whenever I heard noises from Mum and Dad's bedroom, I crept into the passage and crouched down on the floor so that I could listen outside their door. When Dad finally fell asleep, Mum always came out to see if I was there and to reassure me that she was alright before tucking me up in bed again. We both became attuned to Dad's drunken outbursts and knew which nights were likely to be bad ones. On those nights until they went to bed, I kept myself awake by tiptoeing out into the passage and straining my ears for every nuance in Dad's voice, assessing how good or bad his mood was from the tone of his voice and the number of 'Fe farn's'. The fear engendered from listening to

102

what Dad was doing to Mum and being unable to do anything about it, filled my little body with emotions so strong that I physically shook from head to toe and was unable to control the shaking until, once he had fallen asleep, Mum appeared and gave me a strong and unequivocal hug to let me know that she was safe and we could both creep back into our beds and close our eyes and slumber.

Gerald was beginning to crawl around the house and he was becoming fun to play with. He was generally a very happy and calm child but sometimes he would throw a paddy as Mum called it and cry loudly for what seemed like an eternity. Dad lost his temper whenever Gerald began to cry.

"Stop that bloody racket, woman!" as if it was Mum who was making the noise. Mum and I devised a plan between us to keep Dad happy and undisturbed. Whenever Gerald wanted to have a cry I carried the screaming little boy, his arms flailing and hitting wildly against my chest, into the Billiard Room and tried to placate him there. The concrete floor was uncomfortable to sit on but his cries couldn't be heard in our part of the house, so Mum found me some old cushions and pillows which I used to make a comfortable nest behind the door. The Billiard Room had the advantage of being somewhere where few people ever went and, sitting behind the door which opened into it, even passers-by who were going into the Wireless Room wouldn't see me as they walked past. Gerald had several toys which I entertained him with, but his great love was his panda. Panda was almost two-dimensional, he was so flat. Two arms stuck out from his upper body at right angles and two legs stuck out from his lower body at forty-five degrees, all in the same plane. When Gerald was standing in profile, clutching panda to his side, panda almost disappeared. But panda had lovely brown glass eyes and a smiling black mouth embroidered onto his white face and Gerald would not go to sleep or be comforted unless he had panda clutched to his chest.

John had worked through the last few months dismantling the old generator and removing it from the Generator Room into the power station. Now that the room was empty, awaiting the arrival of a table tennis table on the first boat in of the summer season, the new Recreation Room was cleaned, redecorated and prepared for a mid-winter party. Dressed in my best blue net frock, my white open toed canvas shoes newly 'Blancoed', I helped Mum and Betty to lay out the food on top of the heavy canvas cover over the snooker table. The record player had been brought down from Discovery House and as soon as the Norwegians arrived, the party got into full swing. Elvis got us all dancing and Mum and Betty and I stood up for every dance so that all of the men got at least three turns on the dance floor. Happy, tired and exhilarated, I stood in a circle with the adults at midnight as they raised their glasses and toasted the turning point of the winter and looked forward to spring returning to The Point.

For the first time, a ship was coming to South Georgia during the winter. The Falkland Island Company decided to send their new ship, the *RMS Darwin* down with supplies for The Point. She braved the stormy winter seas and we were all very excited as Dad charted her way south. From the moment she arrived and tied up at the jetty, our house was filled with noisy men, all seeming to talk and laugh at the same time. The *Darwin* stayed overnight, just long enough to unload her cargo and for the men to have a party with us at Discovery House. Mum and Betty had been baking for days and they were in their element, soaking up all the news and gossip from Stanley. I was given a huge box of Dolly Mixtures, specially ordered by Mum, and I was in seventh heaven.

July fourth was my sixth birthday and Dad and Mum threw a party in my honour. I woke to a miserable day, grey skies and low, misty cloud. I wasn't going to be able to go out on my skis, so I faced a day indoors playing with Gerald. When I got up and walked into the kitchen, Mum and Dad each gave me a hug and a kiss on the cheek.

"Happy Birthday, Beverley! Your mother and I have a present here for you." On the table beside my plate was a narrow box, covered in brown paper and tied with a piece of string. I sat down and opened the gift. Inside was a watch with a silver face and a black leather strap.

"Thank you Mummy and Daddy, this is exactly what I wanted!" I was ecstatic, this was the sort of present big girls had. I kissed my parents and Dad put the watch on my wrist.

"Her wrist is too small, Pearl. Pass me a sharp knife and I'll make another hole in the strap so that it does up securely." Dad laid the watch on the table in front of him and forced the point of the knife through the leather.

"There! That's better. Now you will always be home on time for your meals and your mother will be able to stop worrying about you!" Now I wouldn't have to rely on my stomach to tell me if it was a mealtime, or on darkness falling to tell me when I should be getting home. Now I had a watch of my very own. I felt very grown up.

For my birthday party, Dad shaved off his beard and Mum baked a rich fruit cake which she iced and surrounded with a frilly paper band. She secured the ends of the band together with a hair grip because the dollop of icing sugar she tried to secure it with wouldn't set. She put six candles on my cake and gave it pride of place in the middle of the kitchen table. I was disappointed, but tried hard not to show it. It was nice that I had a cake, but it looked so bare with just flat, white icing on the top. I didn't want to say anything to upset Mum when she was working so hard to make the rest of the party food, but I did wish that she had decorated it.

At seven o'clock the guests began to arrive. Everyone brought me a gift; all of the gifts were cartons of chocolates, liquorice hats or marzipan bars. I piled them high on the draining board in the kitchen until it resembled a sweet shop. Last to arrive were Uncle Bonski and Uncle Blom.

"Happy Birthday, Beeverley. We bring you Chicklets chewing gum and chocolate," laughed Uncle Bonski.

"And we bring you some special fruits for your birthday cake," said Uncle Blom. He extended a flat, cardboard box towards me and dramatically threw open the lid to reveal fruits of many kinds, apples, oranges, bananas and pears, all made from marzipan. The baker in Pesca had tried his best to colour the fruits with varying degrees of success. The yellow bananas were a light shade of orange, but they looked good. The oranges were a much deeper shade of orange than the bananas, garish and bold. The green apples and pears were a sight to behold. The baker must have found a bottle of green cake colouring somewhere in the back of a cupboard and he had obviously painted the fruits liberally with it. The apples and pears shone bright green and fluorescent in the box like the numerals on a luminescent watch. Uncle Blom and I ceremoniously placed the fruit strategically on the top of my cake. When everyone had arrived and had a drink in their hand, Dad lifted me up to blow out the candles while they sang "Happy birthday,

106

dear Beeverley, happy birthday to you!" Mum cut the cake and I handed it round. On a separate plate I carried the marzipan fruits, hoping that they wouldn't all go and that I'd have more left than just the choicest banana which Mum had put aside for me. I was surprised when only a few bananas and oranges were taken. All of the green fluorescent pears and apples were left for me. It never occurred to me to wonder why!

During the party, Blaze worked his way round the room, being stroked and patted by everyone, purring with pleasure and arching his back to enjoy the stroking even more. Uncle Bonski dipped his fingers into his beer and bent down so that Blaze could lick his fingers dry. This quickly became a party game and, as Blaze wandered around the room, he waited patiently beside each person for their fingers to appear at cat level, dipped in either beer, gin or whisky. Soon the novelty wore off for the adults and Dad pushed back the furniture and put 'I'm All Shook Up' and 'Blue Suede Shoes' on the record player. When we stopped dancing for Mum to pass round her famous Falkland Island sausage rolls, I asked Uncle Bonski to do his party trick for me. He duly sat on the floor, legs outstretched and pulled himself up to a standing position without spilling a drop of his precious whisky.

"But look at Blaze," Uncle Bonski laughed, "he is peessed too! You will see!" He slipped his hand under Blaze's tummy, scooped him up and stood him on the back of the sofa. This was Blaze's favourite place to play, he liked to run along the back of the sofa for its full length then spring off the end on to the easy chair in the corner. Blaze took a tentative step, his front paws slipped and lost their purchase and his head unceremoniously fell forwards and his chin came to rest on the back of the sofa. His rear end and bushy tail stuck in the air for a few seconds, then his back legs gave way too and he was stranded, paws hanging limply on either side of the sofa back. He looked at the surrounding company with glazed eyes, sagging whiskers and an unconcerned air then closed his eyes and lay still, happily purring.

Everyone burst into raucous laughter! Uncle Bonski lifted Blaze back onto his feet and he forced open his eyes and tried to walk again. His legs failed to move forward in any coordinated way and in a sudden rush, they splayed out as he flopped back down on to his stomach. He tried to lift his head but thought better of it. Docile and sozzled, he gave us a sleepy grin then rested his head on the sofa back and promptly fell asleep.

"Beverley, you had better take Blaze and put him to bed in the conservatory," Dad instructed. I lifted Blaze carefully in my arms and carried him to his favourite cushion where he curled up in a furry ball to sleep it off.

During the rest of that week, Mum limited me to eating three marzipan fruits a day, to include only one apple or pear. With only one green fruit, I was still consuming enough food colouring to dye my mouth and teeth bright green. As I was beginning to lose my milk teeth and had a few large gaps in my toothy grin, the green fluorescence added to my ghoulishness and whenever I smiled, all the men pretended to be frightened of me and ran away. After all the marzipan fruits had been consumed, it was still several days before my mouth and teeth lost their greenish hue and returned to their original, healthy pink colour.

A few days after my birthday, we walked out on to the snow with Dad and we watched together as the merest arc of pale orange rose above the mountains behind Pesca then slipped silently away, giving us a tantalising glimpse of the spring that was to come. Winter was drawing to a close. The snow began to melt and skiing became difficult as my skis stuck in the soft snow and wouldn't glide anymore. Unlike the new bungalows which were fully insulated and triple glazed, our old house lost heat and as the temperatures outside began to rise, snow on the roof melted during the day. Huge icicles dripped tears of clear, pure water onto the compacted snow beneath. At night the water froze and huge trees of ice formed all around the house, capturing us inside a forest of thick trunks. Their gnarled and knobbly roots stretched out across the snow like huge hands and the fingers grew longer each day as they searched for prey to capture for the Snow Queen. As the thaw continued, the icicles broke away from the roof and fell to earth with a muted thud. During the winter I had only been allowed to use the ski path around the harbour to Pesca if I was accompanied by an adult, because avalanches happened periodically along the route. Now avalanches were more frequent and Dad banned me from skiing on Mount Duse so I could only ski from Shackleton's Cross on Hope Point. Whenever I heard the loud 'crack!' which precipitated an avalanche, I ran into the conservatory and looked out across the harbour to watch as huge blocks of snow, like icebergs, slid slowly at first, then with increasing speed, down the mountainside. They were followed by a cascade of snowballs, some tiny and others of enormous size. Countless tons of snow came to rest on the narrow path at the base of the mountain, but much of it plummeted into the sea. The harbour lost its neat, circular quality. Instead, the edge of the harbour became ragged with promontories of deep snow which took weeks to melt in the ice cold waters.

When rat-infested sealing ships came down to South Georgia over a hundred years ago, some brown rats escaped ashore. By now, the population had exploded and they lived amongst the tussac bogs, feeding on the succulent roots of the leaf bases which provided them with a plentiful supply of food throughout the year. Our house was built on a brick base with a double floor which the rats used as a running track. At night I lay in bed listening to them as they scuttled about beneath my bedroom floor. As the deep snow began to melt away from the sides of the house, yards of inter-connecting cylindrical tunnels which criss-crossed beneath the surface, became visible. If I stood very still at my bedroom window and waited patiently, I could sometimes spy a large, brown rat as it poked its nose out of the end of a snow tunnel, only to find to its consternation that the remainder of the tunnel which had been there only days before, had now disappeared. With a disdainful twitch of their noses, the rats turned around in the narrow space, momentarily dangling their tails out of the tunnel, before scurrying away into the snowy depths. Walking along by the edges of the snow wall as

110

it continued to melt, I once came across a much wider hole in the snow. As I pushed my face into the hole to look more closely, I found myself staring into a snow chamber, stained yellow-brown, its floor littered with large brown dollops of smelly rat pooh. I quickly pulled my head back and retched as much from the thought of what I had seen as from the actual smell. That evening when we were eating our supper at the kitchen table, I told Dad what I had seen.

"Rats are actually quite clean in their habits," he told me, "what you found was a deserted toilet, which is properly called a faecal chamber. By keeping their waste well away from their nests, the rats keep their homes very clean and free from disease. You should think of what you saw as being interesting rather than disgusting. You can't expect animals to have flushing lavatories, can you?"

"No, Daddy, you can't. I'll try to look at the rats in a better way from now on."

"In a more scientific way, Beverley. Use your eyes and ears and think carefully and logically about what you see around you while you live down here. Remember, living in South Georgia is an experience that few children get, so make the most of it."

"I will, Daddy, I promise."

CHAPTER 6

SPRING AT LAST!

I was playing on the shore one early spring afternoon when I felt unusually warm. The oxygen seemed to have been sucked from the atmosphere and it was stifling. From it being a calm day, the wind began to blow quite strongly down the mountainside. Mindful of Dad's admonishments, I decided I'd better go back to the house. By the time I had reached the conservatory, high winds were tearing down from the mountains, whining and howling and whipping the harbour into a cauldron. Then, in front of my eyes, as if by magic, the snow began to melt. In an afternoon several inches of snow disappeared completely! The white snow path to Pesca was transformed into a grey shingle one; tussac bogs were displayed in all their spiky, green glory and the undulating hillocks which had borne signs of old ski marks were now glistening with damp green moss. Snow still hung on to the top and in the crevasses of Mount Duse, but from our house across to the lower slopes of the mountain, the vista was green. I ran from the sitting room into the Wireless Room where Dad was working.

"Daddy! Daddy!" I waved my arms excitedly in front of him until he took his earphones off.

"Daddy! The wind blew and the snow melted! It all melted right in front of me! It's all gone!" Dad walked to the window and looked out towards the mountain.

"The snow-melt was caused by a fohn Wind, Beverley, F-O-H-N! Weather systems cross the ocean from the Antarctic continent, hit South Georgia and pass over the mountains dropping their snow. The winds then become very warm. By the time they get to The Point, fohn winds can reach gale force and because they're so warm, they can melt snow and ice. Actually, now that you know the explanation behind it, fohn winds are one reason why I want you inside the house when weather systems come in." I nodded in understanding as he walked back to his desk. The wind was still blowing a gale and it had completely transformed the landscape. The fohn wind had given me a new South Georgia to explore. I went back to the conservatory and watched until bedtime, waiting for the wind to blow itself out.

The next morning dawned bright, sunny and completely calm. From my bedroom window Mount Duse sparkled as streams, swollen from the melting snow, fell in cascades down the mountainside. I put on my dress, coat and wellington boots and ran along the new stony path which skirted the shore towards the base of the mountain. About fifty yards from the house, and in sight from my bedroom window, the now fully exposed hulk of a white motor boat rested just above the path, its stern pointing out to sea. The hulk lay on one side at an angle of about thirty degrees. I clambered onboard and walked around the small deck. There was a window space in the wheelhouse where the steering wheel had once been and which looked directly over the bow. The cover to the hatch on deck was loose and when I lifted it and looked inside, I could see that the hull was clean and empty. I could have lowered myself down inside the hull but I couldn't see how I could pull myself up again to get back out. I spent the day being skipper of my own ship. I christened her the *Snowgoose* after Uncle Colin's motorboat

113

in Stanley and I took her for her maiden voyage around the coast of South Georgia to garner essential supplies for The Point. I made brave forays ashore against enormous odds and tore out tussac grass stems so that we could eat their succulent and nutritious bases as Dad told me that Shackleton's men had done. I stored my harvested supplies in piles around the deck.

That night at supper Dad clearly hadn't been drinking, so I asked him if I could please have his permission to play on the boat. He raised no objection so, emboldened by his seeming good humour, I asked him if there was something I could have to stand on to get into and out of the hull. To my surprise, Dad said he would walk over to the boat with me after supper and see what he could do. I sat on the carpet at his feet while Dad drank his cup of instant Camp coffee with three spoonfuls of condensed milk stirred into it and asked him if he knew what the boat was called. He told me that nobody was sure what the origins of the boat were, but she may have been the predecessor to the *Resolution*. He stood up, took me by the hand, which thrilled me, and we went out through the conservatory door towards the boat together. Dad climbed up onto the deck and looked down into the hull. "This would be a safe place for you to play, Beverley, and you could keep out of the wind inside the hull. I know exactly what you need. Come with me!" Holding my hand again, Dad and I walked back to the house. In the support room where the transmitters and spares were kept, Dad also kept cases of beer and a few of whisky which he called his 'working supplies'. He emptied the whisky bottles from one wooden case, took a hammer and banged the nails back into place, once more securing the lid.

"This is just the thing!" Hand in hand again, we retraced our steps back to the boat. I was in seventh heaven! I was spending time alone with Dad and he was chatting happily to me about what games I could play and what name I could give to my boat.

"I would like to call her the *Snowgoose* because she's all white."

"A good name," said Dad, as he dropped the wooden case into the hull.

"Get down into the hull then show me if you can get back up safely, Beverley." I lowered myself through the hatch very gingerly, trying to demonstrate how careful I could be. The wooden case made a secure step to stand on and from it, I was able to pull my upper body back up over the lip of the hatch and wriggle my way back out onto the deck.

 "Do you see those pieces of metal in the ground there, Beverley?" I looked to where Dad was pointing. About four feet in front of the bow of the *Snowgoose*, surrounded by tussac, three large triangles of sharp iron partly buried in the earth and arranged in a circular pattern, jutted dangerously

115

upwards. The tallest piece of metal was about eight inches high, viciously pointed and sharp.

"Yes, Daddy."

"You must always walk round her stern and not the bow so that you keep a safe distance away from those metal shards. If you fell onto either of those pieces of metal, you could be killed or badly maimed. "

"Yes, Daddy. I'll take good care. I promise."

"Good girl! Actually, those pieces of metal are part of an old 'Try-pot' which was used by the sealers to melt down blubber. Interestingly, most of the Try-pots were made in England in a foundry in London then shipped out here. When they are in one piece they look like a witches cauldron. We will see some when we go round to Pesca. Now I'm going back inside. You can play here if you want to." With that, Dad walked back to the house and I was dismissed. But dismissed in a kind way and given permission to stay out for a bit longer! I practised getting into and out of the hold of the *Snowgoose* and soon became adept at it. I returned to the house shortly afterwards, not wanting to annoy Dad by taking advantage of his good mood. Inside, Dad and Mum were sitting together on the sofa, Dad's arm around Mum's neck, listening to a crackly Stanley Radio Station. It seemed a good idea to say that I was tired and that I would get into bed by myself. I thanked Dad again for his kindness and gave him a kiss on the cheek above the shoreline of his bristly beard, then left the room, only rubbing the scratchiness of his whiskers from my face when I was sure that he couldn't see me. When Mum popped in later to give me my goodnight kiss, I observed that Dad seemed to be in a good mood.

"He is, darling, he hasn't had a drink all day. Let's try to keep it that way. Goodnight!" and she went out, leaving the door ajar as always. I went straight to sleep. I had no need to stay awake and listen for them arguing tonight.

I learned to like fohn winds. They could hurtle you from the jetty to a certain death in the icy sea beneath if you let them, but they could be lighter and quite friendly too. When I heard one coming, my favourite game was to run as fast as I could across the stony path from the conservatory to the Snowgoose, stand on tiptoe in the wheelhouse and stick my head out through the glassless window of the bridge, shouting and singing in tune with the wind, at the top of my voice:

"Percy the penguin used to roam
Every day, all alone,
Always on his ownio
Down beside the sea".

Or

"Old McDonald had a farm
Eeeyi Eeeyi Yo!"

The combination of warmth, wind and spume, which sprayed in liberally over the shore from the bubbling cauldron of the harbour, was exhilarating. I was safe from harm but still out in the wind. The *Snowgoose* and I surfed the waves in the harbour, speeding past the seals, whales and penguins sheltering in the deep, protected from the storm. We rescued drowning sailors from certain death as their whale catchers capsized in the mountainous seas; we delivered food and supplies to Shackleton's men on Bird Island, keeping them alive until Shackleton could get back to them on his rescue mission of mercy. When the wind blew itself out, I jumped down from the angled deck of my trusty boat and skipped home for a well deserved glass of powdered milk and a huge slice of Mum's chocolate cake, slathered in thick chocolate fudge icing. If the fohn didn't blow itself out, I was carried along by the force of it towards the house and reached the back door without my feet hardly touching the ground.

I explored anew now that the snow had gone. Birds flew in in huge flocks from their northern feeding grounds to nest and the beach behind the power station hosted a colony which grew day by day until the beach and path around it teemed with feathered souls. Gulls angrily fought for space with the larger, darker skuas. Little storm petrels teetered about uncertainly on thin legs with the gait of a woman wearing over-high stiletto heels, trying to keep away from the larger and more aggressive birds as they screamed and pecked at one other. As I approached them, the gulls flew squawking into the air, and a large skua dive-bombed me, its wing tips skimming my head. I slipped and fell forwards on to the rough shingle, covering my head with my arms for protection. As I regained my feet, the skuas stood their ground, staking their ownership of the beach. As I took a few steps further in their direction, the skuas fluffed up their mottled grey-brown feathers, stretched their necks and extended forwards a clawed foot. Every individual bird turned its beady, malign little eyes in my direction and fixed me with an angry stare. I hesitated. They seemed to be waiting for a signal to attack. I

118

stood rooted to the spot, unsure what to do next. The skuas stared at me malevolently, daring me to take them on. They were only big gulls after all, but they looked so aggressive that I decided that I didn't dare. Logic told me that they would fly off if I ran towards them, flapping my arms and shouting, but their stiff and aggressive bodies gave off a completely different signal. I convinced myself that being near the noisy power station was quite unpleasant anyway, so I nonchalantly turned on my heel and walked away towards the jetty to look at the fish and see if any penguins were coming back into the harbour now that the sea ice had almost completely disappeared.

The melted snow had unearthed another new feature of The Point. A miniature railway line ran from the jetty up over the rise past Discovery House, and on between the other houses up as far as the new bungalow beneath Hope Point. The first time that I followed the railway line, near the jail I discovered a flat-topped trolley. I pushed the trolley and it moved easily. I pushed it a bit harder and jumped on to it and was taken for a short ride. This was a new game and I spent the next hour riding the trolley between Discovery House and the jail. Basil walked past me and said, "I use that trolley to deliver crates from the jetty whenever a boat comes in. You can't use it then of course, but you can play on it to your heart's content until I need it."

"Thank you, Basil, it's good fun! I'll take it home now and show it to Mum."

"You'd better be careful if you take it down to the jetty, Bev. There's a metal turntable at the end of the jetty so that you can turn it around easily. The trolley will pick up speed going down the slope so you'd better be careful that you don't let it go too fast or it and you will be over the end of the jetty in no time."

"I won't go fast, Basil, I promise!" I pushed and rode the trolley down to Discovery House.

After dinner, when I had shown the trolley to Mum, I ignored Basil's warnings and decided that it would be good fun to sit on it while it ran down the slope onto the jetty. With a very small push, the trolley gained enough momentum to travel under its own steam. I leapt on to it and we coasted happily down the small incline. By the time we reached the Post Office at the top of the jetty, we were travelling at speed. I was terrified as all I could see in front of me was an ever decreasing length of wooden jetty and the harbour sitting deep and blue, waiting for me to be flung head first into it. Just before the trolley hit the turntable, I jumped off the back and fell, tumbling, onto the jetty. The trolley careered on for the last few feet until it hit the turntable where it spun round crazily and noisily before it came to a halt. I sat where I was and contemplated my fate. I was safe, but sore with grazed knees and elbows and a small cut on my right arm. The trolley was unharmed but it had spun so madly when it hit the turntable that I was sure that it was going to catapult itself over the end of the jetty and into the sea. The water was very deep there and the trolley so heavy that they would never get it back up once it had sunk and I would be in serious trouble if that happened. I decided that I wouldn't let the trolley run down the rise again, but just use it on the flat. I tried to push it back up to Discovery House but it was too heavy. My fun was over until the next time Basil needed the trolley and pushed it back up the hill.

Early September heralded the opening of the sealing season as sea elephants started coming ashore to breed and Pesca came to life. Before the whalers arrived from Norway for the whaling season, the over-winterers

120

prepared the *Albatross, Petrel* and *Dias* for work. These old whaling boats were now used as sealers. During the sealing season, Pesca was licensed to take six thousand elephant seals from designated beaches in certain areas of the island. Because they are pelagic during the winter and had been feeding in the South Atlantic Ocean for the last five or six months, the oil content of their blubber was at its highest and the blubber from each bull could produce more than eighty gallons of oil. This is what the sealers had been waiting for.

Basil took Betty, mum and me for a trip across the harbour in the *Resolution* to the huge breeding colony of elephant seals at Hestesletten, just beyond Pesca. As we clambered ashore, we found ourselves on a stony beach so crowded with bulls that it was difficult to find space to walk amongst them. Behind the bulls, the cows were beginning to come ashore too, heavily pregnant with this year's pups. This early in the season the cows ignored the bulls and were, in turn, ignored by them too. There were some fights between bulls for control of the harems, but these were lacklustre affairs, neither bull really willing to engage with another and risk injury before the cows had given birth and were ready to be impregnated again. Some of the bull seals were enormous, up to eighteen feet long. They lumbered slowly out of the sea, pulling themselves forwards on their front flippers up the steep banks of the beach. After every few feet, the elephants gave a huge snort, inflated their elongated trunks, then sank into deep thought for a few minutes as they regained their strength. As the biggest bulls weighed up to three tons, hauling that dead weight along a shingle beach was hard work. They found a comfortable piece of beach well above the waterline from where they would be able to watch over their harem of cows, but near enough to the sea to be able to attack unwelcome intruders, then they slept each day away, snoring softly.

Back on The Point, I spent time each day resting with my back against the cairn of Shackleton's Cross, being entertained by a small number of adolescent bull elephants which flopped ashore then lowered their heads for a quiet snooze. After a few hours, or in some cases a few days, depending on how intelligent they were, it dawned on the bulls that they hadn't quite found Hestesletten where it was all happening! On eventually realising their mistake, they lifted their heads, looked around disdainfully, then slowly made their way back to the shore and slipped noiselessly into the sea. With a pronounced sniff of disgust which set their bulbous noses aquiver and sent up a spray of seawater, the lovelorn bulls sank beneath the surface and swam off to continue their search for the female company which the monastic Point had been so spectacularly unable to provide.

Together with the seals, a few penguins came ashore. Around our house, king penguins with their upright stance, tucked their yellow banded necks beneath their flippers and snoozed the day away. Gentoos and occasionally little chinstraps, stood in clumps around the beach, plumping out their feathers in the mild spring air. In the spring gales the penguins fell onto their stomachs and flattened themselves against the ground or hid behind tussac bogs or our house, anywhere which afforded even a little respite from the force of the angry winds.

I watched from Hope Point as the sealing ships put to sea from Pesca, heading out into Cumberland Bay for the designated beaches on other parts of the island. They were away from Pesca for a few days, or sometimes for a week at a time. When they anchored at a suitable breeding beach, the sealers went ashore in a specially designed rowing boat which the Norwegians called a 'pram'. The shallow pram was able to land on the stony beaches and could be hauled up onto the shore quite easily. A man, using a large rod or stick, drove the largest bulls down to the shoreline. There the gunner shot them through the head and a knife was thrust into the heart to stop its blood from circulating. In about four minutes the skin and blubber were removed in one piece. The carcasses were left on the beaches and the single hunk of skin and blubber was attached to a line and towed behind the pram to the sealing ship where it was stored in the hold or on deck until the sealer had a full cargo. When I watched the sealing ships come back into Pesca, their decks were piled high with seal skins, and they sat very low in the water.

Our main introduction to sealing came forcefully through our noses. At intervals during the processing of the seal blubber, the vats and tanks were cleaned out. At these times, the sweet, sickly, acrid smell of heated and melted organic blubber wafted across the cove from Pesca to us on The Point. When the wind was in the wrong direction for us, the waft became a stink and the stink became a stench of the most gut-churning kind. I was unable to play outside when the stench was strong. I was even unable to sit inside the hull of the *Snowgoose* because the organic aroma swirled in, dense and suffocating and lingered cloyingly inside my nostrils. When I walked into the house the smell entered with me and whatever Mum cooked, all of her food tasted as if it had been drizzled over with a thin layer of fish flavoured seal oil which stuck to your tongue and to the inside of your mouth like liquid cement. Not even eating chocolate or chewing gum could mask the flavour of seal. Even when I tried to go to sleep, the dark night itself hung heavily with a rancid air.

A new arrival to The Point at the beginning of the season was Nigel Bonner, who was the Government Sealing Inspector. Nigel had been back to England for the birth of his first child and his wife and the baby, little Martin, were due to come down to South Georgia at the end of the winter. It would be exciting to have another woman and baby on The Point and we all looked forwards to Jenny's arrival. Nigel travelled around the island on the sealing ships to study the elephant seal populations on the coast and to ensure that only a requisite number were killed each season, so that the population remained viable. He was away from The Point for much of the short sealing season but we got to know him better once it was over. With his shock of thick, black hair and long bushy beard, Nigel looked enormous to me, but he was kind, gentle, very knowledgeable and infinitely patient. He was happy for me to trail around after him as he walked the beaches, studying the behavior of the seals and penguins. As we walked, Nigel introduced me to sphagnum moss which covered the large mounds at the base of Mount Duse and most of the plateau behind his bungalow, and the yellow burnett, a plant which hugged the ground and produced burrs later in the summer which stuck to our clothes. Nigel saw King Edward Point as a vibrant, living habitat, full of exotic plants and animals which we were privileged to share the island with. He imparted his enthusiasm to me and I began to see South Georgia through his eyes, not just as somewhere where we happened to have our home, but as a special and integral corner of the planet.

Apart from the *Snowgoose,* the conservatory was my main playroom. On the many days when Dad had had a bit too much to drink, more than just his usual daily quota of beers and whiskies, he walked in uncertainly from the evening sched in the Wireless Room and sank into the sofa in the sitting room, a vacant smile creasing his plump cheeks and narrowing his eyes to tiny slits. This was the sign for me to vacate the conservatory and I gathered up my toys, tiptoed past the sofa and settled down to play on the mat in the hall. As I played, I kept a discrete eye on the sofa, ready to run into the kitchen to Mum if Dad's mood took a turn for the worst. As he drank another whisky or two, Dad usually sang to himself, quite melodically, the chorus of 'The Eriskay Love Lilt. I don't think he knew any more of the words, so he sang the chorus over and over to himself as he slipped into a quieter and deeper reverie. After another few whiskies, Dad became more animated and his voice grew stronger as he declaimed the first of his two favourite poems in a slurred but actorial voice:

"I must go down to the seas again, to the lonely sea and the sky,

And all I ask is a tall ship and a star to steer her by

And the wheel's kick and the wind's song and the white sails shaking,

And a grey mist on the sea's face, and a grey dawn breaking."

Masefield, repeated three or four times, was safe and if he stopped drinking at that stage, we knew that the rest of the night was going to be alright. I watched my behaviour more carefully than usual and played very quietly as his Masefield mood could always erupt viciously into anger, but generally Mum and I relaxed until bedtime and were allowed to go peacefully to our beds.

On bad nights, Dad failed to leave behind the debilitating darkness that his intelligent but troubled mind inflicted on him and he didn't stop drinking after Masefield. If the contents of another glass or two disappeared down his throat, and then he shouted:

"Woman! Get me another bottle!" Mum and I knew that danger was imminent and unavoidable. Mum brought another bottle and forbore to make any comment; if she did, it would just bring forth the inevitable, we would both suffer and he would get the bottle himself anyway. Our hope was that with more whisky inside him, he would fall into a deep sleep and we could leave him snoring loudly in the sitting room. As the second bottle was breached, it became increasingly clear to us both that our hope was a forlorn one if he became even more maudlin and succumbed to Coleridge:

"Water, water, everywhere,

And all the boards did shrink;

Water, water, everywhere,

Nor any drop to drink".

 He bellowed,

"What is the title of this poem, Beverley?" I ran into the sitting room and
stood before him, but at a distance, and smiled my biggest and most winning
smile":

"The Rime of the Ancient Mariner,' Daddy."

 "Who wrote it?"

"Samuel Taylor Coleridge, Daddy."

"This is your father's favourite poem. But you wouldn't be interested in
that."

"But I am, Daddy. Please tell me more about 'The Ancient Mariner'. I love
it when you tell me the story." Sometimes he would be placated and I could
sit at his feet as he told me the tale, repeating himself frequently. But more
often than not he ignored me and lapsed into a brooding silence. After a few
minutes of wondering if he really was ignoring me or not, I took a cautious
step backwards, waited, then took another step back until I was sure that he
had no more use for me. Once I had achieved a safe distance, I retreated
round the back of the sofa then escaped back into the safety of the passage
from where I could keep an eye on developments.

We were reaching the critical point now and I surreptitiously
motioned to Mum every time he refilled his glass. Even at this late stage all
could be well if he confined himself to reciting this one verse and then fell
asleep. But when the last lines of 'The Ancient Mariner' were spat out with
venom and his fist banged the arm of the sofa,

127

"A sadder and a wiser man,

He rose the morrow morn. Fe farn!" we knew that he had slipped into a deep subterranean blackness, peopled by his own demons. No light could enter there, no happy thoughts could penetrate the gloom. Every wrong or slight that he imagined had ever been done to him was being relived and expanded, coloured and magnified, and no one in our house dared to breathe so loudly that we might disturb him. He sat slumped into the sofa, head bent forward, one hand hanging lifelessly down and the other holding on to his glass.

"Fe farn!" He shot bolt upright.

"Fe bloody farn!" His fist rained another heavy blow onto the arm of the sofa. This was it! This was the moment to grab panda and Gerald from his bedroom and carry them into my bedroom and tuck them securely into my bed. If Dad took it upon himself to stagger down the passage and take Gerald from his cot as he had done once before, I could get to my bedroom before Dad realised that Gerald wasn't in his own room. That would give Mum and me a chance to protect Gerald from Dad's wrath. I closed the bedroom door and crept back into the passage to be near Mum and so that I could keep an eye on what was going on. Mum stayed in the kitchen and we both prayed that Dad would fall asleep on the sofa. By now this was a forlorn hope as Dad was rousing himself with louder and louder shouts of "Fe bloody farn!" His fist hit out at whatever was near. His demons were beating frenziedly against the inside of his skull and screaming for release. The silence was broken by a roared,

"Woman! Where are you? Get in here this minute!" Now I was completely on edge, ears straining.

128

"Why don't you come to bed, Peter? It's very late and you've got to be on duty early in the morning."

"Bugger work! All you want me to do is work and get out of your way. I earn the money and you do nothing. You sit in the house all day gossiping with Betty and then you can't even be bothered to look after me when I come into the house at night. Get me another whisky."

"Don't you think you've had enough for today? Let's just go to bed."

"Who do you think you are telling to go to bed? Who the bloody hell do you think you are? Get me a drink or I'll show you who's boss in this house. Fe bloody farn!" It was always safer for me to take things to Dad when he was drunk. He was much less likely to hit me than Mum. I took a glass, not a bottle, and offered it to him, carefully removing the now empty glass from his hand.

"Can I get you anything to eat, Daddy?"

No answer. Nod politely and leave the room.

From here on there was no pattern to his behaviour. He might call for Mum to help him to the bathroom then to the bedroom, where he might fall onto the bed and snore until late the following morning. He might start hitting Mum in the sitting room or in the bedroom with me crouching outside their bedroom door, listening, and Gerald curled up in the foetal position in my bed, clasping panda to his chest for comfort and security. When his attacks on Mum were over and Dad had fallen asleep, Mum crept out of the bedroom into the passage to show me that she was alright. If Dad hadn't been too vicious, we put Gerald into his cot and she tucked me up in bed, giving me an extra-long goodnight hug. If he had been completely uncontrolled and had bruised Mum's face or body, we left Gerald in my bed then went into the

129

kitchen together and put damp tea towels over her bruised flesh, while she drank a cup of coffee. Our lives were slipping into an uncomfortable, unfathomable pattern.

The chickens began to repay Mum and Dad for all their hard work throughout the winter feeding them, cleaning their henhouse out and protecting them from the rats, by laying a few precious eggs. The first egg was ceremoniously collected by Mum, soft-boiled and shared by Gerald and me, Mum feeding us in turn from a teaspoon. As the weeks progressed into spring, hens eggs became plentiful enough for us to eat, but not really plentiful enough for Mum to cook with. That was soon about to change!

Around The Point, gentoo penguins were beginning to lay their eggs. There was no restriction on how many eggs we collected, but we were careful to try to take only one from each nest where two eggs lay cosily side-by-side. Dad perfected the technique of keeping a justifiably angry mother gentoo and her friends at bay with a stick held in his right hand while, with his left hand, he gathered up a single egg and passed it to Mum to lay carefully in her bucket with those he had already harvested. In the kitchen Mum set to work with her usual gusto for cooking. Using one gentoo egg as the equivalent of two hen eggs, she made light sponges and even lighter swiss-rolls which tasted the same as those made with hens eggs, but had a slightly pink tinge. She made melt-in-the-mouth meringues too which she covered with Morfat cream from a tin.

The best fun though was when I was given two hard-boiled gentoo eggs for my supper. The peeled eggs were the size of a large fist. The egg white was transparent, rubbery, unappetising and very easy to peel away from the spherical, bright orange yolk which nestled snugly inside. The yolk was surrounded with a quite strong membrane and when I sucked gently on it, a little protrusion appeared beneath it. I became very talented at sucking my penguin egg yolks just enough to make faces with protuberant eyes, fat noses and hedgehog-like hair. My attempts at making a Pinocchio usually ended in failure as I sucked too hard or for too long in my attempts to make a face with a really long nose. When the membrane burst, a delicious tide of rich egg yolk burst into my mouth. Once I had finished playing with my egg yolks, or we heard Dad's footsteps approaching along the passage, Mum whisked my plate away from me, mashed the yolks with some butter, and gave them back to me to eat with a chunk of fresh Pesca bread.

Once the *Snowgoose* began to lose her charms for me, I ventured further afield towards Mount Duse. I crossed over the tiny wooden bridge, built to carry the path round to Pesca across a narrow, winding stream which ran strongly with clear water, a product of the still melting snow higher up the mountain. I followed the stream around the base of Mount Duse and explored the great mossy mounds which hugged the baseline of the mountain. The sphagnum mounds made an excellent line of houses and I chose the largest one to be my residence. Over the next few days, I carried cups, plates and tins of Dolly Mixture provisions to my house. Sitting amongst the furry brown fruiting bodies of the mosses, I held imaginary audiences with my friends and fed them with delicious morsels, all made and served with great gentility by me. I lay on my back and sank into the moss as the shiny brown spore capsules swayed delicately in the breeze around my head. Sometimes a sooty albatross flew above me, effortlessly gliding on gossamer wings while the peaceful 'lap, lap', of the waves against the shore made me sleepy. More often though my peace was shattered as skuas and gulls squawked and

131

screamed at one another as they wheeled angrily overhead. King and gentoo penguins in small groups on the shore cried plaintively on their one favoured note, and elephant seals snorted and belched in contentment as they rested their huge bulks in the tussac.

Growing in the stream was a green plant whose slender stems swayed in the current as they held aloft small green leaves. When I asked Dad about the plant, he told me that it was called water blink, but that everyone called it watercress and that it was an edible herb eaten by the whalers in bygone days. The next day, I carefully stepped into the stream from beside the bridge, trying to ensure that the water didn't get into my wellies. Lengths of the plant stem were easy to rip off, although the roots were attached very strongly between the stones at the bottom of the stream and I wasn't strong enough to dislodge them. Climbing back on to the bridge, I ate some of the herb. It was surprisingly tasty, a little peppery on the tongue. I had already learned to pull the long stems from tussac clumps and eat the fleshy yellow bases, as Shackleton and his men had done to supplement their meagre food rations. Armed with Dolly Mixtures, tussac grass and watercress, I sat atop my mossy mansion at the base of the mountain, looking out across the harbour, eating my fill from a banquet fit for the Snow Queen herself.

Now that spring had arrived, a flotilla of ships sped southwards, bringing us new supplies and carrying the hundreds of men who would man the whaling stations or continue further south to the Antarctic Bases. The first ship to arrive that season was the *Biscoe*. We all waited on the beach beside Discovery House for her to appear around Hope Point. When she came into sight we gasped at the change in her livery. A grey hull had been too difficult to see amongst the ice so while she had been in the United

Kingdom over our winter, the Falkland Islands Dependency Survey had painted her hull red. We felt that her red hull and white superstructure gave the *Biscoe* extra kudos amongst ordinary grey and black-hulled ships, showing the world that she was a very different and superior being to them. As she skirted the beach and came in to the jetty, the *Biscoe* looked and felt as if she belonged exclusively to us.

Dad had a particular reason for anticipating the arrival of this first *Biscoe* of the season as the man who was to replace Jack as his assistant in the Wireless Room, was arriving on her. The new man was from England and he had signed on for three years as Dad had done. It was going to be important that they should get on well as they were going to work together every day and they would be the only two wireless operators for the winter months. Dad climbed onboard the *Biscoe* as soon as he could. I watched him as he shook hands with the men he knew from Stanley, then I saw him approach the tallest man I had ever seen. This giant was six feet three inches tall and he had to hold his head bent slightly forward, to enable him to fit into the space between the lower deck, where he was standing, and the deck above. He towered over Dad who, at five feet ten inches, was considered to be tall amongst Falkland Islanders.

Mum and Betty were eager to get their post and learn about what their families and friends had been doing in Stanley. Dad and the other men had new stocks of alcohol arriving and I had been sent a case of fruit by grandad. This case of fruit had been brought down from Montevideo to Stanley on the *Darwin* and it was filled with bergamotas, oranges and tangerines. I was disappointed that grandad hadn't sent us any watermelons, but Mum said that these orange fruits contained the vitamins we weren't getting on South

133

Georgia and I should be very happy with what I'd been given. I was happy really, and gorged myself on the sweet, juicy flesh of citrus fruits which I hadn't tasted since leaving Stanley.

The giant was invited by Dad to come to have supper with us that evening, as it was his first day on King Edward Point. He was introduced to us as Ron Carter but in the few hours that he had been on The Point, I knew that the other men had already christened him 'Rubber Bones', and I could see why! As he entered our house, Ron ducked in through the door, his eyes scanning the room for possible dangers which might be projecting downwards from the ceiling. His head was long and oval, and this impression of length was reinforced by his hair, which had been cropped into the neatest possible short back and sides. His body undulated as he walked, giving him a lolloping gait. Large, flat feet protruded from beneath very thin legs. Whenever he took a step forwards, Ron had the appearance of someone who was permanently on the brink of falling over. When he bent his head and upper body towards me to shake my hand in introduction, I was frightened that he might be tipping forwards too far and was going to topple over on top of me. When Ron reached for the salt or took his plate from Mum, each joint in his arms appeared to move independently of the others. I watched as he slowly and carefully lifted his food through that great distance from his plate to his mouth, expecting the food to fall from his fork at any moment while it was in transit. His food was certain to be cold by the time it reached its destination!

In response to Mum's questions about himself, Ron told us that he was married with a young daughter. However, during the war, his wife had left him to go and live with another man but, as they were both Roman

134

Catholics, they couldn't divorce. He had looked at a world map and chose to come to South Georgia to work for three years as a means of putting the greatest possible number of miles between himself and his wife.

"You couldn't have chosen a much more remote spot," Dad remarked dryly.

"Oh yes, I think it will hit the spot very well!" Ron replied. We all laughed politely.

The main topic under discussion between the men on The Point after the *Biscoe* left was the imminent arrival of five new whale catchers which had been built in Holland and whose progress south Dad had been monitoring from the Wireless Station. On the afternoon when the whale catchers were due to arrive, Dad and I walked up to Discovery House and joined the men who had gathered on the shingle beach below to catch their first sight of these amazing new vessels.

"Butler has ordered these catchers to be built to his own specifications. Apparently they have turbocharged diesel engines which make them capable of doing sixteen knots."

"I've heard the Norwegians say that they have a variable pitch propeller which means that they can stop in thirty seconds by reversing the propeller pitch. I've never heard of anything like that before."

"Nor have I. What I do know is that each whale catcher has radar and gyro assisted navigation and direction finders, so that they can plot their own position exactly and send it to the other ships in the fleet. They've set up a new control centre at Pesca which can keep an eye on where each catcher is," Dad said. "Not only that, but when they make a kill they will flag each whale with automatic radio transmitters. There is a course recorder on board which enables them to retrace their course after a kill and retrieve the flagged

135

whales, even at night. Those are pieces of equipment that I can't wait to see."

"Here she comes! I can see the first one coming round Hope Point!" A grey ship, slender and sleek, larger than the old whalers I had seen at Pesca, nosed her way towards us. She was moving at speed, close in to the shore. We got an excellent view as she sped past. The crew, all up on deck, waved energetically at us. I ran down the beach and waved energetically back. "See, Bev, the tall mast at the front has a crow's nest at the very top. That's where a man stands looking out for the telltale sign of a whale blowing. When he spots a whale, he sends a signal to the bridge and the gunner runs along that gangway, which is called the catwalk, from the bridge to the harpoon gun in the bow. That's where he harpoons the whale from."

"They shout 'Thar she blows'!"

"I'm afraid not, Beverley, that was in the days of Moby Dick and Captain Ahab. They use radio telephones now."

"They said that Butler wanted the bow to be built higher to give the gunners a clearer view and to keep them dry in rough weather. He's certainly got what he wanted, the harpoon gun platform is certainly very high."

"There comes the next one!" The second whaler came into view, followed at a safe distance by three more. It was a spectacular sight, five shining new whale catchers cutting effortlessly through the sea, their crews cheering and waving as they came into their home port for the first time. When the last ship passed us, we walked round past the boatsheds to the jetty. On the opposite side of the harbour, the first whaler had docked at Pesca and the second one was manoeuvring in to lay alongside her. Within half an hour, all five catchers were tied together in sequence against the jetty.

"Did you see the designation on the funnels?" Dad asked,

"Yes, they're numbered *R1, R2, R3, R4* and R5. I suppose they are R after old Ryan who owns Pesca."

"I think it's because he's registered them in Panama through one of his subsidiaries and the R comes from that, but you can never be sure about anything in Ryan's companies. I won't forget last year in a hurry," Dad continued, " I arrived here just after Ryan sent down the Harpoon and she arrived with that crew of Argentine nationalists on board ready to take South Georgia for the Argentine. Ryan might be British, but he has worked too closely with Peron and the junta in Argentina for my liking. Actually, in my opinion, he has probably done the Falkland Island Government a backhanded favour by showing the world what the Argies are up to. If the Royal Navy hadn't been in the South Atlantic last summer, I dread to think what might have happened."

"It was a good thing that the *Protector* was nearby with a detachment of Royal Marines onboard, I grant you. I wouldn't have fancied going over to Pesca with our few sports rifles to take the buggers on."

"Nor me neither," Basil replied, "but I thought at one time we would have to. It was a bloody close call!"

"I heard that Ryan was removing his business from the Argentine across the River Plate to Uruguay. Have you heard that?"

"I did hear something like that, actually," Dad replied, "can't say I blame him or that it has come a moment too soon."

Mr Matthews held a party at his house to welcome the Captains of the new R boats and I linked each Captain with his boat. The *R2* was captained by Harald Bordal, a stocky man with a shock of dark brown hair and strong, muscular arms and upper torso, not the sort of man anyone in their right minds would take on in a fight. Harald was someone we grew particularly fond of and it was a real disappointment to me when, at the end of the season, the captain of the *R3* headed the table for the champion gunner and whaler, ahead of Harald who took second place.

On the first of October, the whaling season started officially. At midnight on the thirtieth of September the *R* boats put to sea and we stood on the shore and waved as the five whalers, their lights ablaze, sped out of the harbour. We had to peer through the fog to see them as we had been fog bound for days and we were all beginning to wonder if the weather would ever lift.

Traditionally, each gunner was paid a bonus for every whale he caught. However, Mr Butler persuaded the whalers that if they agreed to be paid a bonus based on the total catch for the season, they would pool resources and increase the overall catch, which would benefit everyone. He ordered the fleet to search for whales over a wide area and, once they had been located, to do the catching then. He left his best gunners at sea to continue hunting and the less skilled gunners towed the flagged whales back to Pesca. The dead whales were secured by their tail flukes to the sides of the whale catchers. Each catcher could haul six whales, three on each side. Each day catchers steamed past The Point, heavily laden and with their decks appearing to be almost at water level because they were lying so deep in the sea. By December, the weather improved and *R* boats and the other catchers were bringing as many as forty-two whales a day into Pesca. Most of the whales were fin or the smaller sei whales, but there were a small number of sperm whales too.

Using Dad's binoculars, I watched the activity in Pesca from the jetty or from my favourite vantage point below the dam on Mount Duse. The whales on The Plan looked enormous and the men swarming over them very small, like ants. It seemed to take the men about thirty or forty minutes to process each whale, with the next whale being hauled up to take the place of the previous one before it had been completely disposed of. From the base of the hosed-down Plan, whale blood created a pink triangular stain in the harbour, the apex of which reached closer and closer towards The Point as the season wore on. Seabirds swam in the pink sea, feeding on the whale

139

detritus in the bloody suspension. As darkness fell, strong lamps surrounding The Plan were switched on and the night shift took over. Sitting on the end of the jetty I could look straight across to Pesca and watch the well-lit whalers as they sped in and out of the harbour, releasing their loads for the men on The Plan to dispatch while we were asleep. The weather continued to be misty and cloudy. On most days I was unable to go out without a coat on, but at least the smell of melting seal blubber diminished once the whaling season began and all the processing was done in newly installed closed boilers. However, when they cleaned out the closed vats at Pesca, the familiar, sweet, acrid stench of melted blubber wafted across the harbour to The Point. We stayed in the house again with windows and doors firmly closed, eating very little as our stomachs turned somersaults at the thought of food. We tried to breathe as shallowly as possible.

On balmy days when the sun shone and a thin cotton dress was all that I needed to wear, I played around The Point, very used to my own company by now. On several occasions, when Dad walked round to Pesca in the afternoon, he let me accompany him. Often he talked to me about his work or what was happening at Pesca; how the whaling season was progressing and what it meant for South Georgia as an island which had to earn its keep, just as all adults had to do. Dad was very interested in local and international politics and linked the progress of whaling here with the wider needs of England and Norway in particular. I wasn't able to understand all that he said, but I listened to the cadence of his voice and tried to follow the breadth and scope of his interests as best I could.

Late one afternoon when we had picked up some bread and pastries from the baker in Pesca and were walking back around the harbour to The Point, Dad pointed up to the sky and said,

"Beverley, look up there. Can you see those structures which look like meringues?" Up above us, against a pale blue backdrop, scattered among some thin and wispy clouds, were a number of quite solid-looking white structures which looked exactly like upside-down meringues. They were narrower at the base and widened upwards in doughnut-like layers.

"Yes, I can see them, Daddy."

"They are actually alien flying saucers which travel through space from the planet Mars and onboard are crews of little green Martian men. They come to South Georgia to check that everything is well here on earth." I walked along beside him in silence, looking upwards with amazement as the Martian craft sailed slowly and majestically across the sky. It occurred to me that Martians visiting the earth might not be friendly in their intent. What if they were to fly down and steal me away or, worse, kill us all?

"Are the Martians bad people, Daddy? Would they do us any harm?"

"Not at all, Beverley! Actually, they are a peaceful people and they look on human beings as their friends. You should just enjoy looking at their spaceships and admiring the fleets as they cross the sky. You will never see Martian spaceships outside South Georgia, this is the only place on earth that they visit." As we neared The Point, the sun began to set and the sky changed colour from blue to a pinkish gold.

"Look, Beverley, the Martians are lighting up their ships! Can you see how they have a special golden glow which emanates from their interior?" I could see exactly what Dad was talking about. The spaceships glowed with a

141

luminescence which was breathtaking in its beauty. Gold, red and orange tinted the sides of the ships and an other-worldly glow surrounded each one. As we reached The Point, I asked Dad if I could stay and watch the spaceships for a little while longer. I climbed on board the *Snowgoose* and made my way around her tilted deck to the stern. I sat and watched the Martian spaceships as they made their slow way across the harbour from Pesca before they flew in a slow, stately procession out across Cumberland Bay.

By now at Hestesletten, the female elephant seals had pups attached to their teats for most of the day as the babies sucked at high speed, extracting every ounce of milk in the three weeks that they were given to suckle before the females mated again and sloped off gratefully into the sea to slake their hunger with tasty squid. When we walked amongst the seals it was interesting and generally safe. The bulls occasionally reared up at me, towering over me by several feet, but they couldn't move quickly and as long as I backed away from them or skipped out of their way, they soon flopped down again, gratefully resting their heavy bodies flat on the beach. The females and their pups communicated with one another in guttural growls. For me, the females saved a deep throated gurgle, accompanied by huge tears which cascaded down their grey faces, leaving a dark trail behind them in the soft fur.

The bulls fought spectacular battles with each other in order to gain control of the forty or fifty females in a harem. The beachmasters, usually enormous, old and battle-scarred, lumbered nosily towards all intruders, their noses inflated and shaking with emotion. On reaching the interloper, in the shallows or on the beach, the two bulls reared up on the back third of their bodies and crashed down with mouth agape, using the massive weight of their upper bodies to drive their short, stubby pointed canines into the flesh of their opponent. Bloodied and beaten, it was nearly always the interloper which backed down the beach and slipped soundlessly beneath the waves, swimming off to find a safe haven where he could recover from his wounds.

King penguins were laying their eggs and Dad collected some for us. Mum cooked with them as successfully as she had cooked with gentoo eggs, using one king penguin egg as being roughly equivalent to four hen's eggs.

One day after lunch, Dad came in from the Wireless Room and said that he had picked up on the radio transmitter that the *R* boats had caught several sperm whales, so he thought that we might go round to Pesca and have a look at whatever was happening on The Plan. Carrying Gerald between them, Dad, Mum and I walked around the cove, enjoying the feeling of warm sunshine on our faces. As we were walking, one of the old whale catchers towed in a full complement of six whales which she released near the foot of The Plan. We walked past the boiler house to the blubber cookery which stood on the front, right-hand side of the Flensing Plan. The Plan foreman came across to Dad and cheerily gave permission for us to stand where we were. He wore thigh length boots with long spikes or nails through the soles. I was fascinated by how easily he walked on them. Down to our left, Eskedal's motorboat picked up a floating whale and towed it by its fluke before a wire rope was attached and a winch pulled it up on to the wide, wooden Plan. Where the whales floated, waiting their turn to be winched up on to The Plan for processing, the sea was red with blood and detritus washed into the harbour when The Plan was hosed down. Flocks of seabirds dived and squabbled over the spoils. Skuas, petrels, gulls, tiny cape pigeons, all swooped and dived and produced a cacophony of discordant noise in the background.

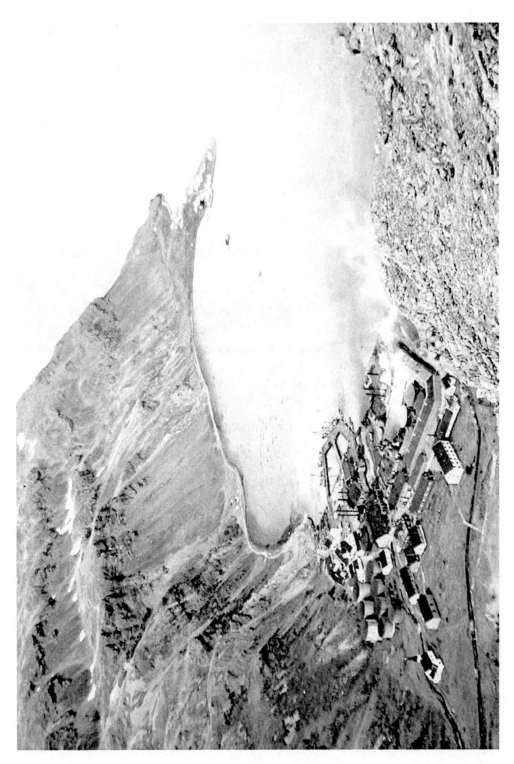

"That is a fin whale, Beverley. You can identify it by the two-coloured marking on its face. As the fin whale came to rest on The Plan, lying on its side, we were looking directly up into its pointed snout.

"The left side of its face is grey and the right side is more white. It looks odd."

"No one really knows why its face has what are called asymmetrical markings, but that is how you tell the difference between fin whales and sei whales. They are both baleen whales which feed on krill and, although the fin whales are usually bigger than seis and are often a lighter grey in colour, it is the facial marking that you should look for." Two men who had been standing beside us, wearing boots with spikes in the soles, collected a frightening long-handled implement each and walked quickly towards the whale.

"Those are the flensers and their flensing knife has a very, very sharp curved blade. The blade will slice through the blubber. You watch!" One of the flensers made a straight incision from the tail to the head of the whale, then he ran easily up on to the whale's back and made another incision along its dorsal length. The second flenser flailed the skin around the head and once he had released a flap of blubber, he attached a steel cable to it and a winch whirred into action, ripping off a huge, eight to ten inch deep sheet of skin and blubber. Chains from a second winch turned the whale over onto its right side and the process was repeated to remove the remaining blubber. The strips were hauled up a metal ramp to the blubber cookery, where it was processed for five hours under steam and pressure, during which time the oil rose to the surface and could be siphoned off into receiving tanks.

Back on The Plan, the Plan foreman measured the carcass and a second team of men began working on the whale. These were the lemmers and their task was to remove the meat and viscera from the carcass. The fin whale was decapitated and a winch dragged its head up a ramp on the opposite side of The Plan to us.

"You see those two ramps, Beverley. The first one leads to the meat cookery plant and the second ramp at the far end of The Plan leads to the bone cookery plant. The lemmers must strip the meat from the bones as closely as possible, as the quality of the meat meal and bone meal which are produced will be much lower if the two contaminate each other." Seemingly effortlessly, the lemmers scythed through the flesh with their flensing knives and huge chunks of whale meat were winched up to the meat loft. The gut and intestines which spilled out on to The Plan were loaded into huge steel buckets which disappeared upwards too. Finally, the bones were hauled up to the bone loft.

"Have you noticed that the ribs were taken to a different loft to the rest of the bones?" Dad asked.

"No, Daddy! But why is that when they're bones too?"

"There is a separate rib loft where the meat is carefully stripped from the ribs before they are sent up to the bone loft for processing so that the meat doesn't contaminate the bone meal"

"I understand, Daddy."

"Good girl, you're learning a lot today." The whole process had taken little more than half an hour.

The Plan was hosed down and the Plan foreman came over to us and said that they had three sperm whales in this catch and they were going to process them all now, as sperm whale oil had to be kept separate from the rest of the whale oil. He bent down towards me and with a smile he said, "You will have a tooth now if you want!"

"Thank you very much, I would like that." I wasn't sure what I was thanking him for, but with Dad nearby, good manners were everything.

When the first sperm whale was drawn up on to The Plan, I was surprised by how different it looked to the fin whale I had just seen. Certainly no longer than the fin whale at about sixty five feet in length, the sperm was dark grey, almost black in colour with an enormous head which made up almost a third of its body length. But it was the shape of its head which was the most striking. It was about ten feet high and six feet across, and it was flat. Big eyes towards the back of the head looked out at us, opaque and infinitely sad. Dad pointed out to me the single 'S' shaped blowhole and the many grey scars marking its head, made by angry giant squid which the sperm whale had delighted in eating.

The process of flensing began as before, then the Plan foreman came over to us and indicated for us to follow him onto The Plan. He took Mum by the arm to guide her. It was greasy and slippery underfoot, but we followed him, stepping carefully, towards the head of the whale. The mouth had been exposed and there, pushing upwards from the long, narrow lower jaw of the sperm whale, were some fifty teeth, each about seven inches high. "Why hasn't it got any top teeth?" I asked.
""There are no top teeth, just sockets in the top jaw," Dad replied.
"I will bring you a tooth from this whale, and for the lady too," said the foreman, nodding his head politely towards Mum; then he led us carefully back to our safe spot, his hand under Mum's arm to guide her as before.

It seemed to be more difficult to process a sperm whale than a fin whale and it certainly took longer. The blubber was very thick, nearly seven inches in depth and much stiffer. The Plan foreman and another man worked at the head to remove the 'case' which contained spermaceti, a precious waxy substance used to make candles, cosmetics, lubricants and pharmaceutical compounds. When the guts were removed, the Plan foreman inspected the intestines for lumps of ambergris, used in medicine and as a fixative in expensive perfumes.

We stayed to watch a second sperm whale being processed then Dad suggested that we leave and call in to the Bakery and get a pastry to see us

150

through the walk on the way home. At the Bakery a new batch of loaves had just been taken out of the oven. Instead of a pastry, I asked if I could have a loaf of bread instead, please? Smiling, the Pesca baker gave me a loaf and two more for Mum, as well as a pastry for each of us. As we walked back round the harbour to The Point, I picked all of the sweet, soft and still warm bread out of the middle of my loaf until I was left with just the crust shell. I threw the crust towards the gulls and skuas and watched as they flew, screaming, towards it and fought angrily over the spoils.

CHAPTER 7

SUMMER

When Dad told us that we were all going to cross Cumberland Bay in the *Resolution* to Moraine Fjord for a special picnic, I was beside myself with excitement. I might see the Ice Palace and even, if I was lucky, the Snow Queen! Mum and Betty began baking meat pies, cheese straws, sausage rolls and cakes in preparation for the picnic and as each morning arrived, I threw back the covers and rushed to the bedroom window to look at the sky. The weather, unpredictable as always, had been behaving badly and it seemed as if we might never get a clear, calm day for our picnic. But when a benign, sunny day dawned, it was agreed that today was the day and we would make an early start!

The little cabin of the *Resolution* was packed with provisions and Betty, Mum, and I sat on the wooden bench, Gerald in his carrycot lying at mum's feet. Mum had brought a large bag of brand new terry-towelling nappies for Gerald.

"Damn it Pearl, are you expecting the little chap to shit all the way there and back? Even then he won't use up a quarter of those nappies!"

"Better safe than sorry, Basil!" Tiny windows around the cabin gave a two hundred and seventy degree view of the world outside. Dad was to follow us in the dinghy with the outboard motor as the Resolution couldn't land us on the beach at Moraine Fjord and Dad would have to ferry us ashore.

With Gerald asleep in his carrycot, we set off from the jetty, around The Point and out into Cumberland Bay. Ahead of us the sea was flat calm and sunbeams danced gaily on the surface. The mountains and the blue glaciers drew closer as the *Resolution*, followed by Dad's dinghy, chugged serenely through the deep waters.

Without warning, as we were more than half way across Cumberland Bay, the surface of the sea lost its lustre. Little white tops broke on small waves and clouds rolled rapidly down the mountainsides and glaciers, hiding them from view. The waves grew taller minute by minute and the *Resolution* began to dance. Basil opened the cabin door and said,
"There's a fohn wind just blowing up. We're going to turn around and head back to The Point. Too unsafe to be out at sea in this!"

The *Resolution* turned round but I couldn't see Hope Point or even Mount Duse through the gathering gloom. Within minutes, the sea had turned wild. The *Resolution* climbed almost vertically up the side of enormous waves and became irresolute. She sat shaking on the crest of each wave while she made up her mind whether or not to go over the top or just slide backwards down into the ocean depths. After long seconds, she held her nerve, time and again, and dipped forward into the deep trough ahead. Sitting in the front of the cabin, my face pressed against the window only feet from her bow, I pushed my little body forward into the window, hoping that my inconsiderable weight would help to tip her forward, over the edge and down into the trough of the next wave. Behind me, Gerald slept soundly in his carrycot but Mum started retching and was soon being despairingly

153

seasick. Mum reached for the nappies. The pile of nappies grew steadily lower. I stuck my fingers firmly in my ears so that I couldn't hear the sounds of her vomity distress.

I had the same view as the *Resolution* of the ferocious seas and I shared every judder of her body and every moment of her indecision and caution, pooling my fears completely with hers. With my fingers in my ears, I rocked my body forwards when she crested a wave to push her over, and leaned backwards when we were in a trough to encourage her to climb upwards again.

"Your Dad, Bev! Can you see your Dad?" Mum asked. Dad! I had forgotten about him. I swayed from window to window, fingers still in my ears, to see if I could glimpse him in the mountainous seas behind us. After about five minutes I spied a small black dot cresting a wave behind us to starboard.

"It's Dad! I can see him! He's alright Mum, he's still following behind us! You don't have to worry, he's alright!" Only I wasn't feeling quite so sure about that. The waves towered ever higher above us and swamped the motorboat every time we dipped into a trough. The wind was howling and Dad was in an open dinghy. We might not even survive, so how could he? Surely his dinghy would be overwhelmed by the waves and sink. I wasn't just frightened, I was terrified, full of fear and certain that the very next precipitous wave powering towards us would swamp us and we would go down. With my fingers firmly pressed into my ears and my body still moving forward and backward in time with the *Resolution*, I began to sing quietly to myself one of the choruses which Doctor McWhan had taught us at Sunday school in the Tabernacle in Stanley:

"A little ship was on the sea
It was a pretty sight,
It sailed along so merrily
And all was calm and bright.

When lo! A storm began to rise
The wind grew loud and strong,
It blew the clouds across the sky,
It blew the waves along.

And all but one was sore afraid
Of sinking in the deep,
His head was on a pillow laid
And he was fast asleep.

'Master we perish, master save!'
They cried, their master heard,
He soon rebuked the wind and waves
And stilled them with a word.

Oh well, we know it was the Lord,
Our Saviour and our friend,
Whose care of those who trust his word
Shall never, ever end."

Over and over again I sang the chorus to myself. If I was singing a song about Jesus, I knew that God wouldn't let us die. Two or three times when we crested a wave at the same moment that Dad did, I spotted the little dot that was his dinghy. God was taking care of us. I began to believe that we would get home safely.

After nearly two hours, we limped into King Edward Cove. The harbour was still rough, but it was sheltered enough for us to tie up alongside the jetty. When Basil came into the cabin to see if we were alright, he found us, ashen faced and wan, a huge pile of nappies full of vomit piled high on the deck beside the carrycot.

"My God, Pearl," he laughed, "I won't forget in a hurry what you think babies nappies are for. I thought you would have had a better idea with two kids of your own!" I walked past the nappies, averting my eyes and trying not to inhale the acrid smell, before I emerged onto the deck outside. The wind caught my hair and whipped it out at right angles to my head. The strength of the wind nearly blew me over, but John grabbed my arm and together, choosing the exact moment when the Resolution was about to be flung against the jetty, we leapt on to its slippery planks. John was afraid that the wind would blow me off the jetty into the sea, so he put his arms round my shoulders and together we fought our way to the house.

"I'll just go back and get your mother now," and I watched as John bent his head into the wind, returning some minutes later with Gerald's carrycot wrapped securely in his arms and with Mum walking beside him, holding tightly to his arm.

"Peter. Can you see Peter?"

"Don't worry, Pearl. You get the children into the house and I'll go round behind the boathouse and see if I can see him coming into the harbour," John said. Walking the sixty or so yards from the end of the jetty had been enough to wet us through to the skin. Mum settled Gerald and changed me into dry clothes. We had just sat down to have a hot drink when John burst in through the kitchen door.

"Peter's fine Pearl! He's tying up at the jetty now"

"Thank God!" said Mum, "I thought I'd lost him forever!"

A few minutes later Dad appeared in the doorway, wet, dishevelled and with the biggest smile on his face I'd ever seen. He was euphoric!

"Get me some dry clothes, Pearl, and get the picnic food on the table. I've invited everyone to come round and have a party to celebrate beating the fohn. God, but that was something! I've never beaten off such odds before. Bloody fantastic!"

Mum was already on her feet and moving towards Dad, her arms outstretched.

"I was so frightened, Peter, I thought I'd lost you."

"Nonsense! It would take more than a gale and a storm at sea to get rid of me! Now, get moving because everyone will be here in a minute." A superficial hug for Mum and no questions about how we had fared. Mum smiled weakly, fought to overcome her still churning stomach and followed Dad to the bedroom to lay out his dry clothes neatly on the bed. Without changing her own wet clothes, Mum put on the tablecloth and began to set out the food for Dad's party. If he started drinking at dinner time, we were in for a very long night.

157

In 1911, ten reindeer were sent down to South Georgia from Norway to provide the whalers with meat. The herd was released at New Fortuna Bay and they established themselves quickly. By the time we moved to King Edward Point, there were two herds, the largest of four thousand reindeer inhabited most of the coastal area to the north east of Cumberland Bay and culls were organised in the summer to provide us with frozen venison for the winter.

For one cull, the *Dias* sailed across from Pesca where some of The Point men, including Dad, joined them. The party landed in Cumberland Bay East, and from there, they walked inland towards the mountains. The mess boys from Pesca were sent onto the mountain slopes to locate the herd. Once found, the boys clambered higher up the slopes until they were behind the reindeer, then they drove them down into a narrow valley. Meanwhile, the shooting party stationed themselves in the hills on either side of the valley with a huge picnic and sufficient beverages (most of an alcoholic nature) to see them through. When the reindeer galloped through the valley, the shooting party loosed their rifles and shot at only the largest animals. However, as they were not wholly sober by then, their shooting was often misdirected and young reindeer and even their fellow riflemen in the hills opposite, were at some risk.

After sharing the remains of their picnic with the mess boys and the crew of the *Dias*, the sealer made her way back to The Point. I waited until she came into view then ran around the beach, keeping up with her and returning the waves of the mass of very merry men who lined her decks. The Point men were put ashore, followed by a reindeer carcass which was heaved unceremoniously from the deck of the *Dias* onto the jetty. This was unusual, as normally the reindeer carcasses were all taken back to Pesca to be prepared for the freezer. Today, though, the hunting had been particularly successful and the extra animal was left for The Point men to deal with.

Mum wouldn't allow me to stay on the jetty while the reindeer was being disembowelled and prepared for the table. Very reluctantly, I walked back to the house and waited impatiently, fuming because something was going on and I couldn't be part of it.

"But I've seen whales being cut up, Mum, why is this any different?"

"I wasn't happy about you seeing whales on The Plan but your father insisted that you should see it as it's the reason why we're all down here. This is a different thing altogether."

"But Mum…"

"No! That is my last word on the subject. Go and play with your brother." I played with Gerald with bad grace for a time, then an idea struck me. I walked innocently into the kitchen and said,

"Mum, do you think you should make some coffee for the men? I bet they won't make them any at Discovery House. I could take them down some coffee and chocolate buns. They'd be really pleased wouldn't they?"

"As they've been working ever since they got back from Cumberland Bay, I expect they are thirsty. Help me to get a tray ready and you can take it down to the jetty." I smiled secretly to myself, I was getting just what I wanted. Mum, always happy to be a hostess and serve food, made six cups of coffee and gave me a plate laden with chocolate buns. I walked down the steps outside the back door and she handed the tray to me.

"Can you manage it, or shall I take it?"

159

"No, I'm fine, Mum. I can manage." I walked slowly towards the jetty, balancing the heavy tray with some difficulty. When I got as far as the Post Office, John saw me and came to take the tray from me.

"Say thank you to your Mum, Bev, this will go down a treat!" I smiled and followed him on to the jetty. Before me lay the carcass of the reindeer, already skinned and disembowelled. The internal organs had been thrown into the sea where a leopard seal circled in the bloody waters around the jetty, bared teeth accentuating its ferocious grin, gorging itself on easy pickings. I stopped suddenly, unable at first to take in what I was seeing. The reindeer, which was obviously female and had been in the latest stages of pregnancy, lay at my feet. Beside her, a fully formed foetus lay on its side in a pool of fluid which looked, to my eyes, like milk. I was dumbfounded. My first instinct was to pick up the baby and take it home, but as I moved towards it, I realised how big it was and that it was most definitely dead and not just sleeping. I screamed,

" You've killed a baby and its Mummy! How could you be so cruel?" and I turned and ran back to the house. I burst into the kitchen, tears streaming down my face, unable to control my shaking body and the bile burning the back of my throat. Mum ran to me and caught me in her arms.

"Let me go! I don't want you! I don't want anyone! You're all murderers and you're going to eat a baby!" Mum hugged me tightly to her chest, whispering calming words and letting me cry it all out. It took a long time before I was calm enough to tell her what I'd seen.

"It's my fault," Mum said, "I shouldn't have let you take down the tray. I didn't think." I knew this wasn't exactly true as I had engineered the whole thing, but this wasn't a time for being honest about unimportant details. I was

160

the injured party and the adults were one hundred per cent in the wrong. They were murderers and were intending to gorge on the fruits of their callousness. This was something I was never going to be a part of.

When Dad came in much later that evening, he called me into the kitchen. He bent down, put his arms around me and held me to him. "Beverley, I know it was upsetting to see a dead reindeer foetus, but it had never been born so it was never alive. When men are shooting at reindeer from a distance, it's not always possible for them to be absolutely certain that it is a stag that they're shooting. Mistakes are made. Now, I'm sorry that you are upset, but we have to eat. Shooting a reindeer is no different to killing a pig or a sheep and you eat meat from both of those animals."

"I'm not eating reindeer. I'm not eating that Mummy or her baby. I won't!"

"The Mummy has been given to Pesca and the baby has been buried. You can eat venison from the other reindeer without being worried."

"Where did you bury the baby? Can I go and see its grave?"

"We gave it a kind burial at sea."

"You mean you threw it into the sea for that leopard seal to get!" I could see by the surprised look on his face that I was right. I pushed myself out from his embrace and looked at him with disgust and hatred.

"You let that baby be torn apart by that stinking seal! I'll never forgive you for that! Never!" I ran into my room, threw myself onto the bed and started weeping all over again. I heard Mum run a bath for Dad and put out his clean clothes in their bedroom next door. She eventually came in to see me and enfolded me like a warm package in her arms, surrounding me with love. "Daddy is very sorry, Bev, but you are a big girl now and you have to understand that things sometimes seem to be bad when they are just the result

161

of circumstances. No one would ever kill a baby reindeer and its mother deliberately, but accidents happen. If no one ate reindeer meat in South Georgia, we would have less food and we have to survive. You know that."

"They didn't have to throw the baby into the sea for the leopards."

"You can't expect them to dig a grave for a reindeer, can you, even if it is a baby? Come to the kitchen now and eat your supper." I wasn't convinced but I knew that Mum was winning the argument, so I held my tongue and said nothing more. I followed her into the kitchen and sat down beside Dad.

"Now, Beverley, tell me about what you have been doing today. Have you got any schoolwork to show me?"

"Yes, Daddy," and I slipped down from my chair and brought my handwriting and sums to show him.

"Very good! Very good! You are progressing really well, Mummy and I can be proud of you!" Far too much praise! He usually forgot to ask about my work or just grunted when I showed it to him. This was an overblown commendation to make him feel better and to placate me. Still, I had to play the game. Without looking at him, I replied listlessly,

"Thank you, Daddy, I'm glad that you're pleased with me." We ate in silence. I toyed with my food, every mouthful made my stomach turn somersaults and I had to fight against bringing it straight back up. If I hadn't hated vomiting so much, I would have. It would have served them right! I think Dad was as relieved as I was when I asked,

"Please may I leave the table?"

"Yes, you may." I went back to my room and read Hans Christian Andersen for comfort.

On Christmas day, 1913, the small, prefabricated, Lutheran chapel at Pesca was consecrated. On every Christmas Eve thereafter, once the men at Pesca and those on the whale catchers had eaten their supper, the two steeple bells were rung. As a group, all of us from The Point walked to Pesca to join the whalers for a service inside the little church. It was a glorious evening, chilly but clear, with a shy moon peeping over the mountain tops. All five of the *R* Catchers were moored in a neat line, the first time that they had been back in port together since they had arrived in South Georgia. We climbed over the wooden bridge which covered the huge mooring rope and walked past the Manager's House, the Bakery, the Slop Chest and the hospital before turning right to join the Norwegians as they walked together in large numbers, following the path past the Kino towards the little white church. Silver moonlight reflected off the cross which crowned the pointed green roof of the steeple and the bells rang in a slightly discordant harmony.

A five minute peal of the church bells reverberated around the mountains and carried us into the building on its wings. We were shown to reserved seats near the front. A sparsely decorated Christmas tree stood to the left of the altar, trying valiantly to lend the little church a festive air. The church had been built to seat two hundred people and it was filled above capacity. Men stood in the aisle and pressed up against the walls. Our combined body heat made the airless room difficult to breathe in and I began to feel quite light-headed. I held tightly to Mum's hand and was about to ask her to take me outside when the Manager walked to the front of the church and the service began. I had missed the moment when I could reasonably leave the church without causing a scene, so I breathed deeply and tried to concentrate on what was happening to keep myself from fainting. The organist played 'Kyrie Eleison' and I listened intently to the music then hung on to every nuance of the address although I didn't understand one word of what was being said. Just being a part of a community which had come together on this one special day of the year to celebrate Christmas, was magical. I soon forgot my queasiness and was carried along by the emotion of the event. We opened our throats and our hearts and sang each carol loudly in English, competing with the Norwegians who sang them in their own language. Then Mr Butler stood in front of the altar and spoke to us about the message of Christmas. I luxuriated in the atmosphere and the uniqueness of the service and remembered back to my last Christmas service in the Tabernacle in Stanley. When it was over, we left the church to the strains of the little organ and were invited back to the Manager's House for coffee. As we walked back home to The Point together, our torches lit the way. Sleeping elephant seals, awakened by our approach, raised their heads, their huge brown eyes shedding tears of annoyance that we should so rudely disturb their seasonal slumbers.

On Christmas morning I woke early. Lying on the foot of my bed was a pillowcase full of presents. I unwrapped sensible clothes which had been sent down from Stanley by Granny McLeod who was obviously aware that I was growing out of my old ones. Grandad Clifton had sent me a tea set; an orange plastic teapot, jug, sugar basin and four cups and saucers. This was better, my dolls and I could have tea together outside in the *Snowgoose* or on my mossy mansion. Then I opened the biggest present. As I unwrapped the brown paper, there lay the most beautiful doll I had ever seen! She had dark, curly hair peeping out from beneath a blue and white gingham hat, securely fastened beneath her chin with blue ribbon. Her dress was made from the same fabric, edged with white lace. When I lifted her up, her long-lashed eyes opened and blue eyes stared back at me. My dolls were baby dolls which I had grown up with and they were very well used, a bit worn really. Here was a pristine doll, beautiful and new, and all mine! I was so happy I carried the doll in my arms into Mum and Dad's bedroom. I woke them both with my cries of

"Mummy! Daddy! See what Father Christmas has brought me!" Through half-open eyes, my parents glimpsed a shining, happy faced little girl, holding out a doll towards them, unable to hold back her pleasure, having to share her emotion with them at that very moment.

"She's lovely, darling," Mum said. Dad asked,

"What are you going to call her, Beverley?"

"Susan, Daddy, after my friend Susan in Stanley."

 "If you go in to Gerald, you can see if Father Christmas has brought him any presents," Mum added. Still clutching my doll, I crossed the passage to Gerald's room. Almost one year old now, Gerald had been crawling for weeks and he could pull himself up and lean against the furniture. He was standing in his cot, holding on to the bars, and looking towards the bedroom door, waiting patiently for someone to come in and release him from his prison. A wet terry-towelling nappy hung suspended between his legs like a hammock from two large safety pins which invaded his vest. I refused to touch Gerald's nappies so I dropped the side of the cot and lifted him carefully out of it, my hands holding him beneath his arms and well away from any wet and smelly bits. On the floor was a pillowcase from Father Christmas so I sat Gerald down in front of it and I reached inside.

"Father Christmas came last night, Ger. Let's see what he's brought you!" There were a few presents at the bottom of the pillowcase, but my hand immediately encountered something big, soft and furry. With difficulty, I pulled it out of the pillowcase. It was a panda, larger than Gerald was! "Look Ger, a big panda for you! Isn't he beautiful!" I sat the panda on the floor in front of Gerald. His soft blue eyes shone with wonder and delight as he reached out his little hands to touch his new toy.

"We'll have to call him Big Panda and call your other panda, Little Panda!" I said. Gerald crawled over to him and I helped him to stand up between Big Panda's splayed black legs. His little hands explored the face then he dropped to his knees and snuggled up against Big Panda's ample tummy. I retrieved Little Panda from the cot and passed him to Gerald. When Mum came into the bedroom, Gerald hadn't moved. Hugging one panda and resting against another, he was in little boy heaven.

I delivered the Christmas telegrams to each house on The Point then, after we had eaten our Christmas dinner, we all met in the Recreation Room. As the adults came in, I introduced them to Susan who they all admired, then they gave me gifts of sweets from the Slop Chest. I thanked everyone warmly and took the boxes of sweets into my bedroom and stacked them carefully in my wardrobe with the others. I would soon rival the Slop Chest itself in confectionery. The table had been taken down and we stood in the large room together, the adults in their party hats, raising their glasses to wish one other a 'Happy Christmas'! Streamers were thrown, the record player was turned up loudly, and the dancing began. I took control of the streamer box and wound my way round the room, unleashing a streamer on each adult and tying them up in its multi-coloured ribbon. The party continued until the early hours of Boxing Day morning. The adults slept late but I walked up to Shackleton's Cross in the grey morning light and watched as the *R* boats left Pesca and sailed back out into the Southern Ocean to re-commence whaling. The Christmas holiday for the Norwegians was a short one, but on The Point, work was kept to a minimum until the celebrations culminated in a New Year's Eve party.

Outside, I shared The Point with a host of adult elephant seals. Males and females came ashore in their hundreds to lie amongst the tussac clumps to moult in single gender groups. Very unattractive now in appearance, their skin resembled moth-eaten velveteen tablecloths, the sort that Granny and all the other old women in Stanley covered their kitchen tables with. The seals created comfortable hollows for themselves between the tussac bogs. Heat escaped from their massed blubber and radiated upwards creating a haze which blurred the outlines of their comatose bodies. They wallowed in their own excreta and, as the weeks passed, the soil became churned up into a wet, smelly mulch, interspersed with pools of stagnant urine. Mum made me responsible for keeping them away from the house and, most especially, from her washing line which was strung out between two long poles outside the conservatory. I took one of Dad's ski sticks and poked the encroaching sea elephants with it. Each one looked back at me, their big brown eyes accusing and tearful, as they nursed their hurt pride and lolloped off towards the beach.

Betty was an exceptional pastry cook, flaky pastry which melted as soon as it touched your lips was her speciality, whereas choux pastry was Mum's. One morning Mum decided that she would try to make flaky pastry, just to see if she could rival Betty's.

She rolled out the pastry carefully, dotted two thirds of it with butter, folded and sealed it carefully and placed it on a dinner plate to rest.

"As I haven't got a fridge, Bev, I think I'll just pop it outside on the top step for ten minutes. It's a cool day so that should do the trick!" She opened the back door and placed the plate on the top step, carefully wrapping a tea towel around it. After about twenty minutes Mum said

"Bev, can you pop outside and bring in the pastry for me, please? I need to add more butter then roll it out again." I opened the back door and almost stepped on the neck of a king penguin lying across it. So tall that he hardly

170

even needed to stretch his neck to reach the pastry on the top step, the king had pulled away the tea towel and was now caught redbeaked in the act of spearing a huge lump of pastry.

"Shoo! Shoo! You naughty penguin!" I shouted, waving my arms in the air, "Get away!"

"What's the matter, Bev?" Mum asked as she joined me on the step.

"That king's eaten some of your pastry, Mum!"

"Damn that bird! Now I'll have to start all over again! Next time I'll weigh the tea towel down with stones. That'll give him something to think about!"

Rubber Bones quickly became a favourite of Mum's and mine, and I had been calling him Uncle Ron almost since the time he had arrived on The Point. When his warship was torpedoed and sunk during the war, Uncle Ron drifted for days in an open lifeboat before being captured and interned in a concentration camp. His maltreatment in the camp left him with skeletal damage, hence his lack of co-ordination. He thought the Rubber Bones nickname was a good joke and often referred to himself by it. Our babysitter-in-chief, Uncle Ron and I spent long hours playing card games together. Incredibly patient and kind, he was happy to take long walks to Pesca with me as I was not allowed to go alone.

On one sunny day, dressed in my favourite red and white cotton dress and wellies, Uncle Ron and I set out on a special expedition. Mum packed us a huge picnic with blackcurrant squash for me and beer for Uncle Ron. Carrying our coats over our arms as a precaution against the changeable weather, Uncle Ron led me by the hand around the harbour, through Pesca and out along the far shore to Hestesletten. Just beyond the sea elephant colony, woolly young king penguins stood silently in their creche, patiently waiting until a parent came ashore and regurgitated partially digested fish into their ever-open beaks. It would be next year before they would moult and be able to join the adults at sea and forage for their own food.

"The baby kings look like teddy bears, don't they Uncle Ron?"

"Yes they do, Bev, but I think they'd be too untidy to sell in any of the big department stores in England! They hardly look very neat do they?" On the beach the elephant seal pups were moulting too, their furry black coats being replaced with sleek grey ones. They snuffled their little black noses at me and a few older ones play-fought with each other, but the beaches were quiet now. No fights were taking place over territory and harems and the pups settled down into a gentle pattern of sunbathing and snoozing, the low guttural sound of contented snoring making a welcome change from the noise and roars which had accompanied the mating season.

Uncle Ron and I laid our coats on the shingle beach and sat down to have our lunch. We had a good view across King Edward Cove to King Edward Point, and the jetty and our house were easy to spot. We watched as two orphaned baby seals tried to make their way to a safe part of the beach, away from the adults who stretched their necks in an effort to bite them as they passed by. While we were eating our sandwiches, Uncle Ron leant across towards me and took my hand in his.

"Don't make any sudden movements, Bev, but there's a leopard seal coming towards us. Stand up quietly, and walk up the bank into the tussac." I did as I was told, not turning round until I was standing well above the tussac line. When I did turn around, Uncle Ron was standing where I had left him. He had reached down onto the beach and grabbed a handful of stones. He aimed each stone at the leopard seal but it was determined to keep coming forwards and it ignored the stones as they bounced off its blubbery hide. This was frightening. I'd seen numerous leopard seals in the harbour, but this was the first one I had seen on land. Elephant and fur seals turned and made their way straight back into the sea if you hit them with a stick or threw stones at them, but not this leopard seal. With its dog-like face and open jaws, it snarled soundlessly at Uncle Ron and I shouted,

"Leave it, Uncle Ron, run up here with me and we can get away through the tussac!"

"Stay where you are, Bev. I don't want this bugger following us!" He reached down for larger rocks and, as the leopard seal moved ever closer, the impact was beginning to have an effect. The leopard stopped in its tracks and it was no longer making headway up the beach. A particularly well-aimed rock hit it directly on its nose and with a snarl, the leopard seal turned and began to move down the beach towards the sea. I was amazed by the speed with which the leopard could move! Elephants moved ponderously, their huge bulk requiring them to stop every few yards for a rest. Fur seals moved relatively quickly on land but this leopard seal seemed to move almost as fast as the dog it resembled. When it had entered the water, Uncle Ron called me back to the shore.

"That was frightening, Uncle Ron, I've never seen a leopard out of the water before! It looked really dangerous and it moved pretty fast!"

"You always treat leopards with respect, Bev, they will attack you if they get the chance. Don't ever get close to one. Remember, they can move as fast as you can over a short distance, so always be on the look-out when you're on the beaches."

"I've never seen one on The Point, Uncle Ron, have you?"

"No, but that doesn't mean that one won't turn up one day. Just be aware of them, that's all."

We walked back through Pesca and called in to the Bakery to beg for a pastry each and some freshly baked bread to take home to Mum. As we walked slowly around the harbour to The Point, we talked about how I spent my days.

"I play on the *Snowgoose* a lot and on the slopes of the mountain. Sometimes I make a house on the top of one of the mossy mounds and take my dolls there. At other times, I just walk around The Point or sit by Shackleton's Cross and look out across Cumberland Bay at the ice floes and the icebergs."

"What you need is a bike," Uncle Ron said, "All girls of your age need a bike to ride. I'll order one for you from England. What colour do you want?" A bike! I was thrilled.

"Oh, a red one please, Uncle Ron! I'll ask Mum to buy me a red skirt to match it!"

"I'll order you a red skirt too, Bev. Won't you look a wonderful sight riding round to Pesca on a red bike!" When I got home I couldn't wait to tell Mum what Uncle Ron had promised to buy for me.

"That is very kind of Ron, Bev, but don't build your hopes up too much, you never know, he might forget to buy it and anyway, getting things down here from England is a difficult business." I tried to take her advice, but I did build my hopes up and I thought about my bike on most nights before I fell asleep.

It hadn't taken long for Uncle Ron to notice bruises on Mum's face and arms. He never said anything to her, and he certainly didn't say anything to me, but on those nights when he and Dad finished their evening sched and Dad had already had too much to drink, Uncle Ron followed him into the house and asked Mum if he could eat with us instead of having to eat the stuff they call food at Discovery House. The food at Discovery was actually very good, but Dad accepted Uncle Ron's word that he didn't think much of it and he regularly stayed to eat with us. Like most of the men on The Point, especially during the long winters, Uncle Ron was an accomplished drinker himself and he could keep up with Dad whenever he wanted to, which was pretty often. However, when he was drunk, Uncle Ron stayed calm and quiet and tended to drop off to sleep in an easy chair. If Dad got angry and started shouting at Mum or me, Uncle Ron woke up and quickly took control of the situation.

"I don't know about you, Peter, but I've had a skin-full! While you go to bed, can I just have forty winks here until I'm able to get my muscles working and can climb the path back to Discovery?"

"Suit yourself! Pearl, help me to get to bed!" But Uncle Ron being in our house was enough to make Dad modify his behaviour and to stop him hitting out at mum. As we got to know Uncle Ron better, however late at night it was when Dad was angry, I pulled on a coat over my nightdress, sneaked up to Discovery House, knocked on his bedroom window until he woke, and asked him to come down to our house for a visit. Uncle Ron became our willing protector.

Mum had ordered some new cushions from Stanley and, when they arrived on the *RRS Shackleton*, she gave me the old ones to put in the hold of the *Snowgoose* to make her more comfortable. Each day, arms filled with dolls, I walked the short distance to the dock where my trusty whale catcher was moored. I was an intrepid Sea Captain, leading the whaling fleet across the Southern Ocean. I appropriated an old broom and tied a wooden spoon to the top of its handle and mounted them in the bow of the *Snowgoose* as my harpoon gun. I stood in the wheelhouse steering her through mountainous seas until I spied a whale blowing in the distance. I steered a crazy course, following the imaginary whale at high speed, hollering,

"Thar she blows!" at the top of my voice. When I had run the whale down, zigzagging across the ocean in hot pursuit, I leapt the few feet across the tilted deck to the bow. Grabbing the harpoon gun, I followed the tiring whale until I was ready to go in for the kill. Once I had harpooned my prey, I hauled it alongside the *Snowgoose* by the fluke and tethered it to the side with strands of tussac grass. Once I had harpooned six whales and had a full complement of three attached on each side of the ship to tow into Pesca, as the leading captain and harpooner in the fleet, I was then able to take a well-earned rest and join my dolls on the cushions in the hold. As I regaled them with a blow-by-blow tale of my latest exploits, I served my dolls afternoon tea from my new orange plastic tea set. From my hoard of Dolly Mixtures which had been sent down from Stanley, I served first an orange and white sweet as bread and butter, followed by pink and white ones as cake. If my dolls had behaved particularly well that day as my jolly crew, I served them a jelly each as a fitting climax at the end of our repast. Even with me clearing their plates at the end of every tea party, a packet of Dolly Mixtures lasted for a long time, as all good captains knew how to make their provisions last throughout the season, and I was the best captain of them all!

Now that it was late in the summer, a few icebergs languished majestically in the calm, opal waters of Cumberland Bay. Jagged ones had torn themselves loose from the three huge glaciers which joined together and forced their way through the mountains into the sea at Moraine Fjord. This summer too, an enormous, flat topped iceberg floated up from the Antarctic Peninsula and joined them. Ice floes floated quietly and leisurely across the bay, changing shape and breaking up as the summer sun melted their superstructures. One day a flotilla of ships approached the entrance to King Edward Cove, their funnels standing proud above their uneven decks. On another day a field of knobbly mushrooms grew on a calm, blue sea.

On the plateau behind Hope Point, sheltered at the base of Mount Duse, a full scale rifle range with mounds up to one thousand yards had been built. This was where Dad practiced his shooting with the .303 ex World War Two rifle which he kept in the Wireless Room. This year's annual competition between The Point and the whaling stations was being hosted by us so Mum and Betty spent several days cooking in preparation. We had been on South Georgia for long enough now not to be surprised by the weather as, even in the summer, storms and gales could rage for weeks at a time. This was one of those times. The wind howled, stirring up white crested waves in the cove and flipping gentoo penguins over onto their backs and sending them scuttling, flat on their stomachs, into the tussac for shelter. It was impossible for the competition to take place so Mum and Betty shared the fruits of their labours between all the houses and for days we sat indoors while the wind threw its might at us, eating vol-au-vents, sausage rolls, cheese straws and jam tarts.

Towards the end of the season, Dad was invited across to Pesca for lunch by Uncle Blom and Uncle Bonski, and at Mum's suggestion, he took me along with him. Holding my hand, Dad and I walked companionably together along the path around the harbour to Pesca. In the dining hall, I sat next to Dad, my back straight and using my very best manners. Beside me was Uncle Blom who drew my attention to a rug on the floor behind us where a small dog was curled up with three black and white puppies nestling against her.

"We have a mother dog with small dogs, you see!" Uncle Blom said, a huge smile creasing his face.

"They're beautiful, Uncle Blom! Please may I play with them after dinner?"

"But yes you must!" Uncle Blom replied. I ate the rest of my meal hurriedly, refusing the offer of cheese and bread that was served to finish off the meal. When there was a lull in Dad's conversation, I tapped him lightly on the arm and asked,

"Please, Daddy, may I leave the table and go and play with the puppies? Uncle Blom says that I can."

"No you may not! You will sit at the table until everyone has finished eating their food. I am angry that you should even ask such a question." I had been publicly admonished and my face reddened. I sat with my hands folded in my lap and my head down, covered in so much shame that I felt that I would never be able to lift up my eyes and look directly at the Norwegians again. After a few minutes when Dad was once again involved in a spirited conversation with Uncle Bonski, Uncle Blom whispered to me.

"I am sorry that I said about the dogs, Beeve, we will wait and you can play with them after a little more time." I glanced up to see not only Uncle Blom looking at me, eyes shining in sympathy, but the other men around the table were looking kindly at me too and giving me discrete smiles through pursed lips. I gained courage from their support and decided to milk their sympathy for all it was worth. I wanted to show up my Daddy for being a horrible and overbearing father. I sat very still, hands carefully folded together in my lap, then I gave a surreptitious, longing glance at the puppies from beneath my long lashes. I was aware that the men noticed. Every so often I repeated my longing look at the puppies, then returned my sad gaze to the contemplation of my folded hands. I could feel that the men around the table were watching me, aware of my desire to play with the puppies and that they thought as badly of Dad as I did. When most had eaten their fill, I looked hopefully towards the puppies once more. Then one whaler, sitting at the far end of the table, reached out towards the cheese board. The man seated opposite me at the table said something in Norwegian, the whaler's hand fell away from the cheeseboard and he looked directly across the table at me. He smiled,

179

forbore to take any more cheese, and the meal ended. I looked up at both Norwegians and gave them a small but heartfelt smile of thanks. I felt particularly gratified that we were bound together by a secret which my father was not only unaware of, but was completely excluded from. Dad and the other men stood up and Uncle Blom put his hand around my shoulders and led me across to the puppies.

While Dad continued his conversations, I cuddled each of the puppies and made friends with their mother. They were tiny balls of black and white fluff, their snuffly noses were black and damp, and their little tails wagged in a delightful way when I patted them. When Dad rose to leave and called for me to come with him, both Uncle Blom and Uncle Bonski said that it would be perfectly alright for me to come back and play with the puppies whenever I wanted to.

"I don't think so, thank you," Dad replied, "Beverley is too young to walk round to Pesca on her own. Actually, she would also be a nuisance here too, so she will have to stay on The Point."   My heart dropped into my wellington boots and bumped along the uneven path as we walked back around the harbour.

I had never climbed up the mountain as far as the base of the dam, but I was growing in confidence and one day, I decided to try to. Reaching the base of the dam was surprisingly easy. The scree on the mountainside gave a good foothold and I scrambled up in good time. From its base, the dam towered above me and I climbed up to the top where the walls of the dam were more than a foot thick and very inviting to walk on. As I walked round the top of the perimeter walls, the deep water inside the dam slumbered chill and dangerous, reflecting a pale sun on its green surface. Once explored, the dam walls soon lost their interest and I looked about me for new adventures. Higher up the mountainside, from just below the snow line, a stream coursed over a small outcrop of rock and fell noisily down a four foot drop into a little pool. I had never seen a waterfall before and was determined to climb up and see it at closer range.

Climbing higher up the mountain was still quite easy, but the scree was thinner and more loose and I slipped several times, grazing my hands and both knees. I thought about giving up and running home to Mum, but I was enjoying the adventure so much that I kept climbing. When I reached the waterfall, my pains were forgotten! The view down the mountain was spectacular. I sat and gazed in wonder. Directly below me, the eight houses and outbuildings nestled together along the length of The Point, their red roofs a bright splash of colour against the green of the tussac and the grey of the shingle. From The Point, King Edward Cove followed a near perfect circle towards me and on round to Pesca at its western end, continuing into Cumberland Bay beyond. From where I sat on the slopes of the mountain and for as far as my eyes could see, mountains and glaciers formed a dramatic and glittering backdrop to the cove. The Ice Palace was too far away for me to see it clearly, but I knew it was there and that the Snow Queen was sitting on her ice throne inside. For the first time since leaving Stanley, I desperately missed having other children to talk to and thought about what they would be doing in school without me. Everything was completely quiet and I felt very alone. The only sound was of trilling water in the streams.

I drew my eyes away from the vista below me and turned my attention again to the waterfall above. Climbing to the top of it was particularly easy as the rocks beside it had been cleared of scree by snow and ice and they shone damply in the sunlight. Looking down over the waterfall was heady. The Point was lit with all the colours of the spectrum as the sun's rays split in the spray. The drop made my head spin as I looked down the cascade directly to the pool and mountain below. I had to grab onto the slippery rocks and lean backwards into the mountain until my vision stopped spinning and the world returned to normal.

I carefully felt my way down to the base of the waterfall. I hadn't noticed before, but the water seemed to fall far enough away from the rock for a small body to creep in behind it. This was a real adventure! I was going to be Shackleton, braving the freezing waters and snowy mountains in my bid to get to Stromness and get help to rescue my men. I flattened my back against the wet rock and slid underneath the waterfall. Before I could get a handhold, my wellies slipped on algal slime and I fell feet first into the freezing pool. Icy water crashed onto my head, forcing me down until I was nearly waist deep. I gasped for breath against the cold and the weight of water which poured relentlessly down on top of me. I couldn't go back and the water was pushing me downwards, my neck felt as if it was breaking and my eyes couldn't see. I was petrified. I felt round the edges of the pool with my hands, desperately trying to find some purchase somewhere. My right hand knocked against a sharp rock and I twisted so that I could grab it with both hands. With all my strength, I tried to pull myself up out of the pool. The water was still beating down on the top of my head, mixing with my own tears to blind me. My knees scraped on the jagged rocks below the water line as I tried to find some way of pushing myself upwards against the might of the waterfall. I was half out of the pool when my welly slipped again and I

182

fell back in, cutting my leg as I fell. My heavy, wet coat hampered me, but there was no time to take it off. I grabbed my handhold once more and pulled myself upwards with all my strength. My knees and wellies together found some purchase against the rocks and I hauled myself out of the pool onto the mountainside. Completely soaked, battered, bruised and feeling very sorry for herself, Shackleton forgot about rescuing her men and wept loudly in pain and disillusionment. Not for long, though. Although it was summer, the weak sunlight held very little warmth. The iciness of the stream water seeped into my bones and I had to get home. I slipped and slid down the mountainside, not caring if I grazed my legs even more. I ran, hobbled and dragged my weary feet along the path to our house. Exhausted by now, I sat on the step and banged on the door crying for my Mummy. Mum threw open the door, gathered me into her arms and took me inside. She stripped off my drenched clothes, wrapped me in a towel and rubbed my skin until it hurt and I cried even more in anguish. She ran a hot bath and the contrast in temperature between my cold body and the warm water as she lifted me in, took my breath away.

When I was warm, comforted and my cuts and grazes had been thoroughly cleaned, Mum asked me what had happened. How had I got myself into such a state? At that moment Dad walked into the kitchen from the Wireless Room, saying he was feeling a bit peckish. His shocked face on seeing me and hearing Mum describe my injuries to him put me on my guard. On my day of instruction about the Golden Rules, Dad hadn't told me not to climb on the mountains, but it occurred to me that that might have been because he never thought I would. Telling him about my walk around the walls of the dam and my scare in the waterfall were likely to make him think that he couldn't trust me to keep myself safe. If I made him cross, his anger would be fierce and long lasting and he would punish me for days. I knew I had to think quickly.

"I was near the big stream at the bottom of the mountain and I was looking to see if there were any fish in it, when I slipped in and got really wet and cold. Then, when I was running home, I fell over on the path a couple of times and cut my hands and my legs. It really hurts Daddy." Looking up pitifully at him and thinking about my stinging grazes helped a few tears to escape to emphasise the point. Mum gave me a hug and kiss and Dad patted me on the head.

"There! There! It's not as bad as it looks you know, Beverley. You'll be right as rain tomorrow. But you must be careful near the stream. Actually, there aren't any fish in there at all. There are no freshwater fish on South Georgia, not even in Gull Lake; they can't survive the winters." He sat down at the table and took a freshly made cinnamon wheel. I breathed more easily. I'd got away with it. The moment of questioning was past. I had explored the mountain! It was my special secret and I was going to guard it from everyone. As Mum often said, what people didn't know couldn't hurt them.

We had basked for two sunny days with temperatures in the low twenties when Dad suggested one breakfast time that Mum should pack a picnic for us and we would walk round to Gull Lake. We walked through Pesca, stopping only at the Bakery to beg for some pastries to help us on our way. Beyond the hydroelectric power station and overlooking the hulk of the Louise, we followed Dad through a low gate in a white wooden fence into the Grytviken cemetery.

" I will show you Shackleton's grave." Dad said and we followed him in a solemn procession.

"The rest of the graves are those of whalers who died here but this," Dad pointed towards the largest headstone standing proud at the top of the graveyard, "is Sir Ernest Shackleton's grave." I stood in front of the granite headstone while Dad read,

"ERNEST HENRY SHACKLETON

EXPLORER

BORN 15TH FEB 1874

ENTERED LIFE ETERNAL

5th JAN 1922"

"I know his wife wanted him to be buried in the Antarctic because that was where he loved to be," Mum said, "but why is there a nine-pointed star on his headstone. That doesn't seem to be very Antarctic to me."

"I'm not completely sure," Dad replied, "I only know that it had some special significance for him and that he had a silver nine-pointed star pinned to his cabin door on the Quest. I think nine was a special number for him in some way." Dad turned to me

"You will notice, Beverley, that Shackleton's grave looks towards Antarctica and out across King Edward Cove where he died onboard the Quest. All of the other graves point east to west which is the normal direction for graves to point."

"I thought Shackleton died at Shackleton's Cross, Daddy."

185

"No. The cairn and cross were built by his companions to commemorate his death, but he actually died on board the *Quest* when she was anchored right about here off Pesca." And he pointed just to the right of the *Louise*. I had always been worried about poor Sir Shackleton dying on Hope Point where it was so dangerous. It was comforting to think that he had died on his ship with his friends around him. With my mind at ease for Shackleton, I followed Dad and Mum out of the graveyard.

We walked up a steep rise to a plateau which stretched, mossy and green, back towards the high mountains surrounding and sheltering Pesca. At the forefront of the plateau a deep lake, navy blue and still, glistened in the sunshine.

"This is Gull Lake," Dad said. "It is one of many glacial lakes which are fed by streams from the glaciers in the mountains. It provides Pesca with its water and as it is so large and so deep, you can see that Pesca will never run dry!" We walked to the pebbly shore of the lake and sat on the warm, dry moss to eat our picnic. After we had eaten, Dad took my hand and we walked together in friendly silence along the shore of the lake while Mum sat in the sunshine playing with Gerald. We were happy and contented together as a family and it was a very happy and special day.

CHAPTER 8

OUR SECOND WINTER

In April, the season ended. There were great celebrations at Pesca as the R boats, together with the new fishing policy which Mr Butler had introduced, achieved the greatest seasonal production of whale oil ever achieved at the Pesca whaling station. Over 94,000 barrels of whale oil had been produced and as it retailed at around £75 per ton for the best grade oil, the total value of the season's production was £1.3 million. Meat and bone meal production also reached a record high and storage of the products was a serious problem. The guano store was filled to capacity and the men had to erect temporary cover for the extra bags of meal before the winter set in. The whalers and the shoremen were buoyant, they were to receive their largest bonuses to date and were straining to get back to Norway to spend it.

We held a party at Discovery House to bid farewell to our Norwegian friends who were going back home to their families for their summer in the Northern Hemisphere. Harald came, smiling and confident, having just completed a spectacular season on the *R2*. Strand and Uncle Bonski were remaining on South Georgia for the winter, but Uncle Blom and Eskedal were going home to spend the summer with their families before returning to South Georgia for the next whaling season. Mum in particular was very sad as Eskedal's weekly visits would end and her excursions to the Kino "kept her sane". The main talk at the party concerned Mr Butler. As an Englishman, at first he hadn't been welcomed by the Norwegians when he had been appointed as Manager. However, under his tenure, Pesca had been thoroughly modernised and was now recognised as being the most efficient and economic land station for whaling in the world. The parent company in Argentina refused to spend any more money to complete the modernisation programme which he had so successfully put into place, so Mr Butler resigned in protest and when his men left, he was going to leave South Georgia with them. A Norwegian was appointed to take over from Mr Butler. Ringdal was a quiet gentleman who often joined our parties on The Point. He had been foreman under Mr Butler and was his obvious successor.

Uncle Blom and Eskedal came to our house for coffee with Mum and I before they went up to Discovery, as our particular friends usually did. Dad was already at Discovery House where the drinking and conversations were well under way. Under his arm Uncle Blom held something, a gift I supposed, wrapped in a piece of old sacking. He held the rough package out towards me and said,

"Here, Beeverley, I have a special gift for you!" I took the bundle which wriggled in my arms. When I drew back the sacking, a little black and white face emerged and around its neck, a fraying piece of red fabric was fastened in a rude bow.

"Uncle Blom! It's a puppy!" I exclaimed in wonder. "Look Mummy, Uncle Blom has brought me a puppy!"

"It is for you to love, Beeve, if your mother likes it. This puppy is one of the ones you met before at Pesca." My heart sank, I knew that Mum didn't agree with pets and that she had said on numerous occasions that she

189

wouldn't have a dog in the house, "Dirty things, always making a mess." I glanced up at her with my best look of supplication. I could see from her face that she wasn't happy.

"Please Mummy, can I keep him? I'll look after him and see that he doesn't make a mess."

"I'm not very keen, Bev. You know I don't like animals in the house. And what would your father think? I doubt if he'd like a dog around the house, getting under his feet." She turned to Uncle Blom and asked,

"Do you know what sort of dog he is, Blom? Will he grow very big?"

"I think he is called a border collie in English, but he could be many things. His mother is a small dog so I think that is what he will be also. He is trained to be clean in the house."

"Can I go up to Discovery and ask Daddy if I can keep him? Please, Mummy!"

"You can. But don't get upset if he says 'No'."

Holding the puppy in my arms, I ran the short distance up to Discovery House. I slipped into the main room and saw Dad talking to Harald. I walked up to them and waited patiently until they noticed me. I didn't disturb their conversation as that would have made Dad wrathful and then he would never have agreed to my having a dog.

"Daddy, Uncle Blom has brought me a puppy. Please can I keep him?"

"A dog? What does your mother say?"

"She says that I can keep him if you say that it is alright for me to do so." This was stretching the truth a long way, but I was desperate to have a puppy of my own.

190

"Well, if your mother says it's alright, I won't object. You must take full responsibility for looking after it though."

"I will, Daddy, thank you very much!" I left the room immediately, before he could change his mind.

Back in our house I told Mum that Dad was happy for me to keep the puppy.

"If your father says it's alright, I suppose you can keep him." I hugged her and then hugged Uncle Blom and Eskedal. The puppy was mine! I had a friend to play with!

"And what name will you give to your dog, Beeverley?" Uncle Blom asked.

"I'll call him Sandy. My friend in Stanley had a dog called Sandy when she lived in England, so I'll call my dog Sandy too." The fact that Susan's dog had been a golden retriever so the name Sandy had been rather more apt, never occurred to me. I missed the party and instead, I played in my bedroom with Sandy. He was an energetic playmate, his little face with its narrow snout had a sweet black button nose at the tip. Big brown eyes sparkled and danced with mischievousness and a lust for life. Sandy scampered around my bedroom, sniffing under the bed and sliding across the polished floor when he jumped on to the mat beside my bed. I pulled him around the room on the mat, pretending that he was on a sled outside in the snow, while he balanced precariously with all four legs splayed apart, trying to stay upright as the mat bunched and stretched beneath him. That night Sandy slept curled up on my mat. He had found a new home, a comfortable bed and a loving owner.

The following day we watched the R boats leave in a line, one behind the other as they had arrived at the beginning of the season, and once more only the over-winterers were left behind to nurse Pesca and The Point through the hardships of winter. I ran around the beach, waving as they steamed out of the harbour, with Sandy yapping at my heels. Back in the house I tried to make Sandy into a living doll. I dressed him in a cardigan which Gerald had grown out of, and it fitted Sandy beautifully, slipping neatly over his front paws and reaching fetchingly across his back, buttoning up neatly under his stomach. However Sandy had other ideas. He objected as soon as I let him go and snapped at the woollen garment with his teeth.

"You naughty dog! Don't tear at your clothes!" I hated any of my things being damaged, I always took great care of all of my belongings. Sandy ignored me completely and snapped at the cardigan ever more angrily, tearing the material ferociously with his teeth, growling more and more loudly as the cardigan refused to budge. In the end, I had to give in and take the cardigan off him. I dressed him once or twice more, but each time the result was the same. I had to accept that I had gained a pet with a definite mind of his own.

John was leaving on the last *Biscoe* out of South Georgia that season to travel back to Ireland to see his family for their summer. When the *Biscoe* came in, Nutt Goodwin, a well-built Falkland Islander with curly hair and a small moustache who dressed habitually in a duffle coat, came ashore to take over John's role and keep the generators working. Nutt was accompanied by his petite wife Dot and their daughter Jackie, who was three years older than me. I felt ridiculously shy and tongue-tied when Jackie came ashore.
"Look, Bev, you've got Jackie to play with for the winter. Go and say hello"
"Hello," I said in a quiet voice, then I looked away and moved back to Mum for support. I hadn't seen any other children for nearly a year and I wasn't sure how to cope with this one. Also she was bigger and older than me and that was a worry. What if she didn't like me? What if she thought I was babyish? I was a bundle of insecurities.

The day after the Goodwins' arrived, Mum and I popped up to Dot's for smoko. Like Betty, Dot had been one of Mum's friends since childhood. Dot was a happy-go-lucky person, quick in her movements and light on her feet. They were living in the Customs House for the winter, a prefabricated Swedish bungalow similar to Betty and Basil's. Underground there was a large cellar for storing food and, with three bedrooms, it was surprisingly roomy.

"Dot and I have got a lot of gossip to catch up on. Go and play with Jackie and show her around The Point." Jackie and I went outside and walked up towards Shackleton's Cross. I was tongue-tied and unsure, but Jackie was a revelation. Confident and ebullient, she chatted about school in Stanley and what she had been doing there; she told me about her friends and what games they played, and where; she was interested in everything she saw and suggested games we could play and plans for filling our time. The winter was going to be fun!

A southerly wind blew for three whole days, keeping us pinned indoors. When the wind changed direction and blew from the east, we were given no respite, it was still far too blustery to venture outside. Once the winds eventually blew themselves out, I cautiously opened the back door and ventured outside. The glaciers had been calving throughout the summer and the high winds had strewn Cumberland Bay and King Edward Cove with brash ice. Ice floes, some as big as cars but many smaller, covered the sea and jostled with one another to crowd the shoreline. Dressed in light cotton dresses, cardigans and wellington boots, Jackie and I stood on the shingle beach down below her house surveying the scene.

"Let's climb onto the ice!" Jackie said, and she put one foot onto a large ice floe which was dancing gently against the beach. She found a handhold in a crevice near the top of the floe and with one heave, hauled herself up on to it. The floe shook and bobbed beneath the force of Jackie's assault, but it stayed upright. Paddling was expressly forbidden by Dad and I knew that it was even more dangerous to play on the ice floes. Floes were really just smaller

194

versions of icebergs with most of their bulk hidden beneath the surface. I had often seen them roll and turn over when the top of the floe melted in the summer sun and they became unstable.

"I think you should get down from there, Jackie. Floes are very dangerous and if it turns over, you'll drown."

"Don't be such a baby!" Jackie said, "It's easy to climb up on one. You try to get on that one there!" She pointed to a nearby floe which was, if anything, bigger than the one she was sitting on. I was very aware of the gap in our ages and I didn't want Jackie calling me a 'scaredy cat' so although I knew that what she was suggesting was foolhardy and dangerous, I determined to follow her lead. I cautiously climbed onto the large floe. The ice was smooth and wet and on my first attempt, I slithered back down the ice, my boots splashing in the shallow seawater. I tried again and by pulling myself upward using grooves in the ice as handholds and footholds, I clambered onto it. It was surprisingly wet and slippery and tilted alarmingly towards me, but by squeezing my hands into two small fissures, I was able to hang on. The ice floe bobbed and I was terrified that it would overturn and throw me into the deeply shelving sea, but under my weight I felt it sink deeper and ground itself more securely in the loose stones of the beach. From my new vantage point, I relaxed a little and began to enjoy the fun of what we had done.

With longer legs than me and with much more confidence, Jackie clambered onto another ice floe. I followed her. We moved steadily from floe to floe. They were unsteady and rocked in the calm sea, and we had to hang on tightly to protrusions and indentations in the surfaces of the ice to keep our balance, as the floes swayed and slithered beneath us. We laughed

195

with the excitement and fun of it all. We worked our way slowly along a short stretch of beach until we got close to Discovery House. Mike stepped out of Discovery and stopped in his tracks. With quick strides he came down to the beach and quietly, but firmly said,

"Girls, carefully come down off the ice, I want to talk to you." With a flourish, we jumped off the ice onto the beach, the force of our feet against the floes sending them spinning and tumbling backwards into the deeper sea. When we were standing together in front of him, Mike deliberately raised his voice.

"I cannot believe how stupid you two girls are! Haven't you any idea how dangerous it is to play on the ice floes? At any moment they can float out into the deeper sea and turn over. If you were thrown into the harbour, you'd be dead within minutes. God, I can't believe how dangerously you two have been behaving!" His face was red and he was obviously having difficulty controlling his temper. We hung our heads, but he hadn't finished with us.

"Beverley, you've been here long enough to know how dangerous the sea is and how quickly the beach shelves. Weren't you thinking? What will your father say when I tell him what you've been up to?" The fun went out of the day. Dark storm clouds gathered around my head.

"Please don't tell my Daddy, Mike, please! I promise I won't ever play on the ice again, only please don't tell my Daddy. Or my Mummy." I added as an afterthought. Dad would be beside himself with anger, not just because I had ignored his Golden Rule about playing on the beach, but because I had been stupid and thoughtless which were the biggest sins of all. I would be in serious trouble for days and when he'd had a bit to drink, he'd take it out on Mum too, that was certain. Mum wouldn't just be upset, she'd worry about me every time I was out of her sight in the future. I hated worrying her but I had to admit to myself that this wasn't all about how she felt. If she was worried enough to make me stay near her at home, my freedom was going to be compromised. It might have been my impassioned plea, although it was more likely that Mike knew how Dad would react; either way, he was mollified and agreed not to tell anyone about what we'd been doing as long as he had our solemn promise that we would never do it again. Quietly we gave our word then sloped off back to Jackie's house and got out her dolls. Then we looked at each other and smiled. We might have got into trouble, but it had been brilliant fun while it lasted!

Gentle snow feathered down from the sky for several days and the topography of The Point disappeared under a neat, white blanket. Being outside was blissful. Jackie and I stood with our arms outstretched and our mouths open, eating snowflakes as they landed on our tongues and walking around like snow-scarecrows. Our coats and mitts were layered white beneath pristine snow and our home-knitted woolly hats were too. We stayed indoors in our own houses when the blizzards came and raged outside. Mount Duse was almost invisible behind drifts of loose snow which the wind gathered up from its slopes and whirled around The Point, creating snowdrifts against the walls of the houses and turning the *Snowgoose* into a large, white hump on the shore. The temperature plummeted and grey skies blotted out the sunlight. The world outside became dark and forbidding. We lived under full electric light and Dad had to keep going outside to dig out the snow which drifted a foot deep in hours against the back door and the door to the Recreation Room. Twice a day, Dad buttoned himself into his overcoat, a long scarf wrapped so many times around his neck and head that only his two green eyes were visible. Head bent against the wind, he trudged then skied his way through deep snow to the henhouse. We watched from my bedroom window as he dug out the door, the pile of discarded snow to his left eventually growing as high as the small wooden shed itself. He checked that the electricity was working and that the hens had heat. There were no eggs to collect, but he took them corn and scraps from the kitchen. As in the real depths of winter, Mum heated the scraps for the chickens, just to give them some added warmth.

Once the snow stopped falling, I took Jackie and Dot up to Hope Point to give them skiing lessons. Jackie picked it up much faster than Dot who was more afraid of falling over so she overcompensated for every bump and lost her balance in the process. Once they could stay upright on their skis, Mum left Gerald in his cot by her bedroom window where we could see him and we took Jackie and Dot onto Mount Duse. The men and I had already been skiing there for several days and had stamped out a piste from the soft snow. Soon Jackie and I were spending long hours on the mountain, skiing down from the dam onto the flatter strand below. It was so much more fun to have a friend to ski with than to ski on my own as I had the previous winter. South Georgia was more exciting now and the days passed quickly.

Dad and most of the other men on The Point were drinking very heavily again. In the morning he would come into the sitting room after his sched and pour a large whisky. If Mum remonstrated with him for drinking so early in the day, he got very angry and remained in a bad temper until bedtime. By seven o'clock in the evening, he was deeply drunk. Mum put Gerald to bed early to keep him out of Dad's way and I played quietly on the carpet, Sandy sitting beside me, tail wagging and his little pointed face watching us all intently.

One evening, Dad stood up to go to the table and refill his glass. He was unsteady on his feet and stumbled forwards, dropping the glass. I picked it up and handed it to him. He took the glass from me without a word and stepped towards the table once more. Sandy thought we were playing a game and frolicked about around our feet, yapping and wagging his tail with glee. Dad looked down at Sandy and shouted,

"Bloody dog, get out of my way!" and with that, he launched a ferocious kick at Sandy, catching him under the stomach and launching him into the air. Sandy flew across the room and crashed into the wall, landing in a small heap beside the table, whimpering in fear.

"Get out of here, you bloody dog!" Dad yelled, his face distorted with anger. Sandy scarpered from the room, still whimpering and with his little tail hanging limply behind him. I stood my ground, unsure what to do. I wanted to run after Sandy, but I was afraid to draw Dad's attention to myself and anger him further.

"Can I get your drink for you, Daddy?" I asked, hoping to pacify him.

"I'll get it myself now I'm up," he growled, as he executed a few unsteady steps before falling heavily into the armchair. After a few minutes, I judged that it was safe for me to leave the room. Sandy was still whimpering pitifully and was being comforted by Mum. I cried in sympathy with him.

"Take Sandy into your room, Bev. I'll watch Peter." I carried Sandy carefully into my bedroom, pulled back the covers and tucked him into my bed. I lay down on the top of the bed beside him and patted his head, talking quietly to him and giving him whatever comfort I could.

Later, when Mum came in to settle me into bed, she told me that we needed to teach Sandy to keep out of Dad's way when he was drunk. Every day thereafter, when Dad was in a bad temper from drink, I made a 'ssshhh' sound and put my finger to my lips. I pointed to my bedroom and Sandy learned surprisingly quickly that this meant that he should go to my bedroom and stay there until I joined him. He was a clever little dog and we came to love one another very much.

The *Darwin* arrived on her now annual mid-winter visit to South Georgia. From the moment she tied up at the jetty, our house was crowded with Falkland Islanders. I was shy and out of my depth. Everyone knew who I was, but I didn't know them. I stood quietly in the kitchen being briefly chatted to, patted on the head and then left alone as a long line of men first congregated in the kitchen talking to Mum, then moved on into the sitting room for a serious chat and an even more serious bout of drinking with Dad.

The *Darwin* was staying overnight so Mum invited her and Dad's closest friends up for a meal. As it was a special occasion, she had planned the meal well in advance and Uncle Bonski brought across a huge number of frozen whale steaks for her to cook. During the whaling season, the butcher in Pesca hung enormous cubes of whale meat inside wire cages to protect it from the birds. Once the oil had dripped out of it and it turned black, he cut off the black meat and sliced the red meat into thick steaks before freezing them. Mum marinated the steaks for an hour in a one-part vinegar to two-parts water solution then she dried them in a tea towel and they were ready for frying. Mum served the whale steaks with lashings of her special onion gravy as we all squeezed up together, elbow to elbow, around the kitchen table. The food was delicious, succulent and tasty as only Mum could prepare it.

"By God, that was as good a steak as I've ever tasted, Pearl!" said Brian, an old friend of Mum's.

"Thanks Brian, I'm glad you enjoyed it!" Mum replied.

"You certainly haven't forgotten how to cook! I didn't know that you could get beef down here. It comes in frozen, I suppose?"

"That wasn't beef, Brian, it was whale meat! You can't get beef down here at all!" Brian stared at Mum, stupefied. His face drained of its colour and his hands flew to his mouth. He started up from his chair, knocking it over in his haste to rush to the back door. He threw the door open forcefully and we heard him retching outside, bringing up his whale meat in large, undigested dollops which fell on to the ground in great splats. I put my hands over my ears so that I didn't have to listen to the disgusting sounds of vomiting, scratching my thumbnails against my fingers to drown out the noise. When Brian came back inside, wiping the cuff of his jumper across his mouth, all of the adults laughed loudly at him. I failed to see the joke.

"You idiot," someone said, "you liked the steak well enough when you thought you were eating beef! What's the bloody difference?"

"I wouldn't eat whale meat if you paid me!" Brian replied in a self-conscious manner.

"Well you bloody well did eat it without being paid and you enjoyed it! At least you did, until you thought about it!"

Dad leaned across the table towards me and said jokingly,

"Actually, Beverley, this is a good lesson for you. This was an excellent example of auto- suggestion. Remind me one day to explain it to you!"

Everyone around the table laughed loudly at Dad's joke. I didn't need to ask him to explain it to me, I had seen enough to understand what auto-suggestion was, thank you very much! Anything connected with vomiting would stay permanently imprinted on my mind.

With his continued drinking, Dad's temper became increasingly uncertain. He was hitting Mum two or three times a week and making her get Gerald and me out of bed. On those occasions, I sat in the armchair cradling Gerald in my arms. If Gerald cried, Dad screamed at him so I started to take him down into the Billiard Room. If Dad wouldn't let me leave the sitting room, I gave Gerald my finger to suck and held him and Little Panda close to my chest, both to comfort him and to smother his cries. The nights after parties were always the worst as Dad drank copious quantities of beer, followed by a mixture of spirits, at every party. Mum and I sat together in the kitchen and had a serious talk together before the mid-winter party at Discovery House.

"Bev, I've been thinking. When your Dad has had a few to drink, he always asks you to go to the bar and get his drinks for him. If you go to the bar and say that he only wants a bitter lemon without the gin, whoever is behind the bar will think that's what your Dad asked for and give it to you. He will never know. That way, we can keep his drinking down and he'll be better when we get him home."

"But Mum, what if Dad finds out that I've done that? He'll be really angry with me and give me the biggest hiding I've ever had."

"By the time he's drunk his beer and had a few gins, he's lost any idea of what's going on around him and he doesn't taste anything. Try it tonight. It'll work, you'll see."

As the party progressed the adults, with the one exception of Mum, became increasingly tipsy and the noise level rose.

"Beverley, come over here and get me another gin!" This was the instruction I had been dreading. I did as I was told, of course, and took Dad's empty glass from him. I crossed the room to the bar and deliberately made sure that my back was turned to Dad. In a quiet voice I asked Mike, who was taking his turn behind the bar,

"My Daddy would like a bitter lemon without the gin, please." There was a deep silence amongst the men near the bar and they all looked at me. I froze. What if one of them made a joke to Dad about him going easy on the booze or 'losing his drinking arm'? Mike picked up the gin bottle and put it on the bar, directly in Dad's line of vision. Then, he took the glass in his hand, bent down behind the bar, and poured in the contents of a bottle of bitter lemon. He passed me the gin-free glass and said,

"There you are, Bev, your Dad's gin and bitter lemon!" I felt interested pairs of eyes boring into my back as I crossed the room back to Dad. I caught Mum's eye as I walked and she gave me a little nod of encouragement.

"Daddy, here is your drink," I said. I didn't dare to say "Here is your gin and bitter lemon," because that would have been a lie and I wasn't good at telling lies. Mum always told me that I had to tell the truth because she could see

204

lies clearly written across my face, and I believed her. Fortunately, the ruse worked. Dad drank his bitter lemon without a word. When he called me back to refill his glass, I did the same thing again and Jimmy, who was on bar duty this time, made a show of displaying the gin bottle but gave me a glass of bitter lemon only. Once again, Dad didn't notice. I saw several of the men smiling when I asked for the new drink for Dad, but I felt that they were smiling in a kindly way. Mum's black eyes and bruised arms couldn't always be hidden in such a small community and, although no one ever said anything, she and I were always treated with the utmost care and friendliness by all the men on The Point, and by the Norwegians. That night was a little victory for us. Dad never found out what we were doing, and it was a little ploy which we used at most parties thereafter. We won a partial battle, but we both knew that we were never going to win the war.

Jackie and I were stuck indoors for days by misty, cold and dismal weather. We cut up most of Mum and Dot's retail catalogues to make paper dolls. We chose ladies in the skimpiest lingerie possible, preferably standing straight on to the camera, with two arms, one clearly visible on either side. We got Mum to stick them on to cardboard with flour-and-water paste before cutting round them very carefully.   The dolls were now stiff enough for us to be able to cut out dresses and coats and hang them around their necks. We cut out fridges and ovens, mats and chairs, beds and bookcases to make beautiful homes for each of them. Then we dressed them up to go visiting each other and to go to parties and dances. My bedroom was a sea of paper so the window could never be opened in case the carefully designed rooms and wardrobes were blown away. But after days of being housebound, even playing with paper dolls lost its allure. Real dolls weren't much better and

Gerald could only be kept amused for so long. As the days wore on, we looked for more excitement.

Just before Jackie went back home for her supper, she had an idea. "I know! Let's have a midnight feast!" She led the way into the Billiard Room and told me to help her to take the cloth off the table. The billiard table was covered in a heavy-duty green canvas cloth which was always left folded in half as it was still large enough to cover the table top. When we unfolded the cloth to its full size, we pulled it over the table and it fell to the floor on all four sides.

"Come under here," Jackie said, lifting up the cloth and crawling under. "We could leave our food here for our midnight feast then, when Mum sends me to bed, I'll climb out of my bedroom window and come down here. You can get here too and no one will know. Then we can have our midnight feast!" It was a brilliant plan and it was sure to work! I went into the kitchen and asked Mum if we could have some cake; we went into my wardrobe and collected packs of chocolate, liquorice hats, chocolate-covered marzipan logs and chewing gum. We took our hoard back to the Billiard Room and stored it under the table.

"We'll need something soft to sit on," Jackie said.

"Let's bring our pillows tonight, they'll be good!"

Dad came in from the Wireless Room very drunk, too drunk to eat. He took himself into the bedroom and Mum helped him to get into bed. "He'll sleep all night now, Bev, so we'll have a quiet time," Mum said as she gave me a hug before supper. Mum fed Gerald then we ate our pork chops, with mashed potatoes and tinned peas, before Mum tucked Gerald into his cot. Mum and I sat and listened to Stanley Radio for a while before I feigned tiredness and went to bed. As always, Mum came in to tuck me up and give me a big goodnight hug and kisses.

"Goodnight darling. Sweet dreams!" and she put out the light and left the room. I waited patiently for what seemed like a long time then I got out of bed, put on my coat over my nightie, took my pillow and carefully opened the bedroom door. The passage was empty but there were lights on in the kitchen so Mum must still be in there. Furtively, I crept along the passage toward the dividing door with the Recreation Room. The door creaked protestingly on its hinges as I pushed it open and, as I went through and turned back to shut it, there was no sign of Mum, so I was safe! I ran into the Billiard Room and crept in beneath the cloth. Jackie was already there! Our adventure had begun.

It was a very dark, clear night. We sat on the billiard table looking out of the window towards Pesca. Silver streamers emanated from the reflection of a full moon on the harbour and the mountains towered serenely above the sparkling display. In the clear sky, bright stars clustered around the Southern Cross and twinkled brightly. We whiled away an hour choosing stars amongst the southern constellations to give as a special present to everyone we knew, then, growing tired, we crept under the tablecloth to commence our midnight feast.

We hadn't been eating sweets for very long when we heard voices. We both went "Ssshhhhh," with our fingers against our pursed lips, and we sat stock still. Footsteps entered the room; there were several men's voices and Mum's voice too.

"I'm sorry I had to come and get you, Ron, but Peter's asleep and I'm so worried about Bev. She wasn't in her bed when I went to check on her. I've searched the house and I can't find her anywhere. I can't think where she might have gone."

"Don't worry, Pearl, we'll find her. She can't have gone far. Where does she like to play?"

"Over in the old boat over there. She calls it the *Snowgoose*. I didn't think to look in there. That's probably where she is."

"I'll go and have a look," said a deep voice, "you stay here with Ron." Jackie and I looked at each other, still keeping quiet. I wasn't sure how to deal with this unexpected turn of events. I suppose I should have thought about Mum coming back in to my bedroom to check on me before she went to bed herself, but the thought had never crossed my mind. I felt very uneasy. I signalled to Jackie, lifting up the edge of the cloth and pointing, indicating that we should go out. She shook her head. She was probably right, we would get into serious trouble if we were found. Better to sit it out. Mike, who had gone out to the *Snowgoose*, came back.

"Sorry, Pearl, no sign of her there. We need to think about how to go about this. Perhaps we should cover The Point and search it systematically? What do you think?" Before he could receive a reply from the other men, Mum burst into tears.

"My Bev could be in the harbour by now, drowned! If anything happened to either of my babies, I couldn't live myself. I just couldn't get up every day if I didn't have both my babies."

"There, there, Pearl! I'm sure Bev is fine. She probably just wandered off into the night for a little walk. She's a sensible girl, she won't come to any harm. Don't you worry, we'll find her!" I couldn't bear it. Mummy was crying and it was all my fault. Without another glance at Jackie, I crept out from underneath the tablecloth and ran to Mum, flinging myself into her arms.

"I'm sorry Mummy, I didn't mean to make you cry. I'm alright! Jackie and I just wanted to have a midnight feast, that's all!" Mum held me close to her, stifling her sobs and kissing my head as if she might never hold it again.

Mike lifted up the edge of the tablecloth to reveal Jackie, our pillows and the remains of our feast.

"Well! Well! What have we here then? It looks like a real feast. Can we all join in?" Jackie crawled out and offered everyone some of our goodies. No one was angry and no one reproached us in any way until Uncle Ron said, "Jackie, I'm going to take you home to your Mum. I don't think either of you should do anything like this again unless your Mums know where you are."

"We won't!" we both promised. As the men turned to go, Mum said, "Thank you all very, very much for coming out to look for Bev, I'm very thankful. I just wonder, could I ask you not to say anything to Peter about it? He's asleep now so he doesn't need to know, and he will be very cross with Bev if he finds out."

"Of course we won't say anything to Peter, Pearl. There's no point in getting Bev into even more trouble is there? I'm sure she'll never do anything like this again, will you Bev?" Mum and I knew that it wasn't only me that Dad would be angry with. In his present state of mind, we would both feel his fists. I shook my head in assent. I had learned a very hard lesson.

When Mum tucked me into bed, I held her tightly around the neck and wept.

"Mummy, I'm so sorry that I made you cry. I promise I'll never do anything like that again."

"It's alright, darling, you just know how your Mum gets if she thinks anything has happened to her babies. I couldn't bear it if anything happened to you or to Gerald. But you have to think a bit more about how Daddy is too, and you mustn't do anything that will upset him either." She didn't have to say anymore, I knew exactly what she meant. I needed to be good and to think all the time about what would keep Dad happy and stop him getting into a temper with us. I was nearly seven and it was about time I acted more like a grown-up.

Part of that growing-up was the greater responsibility I felt for Gerald. He was a glorious little boy, blonde haired with enormous blue eyes and a sweet smile. He was walking, albeit unsteadily sometimes, and he was experimenting with his first words. When Dot came down for smoko, Jackie and I played cars and lorries with Gerald, and on days when the blizzards were particularly fierce and we were housebound, I took Gerald into the Recreation and Billiard Rooms and we played 'chase' around the tables or made a den under the billiard table, just as Jackie and I had done so disastrously several weeks before. He had a gentle nature and was learning quickly to stay silent whenever Dad shouted, and to scramble to my side, leaving Mum to cope with Dad's temper while we watched developments from a safe distance.

Jackie had her tenth birthday in June and I was going to be seven on July the fourth. Mum and Dot hosted a joint midwinter and birthday party for us together at Discovery House on midwinters day, the 21st of June. Once again, I dressed in my blue net dress and white canvas shoes. Together,

Jackie and I welcomed all the over-winterers from The Point and Pesca and graciously accepted the kind gifts of cartons of sweets and chocolates which everyone brought for us. Most exciting of all were the joint gifts from Strand and Uncle Bonski. They had asked the carpenters at Pesca to make Jackie and me a dolls cot each, an exact replica of the one which they had made for Gerald when we arrived on The Point. I was thrilled as I now had a bed for my other dolls to sleep in. Susan had no need of a wooden cot because my present from Mum and Dad was an oval crib of lace-edged, pink flowered fabric with a hood which could be raised and lowered to shade Susan's eyes from the light when I put her down for her daily naps. By the end of the evening I was so fired up that is was impossible for me to sleep, even if I had wanted to. As usual I listened for sounds coming from Mum and Dad's bedroom, but this night all was quiet. I climbed out of bed and gazed through my bedroom window at the full moon shining on the snow and on the pack ice in the harbour. Mount Duse rose mighty and dark in the background, it went up and up and I had to bend my head backwards so that I could see the fluffy hat of clouds sitting on its head. Sheltered in its lee, The Point lay protected in a cascade of silver moonbeams, reflected back by the crystalline crust of the snow into my room, lighting my face in its glow. It was the most beautiful night I could ever remember, and I stood at the window for more than an hour, while the peace and tranquility bathed my soul with its healing.

Even though Mike was teaching Jackie and me multiplication and division for a few hours each week, Dad listened to me read on a few occasions, but he had a short attention span for fairy stories. Generally, he took my Hans Christian Andersen book, allowed me to choose a story and barked a few questions.

"What is a botanic garden?"

"Spell 'crocodiles' and explain to me what type of animal they are and which part of the world they are found in."

"Spell 'restraint' and put the word into a sentence."

"Spell 'illuminating' and describe something to me which you think is illuminating." In preparation for his questioning, I read a new story again and again with great care and learned very quickly to ask Mum the meaning of words that I was unsure of. If it was a word that Mum didn't know, I asked Dad when he was sober and seemed to be in a good mood. I took pains to learn how to spell the long words, as those seemed to be the ones that Dad questioned me on. Where Dad was excellent, was in making up sentences for me with the chosen word embedded in it and which made its meaning completely clear.

With Eskedal home in Norway, our visits to the Kino in the Pesca motorboat had been severely reduced. We were not such close friends with Eskedal's replacement so we skied round to Pesca more often. One evening Mum and I went to the Kino with Betty, Jimmy and Mike. As it was late in the winter and the spring thaw was just beginning, we didn't talk and skied neatly behind one another like a troupe of ducklings, silent and careful not to set off any avalanches.

On our return from the Kino a glowing white full moon hung low in an ebony sky. We skied back home, our way lit by moonbeams reflected off the snow. We soon found our route around the harbour blocked by an avalanche which had obviously occurred while we had been watching the

212

film. Snow had swept down the mountain in such a mass that a new spur of the mountain seemed to have appeared which pushed out into the sea. We had to scale the spur of loose snow so Mike led the way with Betty behind him, then me, then Mum and behind her, Jimmy. We climbed up the side of the snow hill, carefully placing our skis in Mike's tracks to compound the snow beneath them. At the top of the rise, we skied silently, following in Mike's tracks over uneven and very soft snow, skirting headless snowmen which surrounded us like a frozen army in the silver moonlight, their shadows pointing like stubby fingers up the mountain from where they came.

Suddenly, Mum gave a little, startled cry and as I looked behind me, she fell away beneath me, carried on top of a huge slab of loose snow which had dislodged itself and continued its downward slide. Coming to rest on the avalanche snow which was jutting out into the sea, Mum stayed silent and still, holding her nerve and looking up at us with pleading and terrified eyes. I wanted to cry but I bit my lip and tried to quieten the noise that my heart was making as it pounded inside my chest. Silently, Mike, Jimmy and Betty made a human chain. Mike carefully edged his way down towards Mum, then Jimmy followed for a short distance, and Betty anchored herself by digging her skis deep into the snow and leaning back into the mountainside. Mike got just close enough to Mum to grab the ski stick she held up to him. With his other hand, Mike held his ski stick up to Jimmy who repeated Mike's actions and held his stick up for Betty to grab. Slowly, carefully, without a word, Betty began to pull on Jimmy's stick, he pulled on Mike's and Mike pulled Mum inch by inch, up through the soft snow back to where Betty and I were waiting. In the moonlight I could see that Mum was shaking but there was no time to comfort her. Again without exchanging a

213

word, we lined up and followed Mike across the avalanche and back round to The Point. When we reached the door of our house, we all started to talk at once. Now that the danger had passed and we had returned safely, our voices lifted and words tumbled out of our mouths in a sheer torrent of noisy relief. What we said was unimportant. The fact that we could say anything at all and were unhurt and safe was enough. We drank coffee or whisky with Dad around the kitchen table and ate huge slabs of cake. The film was forgotten, only the escape from the avalanche filled our minds. Mum, still shaking but remarkably stalwart fed us all, her eyes shining with either unshed tears of relief or the sheer joy of just being alive.

Most Argentines crewed ships like the steam tanker the Conquistador, and were itinerant. Carlos, a short, round man with neatly cut black hair and an even more neatly trimmed narrow moustache, was one of the very few Argentinians who were based at Pesca. As most of the men allowed their beards and hair to grow straggly and long, especially during the winter, Carlos's fastidiousness of dress and appearance caused him to stand out. He spoke very broken English, but his love of food and cooking overcame any communication problems. His favourite pastime was sitting in the kitchen with Mum, discussing food and looking at her one recipe book. During one of their chats, Carlos persuaded Mum to let him come round and cook her a 'mondongo' which he assured her was a great Argentinian delicacy. Two days later, he knocked at the door at smoko time and dropped a very full sack on the kitchen floor. From this sack rolled numerous catering sized tins of baked beans, tomatoes and tomato puree; fresh onions, garlic, carrot, potatoes and apples from the Pesca cold store; bacon and bay leaves, and from the depths of the sack, a mountain of pork tripe. Enthusiastically, Carlos cut up

214

the tripe into small pieces on the draining board while he directed Mum to work on the onions and garlic. In her biggest pan he put the tripe on to cook in a broth of bacon, onion, garlic, apple, carrot, bay leaves, tinned tomatoes and tomato puree.

"You have more?" Carlos enquired, pointing at the saucepan. Mum showed him her three smaller pans.

"No good. Big! You got big?"

"He wants another big pan, Mum. Shall we go and ask Dot if she's got one?"

"No, go up to Discovery House, they'll have big pans up there." Jackie and I jumped onto our skis and whizzed up the slope to Discovery House. We returned minutes later dragging a huge pan between us like a sleigh. In the kitchen, the two large pans of tripe simmered away for four hours. When Dot called in for an afternoon cup of coffee, she was greeted by Mum and Carlos preparing mounds of potatoes and fretting about how he was going to cook it all.

"You'd better come back with me, girls, and I'll lend you my biggest pan, too," Dot offered.

"Will you and Nutt come down for supper?" Mum said, "It looks as if we're cooking enough for the whole Point!" Jackie and I skied up with Dot. She attached a length of thin rope to her largest pot and we dragged it behind us through the snow back to Carlos. He was happy now, in his element, surrounded by billows of steam and cooking for glory.

As the cooking progressed, the sheer quantity of mondongo that Carlos was preparing became evident. Piles of potatoes tumbled into the pots and Mums' eyes opened in surprise. She whispered in my ear

"Go down to the Wireless Room and get your Dad." When Dad walked into the kitchen, Mum put on her brightest smile and said

"Look, Peter, Carlos is making us his mondongo. I've invited Dot and Nutt but, since there's so much food to go round, shall we invite Betty and Basil and the men from Discovery House too?" Never slow to take in information and with the three huge, steaming pots giving him a particularly cogent clue, Dad sent me up to Discovery again to invite everyone to a mondongo party. Then I skied up to the door of the Magistrate's house and knocked loudly.

"We're having a mondongo party, Mr Matthews. Mum says would you like to come down and join in?"

"A 'what' party, Bev?"

"Carlos is cooking a dish from Argentina called a mondongo, you've got to come and try it. He's cooked enough to feed us and the whole of Pesca together!"

As everyone arrived, Mum handed them a plate or a bowl and a spoon. Dad had set up a bar in the passage. With our implements at the ready, we queued up in the kitchen while Carlos ceremoniously ladled out his mondongo. Lumps of tripe, vegetable and apple plopped into our bowls, swimming delectably in a tomato sea. Mum dropped grated cheese on the top and we all tucked in. Despite its humble beginnings, the dish was delicious! Tasty, hot and satisfying, it cheered and warmed us on a bitter winter's night when we hadn't seen the sun for weeks. After everyone had had seconds and had eaten their fill, we still had a whole pot left over, enough to feed the whole Point for another day.

CHAPTER 9

SPRING AND SUMMER

With the onset of spring came the melting snow and avalanches again. Jackie and I broke icicles off from the side of our house and had sword fights with them. We gave up skiing and played indoors most of the time. Gerald played near us with his lorries and cars, but I wasn't very keen to play with him as I knew that Jackie was leaving on the Shackleton, which was due in very soon.

The first ships of the season arrived bringing back Uncle Blom and Eskedal, together with a full complement of whalers. The first *Conquistador* brought down fresh fruit from Argentina and, on board, were Nigel's wife and new baby son. On the morning that she was due to arrive, thick fog enveloped The Point and Pesca and even the harbour was completely obscured from sight. After dinner Eskedal came across from Pesca to collect Nigel and we stood on the jetty, peering into the gloom until the ghostly outline of the Pesca motorboat emerged from the swirling mists and Nigel was able to clamber on board. The *Conquistador* couldn't be seen, but we were able to hear her foghorn as she crept nearer, navigating by radar alone. Jackie and I stood in the doorway of her house, looking out across the bay, growing more and more excited as the foghorn sounded louder and louder until, as if she were the *Marie Celeste,* the ghostly outline of the *Conquistador* slipped past us silently, seemingly devoid of crew or passengers. About an hour later we assembled on the jetty to welcome the new arrivals to The Point. By now the fog had cleared and a snowstorm was being carried in on the back of a driving wind. Nigel handed his wife, Jenny, into the waiting arms of the men and then he carried the baby ashore. Jenny was very pretty, slender and smiling with dark, wavy hair peeping from beneath a scarf tied very securely under her chin. Jackie and I stood apart from the landing party, shy and tongue-tied, as Jenny's luggage was loaded on to the trolley and Dad and the others bent their backs to push it up over the rise, past Discovery and the other houses to the little green-roofed bungalow which nestled beneath Hope Point at the farthest end of the settlement.

When the *Shackleton* arrived from Stanley, even the parcel of school work and a new dress sent down by Grandad failed to lift my spirits. John arrived back from his holiday in Ireland and, although he was a lovely man and it was nice to have him back in South Georgia, the *Shackleton* was taking Nutt, Dot and Jackie back to the Falklands now that Nutt's contract was complete. I stood on the jetty, tears streaming down my cheeks, as I waved goodbye to my friend. As I ran around the headland, waving manically to her as she waved back to me just as hard, sobs racked my body and my heart was full of bitter regrets that I was still on The Point alone, while she was going back to Stanley to start school again and play with all of the friends who were waiting there for her.

Later, when I walked into the kitchen, Mum saw how upset I was. She wrapped me in her warm arms and hugged me tightly against her ample bosom.

"I know you'll miss Jackie, Bev, but you'll soon get used to being on your own again and Gerald is getting bigger now and much more fun to play with." I looked at Gerald's golden head, bent over his lorries as he concentrated on filling the tippers with Dolly Mixtures from our newly arrived annual supply. I loved my little brother, but he was no substitute for someone of my own age to play with.

"I know, Bev, why don't you have a look at your new school books. Go and sit at the table and I'll bring you a nice glass of cordial to help you to concentrate on your work. Then I'll make some chocolate buns just to keep you going!" Dear Mum, food and hugs were her answer to everything. Still, it seemed to be a good idea and it would at least give me something to occupy my mind.

Jenny settled in to her bungalow quickly and soon she was having coffee regularly with Betty and Mum. A biologist herself, Jenny was keenly interested in Nigel's work. They bought a Linguaphone course in Norwegian and spent an hour each day learning the language so that they could converse more easily with the Norwegians on the island. Before she left England, Jenny was worried about Martin's diet on South Georgia so she wrote to the Heinz Food Company to ask them how many tins of baby food she would need to take with her, and they replied that she would need twelve hundred tins, which was the equivalent of eighteen months supply! Heinz offered to give her the tins of food free in return for allowing them to use her story for publicity. Jenny agreed to this and a photograph of her and Martin, together with a short article, appeared in several British newspapers. Jenny generously shared some of the cartons of baby food with us. Even though Gerald and I certainly didn't need pureed food, we tucked into the tins with relish, especially the chocolate semolina and rice pudding.

Now that the sealing season had begun, Nigel once again organised to go out with each boat in turn. Jenny's first experience of having him go to sea with the sealers was terrifying for them both. Because the waters around South Georgia were largely uncharted, the old sealing boats had to navigate rough seas and treacherous inlets unaided in order to get close enough to the shore to land the prams. On the first trip of this new season, Nigel went out with the Albatross. Unusually, this winter the pack ice stretched from the Antarctic peninsula right up to the southern shore of South Georgia, so two-thirds of the beaches where sealing was licensed were inaccessible. The Albatross tried to negotiate her way into a particularly rocky cove about a mile around the island from The Point, but she ran aground on submerged rocks and began to list heavily. In response to her distress call, the *Dias,* which was nearby, steamed back into Pesca at her top speed of seven knots.

We watched from the jetty as Eskedal, in his motor boat, met her in the bay, handed across a long towing rope, then she turned tail and steamed out to sea to rescue her sister sealer.

Dad was monitoring the exchanges between the sealing ships and Pesca while Jenny nervously waited at home, terrified that, at any moment, the ship would move with the tide, slip on the rocks and turn turtle. When the *Dias* reached the *Albatross*, she reported back to Pesca that she was still listing heavily, but the hull appeared to be intact and she wasn't taking on water. Happily no one on board had been injured and the crew and Nigel were in no immediate danger. The *Dias* attached a towing rope to the *Albatross*, but being a smaller ship, and already fifty-six years old, this little old lady was unable to accomplish the task alone. The third Pesca sealing ship was too far away to be of any practical help, so the *Bouvet* was dispatched from Leith Harbour and steamed in to join the rescue. At high tide that evening, the *Dias* and *Bouvet* between them, managed to refloat the *Albatross* and we watched for her lights as she limped back home into safe harbour with her crew and passenger unscathed. There was still snow on the ground so when Nigel got ashore, he had to ski around from Pesca in the dark, his skis running in the deep ruts we had created during the winter. After the drama of that night, Jenny felt completely unnerved whenever Nigel was at sea.

Strand was keen that I should pursue my education and whenever he came to our house, he would take me to one side, peer at me over his spectacles and ask,
"And now, Beeverley, what have you done for your school?" I always exaggerated what I had done, but with Mike having been our tutor during the

winter, it had been much easier to field his questions. To encourage me in my studies, Strand asked the carpenter in Pesca to make me a desk as a surprise gift. He brought it round to The Point in Eskedal's motorboat and, together, they struggled up the path from the jetty to our house. When Mum opened the door to them, Strand, holding the desk aloft, presented it to me with his usual kindness and huge smile. Behind him, Eskedal carried a wooden chair to complete the set. It was a particularly solid and heavy desk with a sloping lid which opened on quiet hinges to reveal a storage compartment inside for my books. Now that my school package had arrived from Stanley, I opened the lid and slipped three of the four workbooks inside. With pencils sleeping in the groove along the top of the desk and an India rubber at the ready, I opened the first English workbook and began to read. Short extracts from famous books were followed by comprehension exercises. Creating sentences, which illustrated the meaning of new words, was easy as they were far less complicated than those Dad gave me to work with. I sat at my desk and worked through the book with real enjoyment, but I couldn't help thinking how much nicer it would be if I could be doing this work in a classroom with other children, so I invented some classmates and held two-sided discussions about our work and what we would do when we went outside to play. Now that Jackie had gone back to Stanley, I felt my isolation much more keenly and at times, I felt lonely and a little bit lost. When I had completed all of the exercises in the first English book, I opened the cover of the first arithmetic book and received a shock. The sums were multiplication and division again, just as the last ones had been, but these were different. Instead of multiplying or dividing by numbers up to twelve, the multipliers and divisors were all numbers greater than twelve. What did that mean? I looked at the calculations in the back of the second book. There was a divisor of 46 in one question. Was I going to have to learn multiplication tables up to 46?   It seemed like a lot of learning to have to do and my spirits slumped.

Dad and Uncle Ron were working long scheds now as they were in regular contact with the cargo ships, whale catchers and factory ships which were lumbering their way down through the Southern Ocean. Uncle Ron often ate with us while these long shifts were taking place. When Dad and Uncle Ron came into the kitchen for their evening meal, I stood beside Dad's chair and proffered my new arithmetic books.

"Daddy, I can do the English work which was sent down from Stanley, but I don't understand the arithmetic. Do I have to learn more multiplication tables to do these sums?"

"Not sums, Beverley, calculations."

"Sorry, Daddy! Calculations."

"Actually, Beverley, these are forms of arithmetic called long multiplication and long division. The whole point of this work is that you are able to complete multiplication and division calculations without knowing more multiplication tables in your head. I am much too busy to teach you now, but I'll show you what to do another time."

"Thank you, Daddy." I was crestfallen. I had got into the swing of schoolwork again and I wanted to complete it all before the next boat left. I wanted to send my work back to Stanley quickly so that the teachers at school would be pleased with me. Now it might be months before Dad taught me, if ever. His patience for teaching had been worn out a very long time ago. Uncle Ron must have seen the disappointment on my face.

"You know, Peter, now that Mike is going down to Antarctica on the next Biscoe and Bev doesn't have a teacher, what about if I teach her for an hour on three afternoons a week as Mike has done? I think I could just about manage to teach her long multiplication and division. It would break up the day and give me something to do."

"Well, if you don't mind, Ron, that would be a help. Actually, I don't enjoy teaching Beverley, probably because she's my daughter. I'm sure she would learn better from you than from me anyway."

"Well, that's settled then", said Uncle Ron, "Tomorrow is Wednesday so you come over to my room after dinner, Bev and we'll make a start!"

"Thank you, Uncle Ron, I'll look forward to it!" And I did look forward to it. I loved learning and I was incredibly fond of Uncle Ron. Mike was a more distant character, although very kind and patient. Uncle Ron and I were close and being with him would be fun.

The following afternoon, once we had finished our dinner, I collected my arithmetic books and walked the short distance to Discovery House. I knocked politely on Uncle Ron's bedroom door and entered in response to his

"Come in, Bev!" I had never been in Uncle Ron's room before. A single bed rested against the left wall with a small locker beside it. A large, glossy, black lacquered box, lavishly decorated with red roses and twirling greenery stood on a square table behind the door.

"Uncle Ron, what a beautiful box!"

"That, Bev, is my Black Box, the best radiogram you will ever hear! When we've finished our lesson for the day, I'll play you one of my records as a treat!"

"Thank you, Uncle Ron! I'll really like that!"

"Well, sit down on the chair," and he gestured towards the only chair in the room, nestling beneath the window, "and we'll begin!"

The hour of my lesson flew by. Uncle Ron was a good teacher, logical and fluent. We worked through examples of long multiplication patiently and thoroughly. He set me a page of calculations to do on my own before our next lesson on Friday, then said,

"Alright, Bev, now for a treat! I'm going to play you a song by the greatest singer in the world. You won't have heard of her, but her name's Pearl Bailey. She sings the blues like no one else. Sit back, close your eyes, and listen to this!" With a swirl of his hand, Uncle Ron delivered a record from within a brown paper sleeve, laid it reverently on to the turntable, and sat down on the edge of his bed. I sank back into the upright chair as best I could, closed my eyes and listened. After a short orchestral introduction, a deep, dark voice sang:

"Takes two to tango,
Two to tango,
Two to really get the feeling of romance.
Let's do the tango,
Do the tango,
Do the dance of love…"

I listened, rapt, to a melodious voice as it breathed life into every syllable of every word of the song. I had never heard such depth of expression before and I felt bereft when it ended.

"That was wonderful, Uncle Ron, not like any of the records we play! It's not like Elvis or anything."

"It's the blues, Bev! This music comes from the Deep South of America. It's the music of the American Negroes!" I didn't understand who Negroes were or where the Deep South of America was, but I did know that I was tingling with emotion.

"Why don't you play your Pearl Bailey records at parties Uncle Ron, or at our house?"

"This music isn't to everyone's taste, Bev, so I prefer to keep it to myself. And I'm afraid that someone might scratch my records when they've had a few at a party, so that's another reason why I keep the records safely in my room. The Black Box and Pearl Bailey will be our secret!" I had seen enough of how adults behaved at parties for myself to recognise the wisdom of Uncle Ron's words. I left his room looking forward to our next lesson so that I could hear Pearl Bailey sing again.

On her way to the Antarctic bases, the *Biscoe* called at The Point, but she only stayed for a few hours while she offloaded supplies and post for us from Stanley. As I walked back up the path towards our house after she set sail, Uncle Ron came out from the Recreation Room door and called me. I walked inside and found him and Dad standing beside a very large cardboard box.

"I've got you a present, Bev," Uncle Ron said, "come in and help us open it." The cardboard was stiff and very strong, it took several minutes for Dad and Uncle Ron to tear it enough for me to get a glimpse of what was inside.

"It's a bike! Oh, Uncle Ron, it's beautiful! I can't thank you enough!" I ran to Uncle Ron and threw my arms around his waist. He bent almost double and wrapped his long, spindly arms around me to give me a hug.

"Now you can get round to Pesca in a few minutes, Bev! We won't see you for dust now, will we?" As the bike was revealed in all its glory, my heart sank a bit. The bike was shiny and new, but it was blue and white and not red. Also, there wasn't any sign of a skirt to go with it as Uncle Ron had promised when he mentioned a bike to me when we were walking home together from Hestesletten last summer.

"Beverley," I thought to myself, "you're being greedy and unkind. This is the best present you've ever had and you're still not satisfied. Be grateful!" I banished my disappointment and ingratitude and took hold of the handlebars. It was truly a magnificent machine.

"Look, Bev, it's got a shiny bell so that you can scare the seals and penguins out of your way!" Uncle Ron joked.

"Get on to the bike and let's see if you can ride it," Mum said, as she came in to the room from the house, Gerald gripping her hand tightly as he waddled unsteadily beside her. I got on to the bike but, as soon as I put both feet on the pedals, I toppled over and had to put one foot on the ground to steady myself.

"Careful!" Dad said. "I'm going to hold on to the saddle and you ride slowly around the table. You'll soon get the hang of it." For an hour, Dad patiently circled the table tennis table with me, building up my confidence and helping me to get my balance. Once he had completed the afternoon sched, he spent a second hour with me. He never once raised his voice and we laughed together when I wobbled and had to struggle to stop the bike from falling to

227

the floor. By bedtime, I was riding my bike in wobbly circles around the room, clutching the table to stop myself from falling off whenever I lost my balance.

"You have really done very well, Beverley! With a bit more practise tomorrow morning, you should be safe to take the bike outside. Now, I'm going into the house for supper. Don't be long!" As he left the room, Dad turned back towards me and said,

"Actually, there is one thing you should remember. Ron went to a great deal of effort to get this bike for you and it cost him a lot of money. I expect you to look after it and keep it as new. If I ever find that you have left it outside in the rain, I will take it away from you and you will never see it again."

Now that I had my bike, I discovered a new freedom. With Sandy yapping at my heels, I rode around The Point and around the harbour to

Pesca, but usually only as far as the huge mooring rope. Beyond it, Pesca was working twenty-four hours a day again, processing the whales which were being towed into the whaling station with the utmost regularity. I knew that I wasn't allowed there without an adult and, anyway, I was much too shy to ride past the men on my own. Each day I took Gerald for a ride on the bike. I perched him precariously on the saddle and held on to him around the waist. With my right hand, I steered the bike and together, we made our wobbly way to the *Snowgoose* where we played Sea Captains and Crew and feasted on Dolly Mixtures, snug amongst the cushions in the hold.

In Mum's pantry were two food items which we pilfered whenever the chance arose. Gerald and I had developed a taste for icing sugar. We sneaked into the pantry when Mum was in another part of the house. We licked our fingers, stuck them quickly into the packet of icing sugar, then ran out through the back door. I plonked Gerald into a tussac bog then leapt into a nearby one myself and we sat in comfort and licked the sweet confection, making it last as long as we could. The other thief of food from the pantry was Sandy. He had developed a taste for raw potatoes. Whenever the pantry door was left open by mistake, Sandy ran in, worried the potato sack with his teeth until a hole appeared, then rolled out a potato. Knowing that he was stealing, and remembering a few hard smacks which he had received from Mum in the past when he had been caught red-handed, Sandy became an expert potato stealer. With the prize in his mouth, he ran into my bedroom and devoured his tuber beneath my bed. If I disturbed him while his jaws were chomping on his potato, he gave me a little snarl, his lips curling up to bare his teeth. I don't know if Sandy would have bitten me had I tried to relieve him of his contraband, but as it was only an old, chewed potato, it

229

never mattered enough to me to try. We had our icing sugar and Sandy had his spuds. It was only fair after all!

The Captain of the newly arrived *Conquistador* came to visit us with Carlos. An ugly, ungainly modified tanker, this Ryan steamship carried oil and men between Argentina and South Georgia. The Captain spoke excellent English and we got along very well together. Our reward for our hospitality was an invitation to have lunch on board. Gerald and Sandy were left at home with Uncle Ron while Dad, Mum and I walked round to Pesca on a chilly but sunny day. We were given a warm welcome by the Captain who shook our hands energetically in turn, before leading us down, deep into the bowels of the ship. Carlos had warned us that it would be a long meal with perhaps seven courses, so Dad had prepared me well. I knew that I must eat a little of each course and not give any indication at all that I wasn't enjoying myself to the full, even if the afternoon proved to be a long one.

The first course was soup. Mum was served hers first and I noticed her eyes widen as she glanced down into her bowl. I was served mine next and I realised immediately why Mum was staring directly at me and giving me her 'Don't you dare to say anything!' look. Nestling comfortably in a deep pool of thick, white liquid were two glistening orbs. Two codfish eyes stared directly up at me from their central position in my bowl. I glanced at Mum and saw that she was still observing me from across the table, so I sat meekly, hands crossed in my lap, and tried not to look at the fish eyes which, to be fair to me, was a difficult feat to achieve. Mum was lucky, she only had one eye, but I had two, bobbing serenely. Mum looked across at Dad and when he had been served his soup and realised what was concerning her, he said,

"There might be too much soup for you to eat, Beverley, and probably for you too, Pearl. It is alright to leave what you can't manage. I am sure that you will be excused."

"Thank you, Daddy," I replied and picked up my spoon. The soup tasted quite nice in fact. What was disconcerting, as I moved my spoon around the bowl, was that it set up a current in the liquid and the two eyes, in neat procession, followed closely behind the heel of my spoon. By dipping the spoon quickly into the soup, I could raise eye-free liquid to my mouth. I tried not to notice the two glassy orbs as they stared at me in a disfigured duplicate, chasing one another around the bowl in a crazy pattern which made my head swim. I pushed them down to the bottom of the bowl but they popped straight back up and gyrated on the surface. I tried to turn them over so that they wouldn't stare at me, but they were like wobbly men and turned themselves the proper way up again. I ate the soup very slowly, and said a polite and heartfelt 'thank you' of gratitude as the steward cleared away the offending bowl and the eyes fixed me with a final, glassy stare.

The Captain and officers kept their cutlery at the end of each course, but we were given clean cutlery as each new course arrived. We ate gastronomic South American dishes, followed by a huge beefsteak served with salad. It was a very long and delicious meal, spoilt only by the imprinted image of two gyrating fish eyes staring at me from behind my retinas as I closed my eyes to sleep that night.

The underground alcohol trade in Pesca was a frequent talking point for Dad and the other men on The Point. As they had plentiful supplies of alcohol, which they freely imbibed, the activities of the whalers across the harbour provided an endless source of amusement. The main joke was that the *R* catchers were the cleanest ships on the planet because their crews ordered cases and cases of Brasso, supposedly for the express purpose of keeping the brass of the new ships clean in poor weather conditions! The men put the Brasso into freezers or out in the snow whereupon the main contents froze but the alcohol floated to the top and could be poured off. Rice and sultanas were heavily ordered foodstuffs too. Home-made equipment for making rice or sultana wine was hidden in ingenious places all around Pesca.

'Soup' was made from a mixture of yeast, sugar, raisins and potatoes, or potato peelings. The soup was hidden in a cupboard or wardrobe with a cloth over it and a bulb beneath. As the mixtures fermented, a dense stench of yeast and decaying vegetables emanated from various bedrooms into the corridor of the New Barracks. The smell was stronger and more disgustingly potent even than the smells from the blubber cookers. At intervals the 'vintners' lifted the cloth, dipped a cup in and tasted the liquor. At the weekend, the 'wine' was siphoned off and stored in old, well-used glass bottles and used liberally to lubricate dry throats. For even greater potency, the tinsmith made stills. Once the soup had fermented and was really stinking disgustingly, it was poured into a still and heated from beneath. The 'steam' when condensed was amazingly pure alcohol. It was one of the Manager's frequent duties to go on rice-wine and still hunting expeditions. On one occasion a still was discovered containing 95% alcohol!

Puro however, was a different thing altogether. It was a contraband alcohol brought down by the Argentine crews and sold to the whalers as a way of making a little extra cash on the side. Puro was carried south in half-litre

232

bottles and was nearly pure alcohol. The whalers either drank it diluted with water or with some fruit cordial added to it to improve the flavour. Dad and Basil brought back stories from Pesca of whalers who went on board the *Conquistador* fully dressed only to stagger ashore later without their watches, razors, radios, or even most of their clothes, hugging a bottle of puro! No one on The Point would touch puro. 'Gut rot' is what Dad called it.

Whenever a ship came in to Pesca from Argentina, Basil dressed in his policeman's uniform and in his role as customs officer, went round to check the ship for puro and other contraband. When he boarded the ships, the crew 'forgot' their English and failed to understand anything that he said. When he came upon a locked cupboard or cabin, it took ages for the key to be found and when Basil eventually got to look inside, there was never any puro in sight. Sometimes he spotted a member of the crew rushing along the deck carrying a full sack. When Basil asked to examine the contents, the sack was inevitably found to be full of rubbish. He always found some bottles of puro and brought them back to The Point where he either poured it into the sea or we used it as window cleaner.

"They deliberately leave some bottles for me to find I think, just so as I'll go away happy!" Basil said. "But did I tell you about when I went aboard the *Harpon* when the Argie nationalists brought her down? No? Well I had a bloody good day, Chay! I found fifty-six bottles of puro hidden around the ship, and I threw the lot overboard because there was too much to bring back to The Point here. The crew were beside themselves and almost lynched me! They threatened to throw me overboard and said they'd murder me if I ever set foot on the *Harpon* again! Knew enough English to say that, the buggers!"

233

On the day of the Inter-Station Football Tournament, which was being hosted that season by Leith Harbour, the *Sabra* collected the men from Pesca then drew up alongside our jetty so that we could hop on board. It was a beautiful day, sunny, warm and flat calm so I was able to stay up on deck and position myself away from the diesel smells which on the Sabra were so potent that they had turned my stomach on our first trip to the Winter Sports. When we arrived at Leith Harbour we were met by the Manager, Sverre Asketh, and given a delicious breakfast before the tournament started. Husvik also had a football team and as each team played both of the other two, the tournament went on for several hours. I soon got bored and Mum said,

"Bev, I want to walk over to the graveyard. My Uncle Dick is buried there and I promised your Grandad that I would visit his brother's grave while we were down here. I asked Peter to find out where his grave is and apparently it's in what they call the 'new' graveyard. The original one is here in the middle of Leith because a landslide caused them to rebuild around it, but the new one is somewhere out beyond the oil tanks, so let's go and see if we can find it." Clasping Gerald to her shoulder, Mum and I walked past drab buildings along Pig Street towards the flat shore and on towards the twenty or so huge oil tanks, similar to those at Pesca. As we rounded the oil tanks, a little stream ran down to the sea and above it sat the graveyard. There were four rows of graves. As we walked between them, there were several which were clearly quite recent and I wondered to myself what had happened to these men. No one had died at Pesca to the best of my knowledge and I was surprised that men had died at Leith.

We walked along the rows of graves then,

234

"Here it is Bev! I've found it!" Mum stood at the foot of a grave in the middle of the third row. On the headstone was a small plaque which read:

RICHARD CLIFTON

PORT STANLEY FI

DIED 4-3-1933

AGED 28

Mum stood quietly, staring at the gravestone, lost in her own thoughts. When I thought it was alright to talk to her, I asked,

"Mum, what did he die of? Was he a nice man like Grandad?"

"He was a lovely man, Bev! He came down to South Georgia to make enough money to get married. But while he was here, he died through lack of cabbage."

"How do you mean, through lack of cabbage?"

"He died because he didn't get enough vitamins in his food. That's why we always buy cabbage from Pesca. It's very important that you always eat your cabbage!"

On Christmas Eve we attended the Christmas service at the little church in Pesca then went to a party at Discovery House. As usual, Dad got very drunk, but so did everyone else, with the exception of Mum of course, who still refused resolutely to ever try a drop of the stinking stuff! When we got back to our house, I undressed quickly and got into bed. Because Dad was so drunk, I stayed awake as always, ready to slip out of bed and sneak into the passage and wait outside their bedroom door so that I could listen to what was going on between him and Mum. By now I had developed a wide range of strategies which allowed me to push open their bedroom door and intervene when Dad began to use his fists. Nightmares was my best ploy, and by the time Mum had taken me back to my room and 'comforted' me, Dad had usually fallen asleep, grumpily and aggressively snoring like a sea elephant.

I knew that my sack of presents was going to be left on the foot of my bed because Father Christmas and his sleigh visited every child in the world, even if they lived on remote islands like South Georgia. That Christmas Eve night I was anxious to get to sleep because I knew that Father Christmas only came when children were asleep and, if I was awake when he happened to come to The Point expressly to deliver presents for Gerald and me, he wouldn't leave any for us at all. The idea that he might fly over South Georgia several times in the hope that I might have dropped off was unthinkable, so I was desperate for Dad to go to bed quietly and not be in one of his aggressive moods.

Instead of going straight into his bedroom as he usually did, Dad pushed open the door to my bedroom and fell headlong across the foot of my bed. I pretended to be asleep although how anyone could believe that I hadn't been awakened by such a crash, I couldn't understand.

"Fe bloody farn!" he said, and tried to push himself up.

"Be quiet, Peter, or you'll wake her," Mum said.

"Don't you tell me what to do, woman! I want my daughter to get her presents from Father bloody Christmas and that is what she'll get!" With that, Dad plonked a pillowcase of presents lumpily across my feet and staggered his way out into the passage again, breathing heavily and hanging on to the doorposts for support. I listened as Mum got him into bed and breathed a huge sigh of relief when I heard him begin to snore. A little part of the spirit of Christmas died inside me.

I sat up in bed and wondered what to do. I was confused about what Dad had said about 'Father bloody Christmas'. It was clear to me now that Santa must be a fairy story and not a real person as I had believed him to be, but my difficulty was that Dad clearly expected me to still believe in him. Mum hadn't come back into my room so I couldn't ask her advice. I thought I might as well open my presents. I was anxious to see what I had been given and felt too excited to sleep. Then I thought again! What if I opened my presents now and Dad found out? He would know that he had woken me up and he would be furious. I resolved to try to go to sleep and pretend that I'd heard nothing.

When I awoke early on Christmas morning, I opened my presents to find a children's encyclopedia, full of facts arranged in alphabetical order and illustrated with small, coloured drawings depicting the wonders of the world. It was a marvellous book and I sat up in bed reading it, beginning with the 'aardvark' which was an African animal, as exotic in nature to me as its name. When I heard Mum and Dad stir next door, I grabbed my encyclopedia and rushed into their room.

"Mummy, Daddy, Father Christmas has been! Look what he brought me, an encyclopedia! Isn't it the best book you've ever seen?" Mum and Dad smiled at me and talked to me about my other presents. Then Mum brought Gerald into the bedroom and together we all helped him to unwrap his toys. Neither Mum nor Dad mentioned the previous night, and neither did I. I made sure that I mentioned 'Father Christmas' once or twice in Dad's hearing as we talked to friends during the day. I didn't want his vanity to be hurt.

That Christmas was a 'Noddy Christmas' as far as Gerald and I were concerned. He fell in love with the two Noddy stories 'Father Christmas' had brought for him and we sat together, resting our heads on Big Panda, Gerald holding his Noddy car. While I read the stories over and over again, Gerald made the 'parp, parp' noises of the car whenever they were required and even when they weren't.

My lessons with Uncle Ron continued and while they were instructive and we often chatted about facts I had gleaned from my encyclopedia, the best part of my lessons by far continued to be the blues music which we listened to together once the school work had been done. As time wore on and I could play with longer and longer multiplication and division sums, he left me more and more to educate myself from my encyclopedia. Uncle Ron and I spent most of our hour together sitting back, closing our eyes, and being carried away by the velvet tones of Pearl Bailey.

Uncle Ron had other L.P's too, primarily by another blues singer, Ella Fitzgerald. He had a double L.P. called 'Ella Fitzgerald Sings The Cole Porter Songbook'. When he started to play me tracks from these records, I fell more in love with Ella than with Pearl. 'I Love Paris' and 'Always True To You In My Fashion' became my favourites and I hummed the tunes as I wandered around The Point. As Uncle Ron was so enamoured of Pearl Bailey, I thought it would be unkind of me to tell him about my preference for Ella. I thought that he might get upset and stop sharing his records with me, so I held my tongue.

The weather that summer frequently kept me in the house. Warm, calm days sometimes reached a temperature of fifteen degrees Celsius, rising higher when a fohn wind blew. Then, suddenly, the weather would break and thick clouds descend. On most days there was some rain or drizzle, but usually not enough to send me running home. Gales, usually but not always short-lived, were frequent. The weather often changed, sometimes from hour to hour. Sunshine, rain or snow squalls, gales and everything in between were packed into a single day. The weather patterns were so completely unpredictable that I was unable to go far on my bike because the weather broke with such speed and frequency that I needed to stay within easy reach of the house.

On one particularly sunny day when I was feeling fed up with being stuck on The Point by the weather, I decided to find something exciting to do

so I ventured further than I had ever done before. Beyond Hope Point the
mossy hillocks soon gave way to shale slopes at the north-easterly extent of
Mount Duse. I climbed the lower slopes with difficulty as the loose shale
and stones fell away beneath my feet and I frequently slipped back down the
mountainside as quickly as I tried to climb it. As I progressed further along, I
noticed pretty coloured stones in the shale, survivors of volcanic activity in
the ancient past. As I looked more keenly, I found brown, green, yellow and
reddish stones, some worn to glass, shiny and reflective. I had found
precious jewels! They became rubies, emeralds and diamonds in my hands!
Keen to find more, I ventured further and further up and along the slopes,
away from The Point. I was Snow White leading the dwarves to their mine
to dig in the dark depths of the mountain for treasure. I needed somewhere
safe to store my jewels and looked around me. About a hundred yards
further on and higher up the mountain there was a fairly large overhanging
rock. I made my way with some difficulty across the steep and slippery
terrain but I wouldn't give up and I eventually reached it. The rock was
firmly embedded in the mountain and was never going to fall away, even
under the force of the strongest gales or heavy snow. Crouching beneath the
overhang, I used a large piece of flat stone to scrape away a ledge beneath it
then sorted my jewels according to their size, colour and clarity. Completely
intent on hoarding my treasure trove, I forgot the Golden Rule and never
once turned round to look across Cumberland Bay or up the mountainside for
weather systems sweeping in. Suddenly, without any warning, it turned cold.
A dense bank of heavy cloud had rolled rapidly down the mountainside and it
enveloped me in its dank mist. Suddenly shivering, I turned to my left and
looked back towards The Point. It had disappeared completely. I couldn't

240

see it anymore. I crept beneath the overhang of the rock as the wind was blowing strongly by now, flinging glacial sleet horizontally into my face. There was no shelter anywhere to be found. I had gone out to play wearing only a summer cotton dress, white ankle socks and heavy leather shoes. I hugged my arms around my body trying to keep warm, but my light dress was already soaked through and clinging to my skinny limbs. Cold, frightened and unable to see more than a few feet in front of me, I decided that I had to walk back towards The Point. The weather could change rapidly again but it could also set in for the rest of the day. I slid unseeingly down the mountainside to the base until I could feel moss beneath my feet. I knew that if I walked westwards and kept the mountain slopes on my right, I would eventually reach the path to Pesca and then I would be near home. For over an hour the winds buffeted me and the sleet flew. My progress was painfully slow. If I climbed a bit higher up the mountainside, shale footholds gave way under my weight and I was shivering so much that my footsteps were unusually unsure. If I stayed on the moss, in the mist and sleet I could easily wander away from the mountain. If I did that, I was frightened that I might stray towards the sea and fall over the cliffs. Cold, miserable and wretched as I was, I was more worried about the reception waiting for me when I eventually did get home that I was for my own safety. Mum would be beside herself with worry. I imagined her standing at the window, staring out at the grey mist, tears streaming down her face for her lost little girl. Then I thought about Dad. If he knew I hadn't got home before the weather came down, he would be furious with me. I had forgotten the Golden Rule. I trembled to think what he would say and prayed that Mum would be able to keep my absence from him.

Before I reached the path to Pesca, the wind dropped, the sleet stopped and the clouds began to lift. My plan had been a good one and I could see the cove curving to my left towards our house. By the time I had run the last quarter of a mile home, my dress was beginning to dry out and the world looked peaceful and calm once more. As I got near to the house, Mum ran out through the conservatory door towards me and gathered me into her arms.

"Where have you been, Bev? I have been worried to death because you weren't here for your dinner when the weather came down! What happened to you? You know you should always get home before bad weather comes in."

"Sorry, Mum, but the storm came down so quickly I just sheltered under a rock until it went over."

"You'd better go into the Wireless Room and tell your Dad that you're alright. He was very cross with worry because you didn't do as you were told, so say sorry to him nicely and show him that you're alright. I'll get you something to eat." With mounting trepidation I walked slowly through the Recreation Room to the Wireless Room, thinking about what was the best thing to say and how to say it. Deciding on the 'happy' approach I ran up to Dad's chair and put my arms around his shoulders.

"I'm very sorry if I worried you by being late, Daddy, but the clouds and sleet came down so quickly that I thought that it was safer for me to shelter under a big rock until it went over. That is the right thing to do when the weather is bad, isn't it? I couldn't see far enough to walk home safely."

"Your mother and I have been very worried about you, Beverley. You have been told time and again about keeping a lookout for changing weather. You know the Golden Rule. You know full well that you must always get home before the weather changes. If the weather hadn't changed again I would have had to have called out the whole Point to go searching for you. I've always told you to get home before the weather breaks and the gales come. Where were you?" This conversation was straying onto dangerous ground. I hadn't been told not to explore the mountain beyond Hope Point and I wanted to go back there again to find more treasures, but Dad might stop me from going there if he knew the truth.

"I've made myself a house on a moss hill over near the base of the mountain but when the cloud came down all the moss hills looked the same and I couldn't see where the houses were. There's a big rock there and I crawled

243

under it until the weather got better. I know you told me to come straight home if the weather got bad, Daddy, but this was so quick that I truly didn't see it coming, then it seemed better if I just stayed where I was. I'm sorry if what I did was wrong and that I've made you angry with me." I held my head low, crossed my hands in front of me and looked down at the ground. "Perhaps, in the circumstances, you made the right decision. However it is very unusual for you to get no warning of cloud coming in. On this one occasion I will overlook it, but you know the Golden Rule and I don't ever expect to have to talk to you like this again."

"You won't have to, Daddy, I promise. I'm so sorry about today. It did all happen so fast though."

"The speed at which it changes is a well-known feature of South Georgia weather. It is something you should have to get used to by now and have to be on a constant look out for. Now go back to your mother and have something to eat."

"Yes, Daddy! Thank you, Daddy!" I quickly left the room before he could think of anything more to say.

"What did your father say?" Mum asked when I walked into the kitchen.

"He told me to always be sure to get home before the weather changes in future. But it did change so fast today Mum, honest."

"Well you're lucky that he let you off so lightly this time. I thought a slap across the back of the legs was the least you'd get because he was so cross. Now look what I've made for you, a nice plate of hot stew." I tucked in with relish.

In April, a new Ryan ship sailed into Pesca. She was called the *Calpean Star*, and she was the most attractive ship I had ever seen. She had been built by Harland and Wolff in Belfast in 1929 and launched as a passenger ship called the *Highland Chieftan.* She had twin screw propellors and was able to carry nearly seven hundred passengers, a hundred and thirty five of them in first class. She had six holds for carrying refrigerated cargo so she was a perfect choice for carrying the Pesca whalers and a cargo of meat and bone meal back to England. When we were invited onboard, I was overwhelmed by the grandeur of the interior. The first class public rooms and the dining room were lined with oak and heavy oak beams stretched overhead. Coloured glass panels decorated the doors and as the sun shone through them, they threw crazy beams of colour across the carpeted floors. We were taken up to the bridge which was large and spacious. When I sat in the Captain's chair and looked out across the harbour, the bow seemed to stretch far into the distance before me.

As we walked back around the harbour after our visit to the *Calpean Star*, I kept glancing across at her clean and sleek lines as she floated gently on the slight swell. Two squat funnels sat attractively above her white superstructure and she gave me the impression of being a grand lady of the sea. Compared to the *Conquistador* with its riveted metal plates, hastily erected on deck to give more accommodation for the whalers, the *Calpean Star* was clearly the jewel of the Ryan fleet.

Radio reception on The Point was poor at the best of times, and during storms, we were unable to hear anything at all. Each evening when Dad walked into the sitting room, he switched on the wireless and started twiddling the knobs to get the clearest signal possible to listen to the World Service from the BBC. At this point, Gerald and I chose a toy each, walked out into the passage and sat on the rug so that our presence didn't disturb Dad in any way. We wouldn't have made any noise, but he got so angry if one of us sneezed or made any sound during any programme, especially the News, that withdrawing physically from the room was the wisest thing to do. Once the News was over, Dad left Stanley Radio playing, especially if an episode of 'The Archers' or 'The Navy Lark' was being broadcast. Beyond that, he had little interest in local programmes from Stanley and often he read or left the room, leaving Mum to listen to whatever programme was on. On one of Mum's programmes, I heard a man singing the blues!

"I've cried so much,
Since you've been gone,
I guess I'm drowning in my own tears…"

"Mum, who is that man singing?"
"It's Ray Charles, Bev. Wonderful singer!"
"What's the song called?"
"'Drown In My Own Tears', I think. It makes you want to cry too." I listened, rapt, to his voice. It made the hairs stand up on the back of my neck. Every phrase cut through me, every note and pause accentuated the emotion of the song. I couldn't wait to tell Uncle Ron! I wasn't allowed to go up to Discovery House on my own at night, so the next morning I waited by the outdoor entrance to the Recreation Room for Uncle Ron to come in to work.
"Uncle Ron!" I called as I ran towards him, "Uncle Ron! I heard a man singing on the radio last night. His name is Ray Charles and he sings the blues like Pearl Bailey!"

246

"I know Ray Charles and he's a good singer, but he isn't a patch on Pearl Bailey. No one is!" Uncle Ron would never like anyone better than Pearl Bailey, however well they sang, I was certain of that. I knew too that I liked Ray Charles more than Pearl Bailey and even more than Ella Fitzgerald too. This was clear blasphemy on my part so I decided I had better not say anything more to Uncle Ron.

On Saturday evenings, Gerald and I listened to 'Children's Corner' from Stanley Radio. Falklands Island children always had a request played for their birthday and we all waited expectantly and with much excitement for the instruction... and you will find your present 'under the stairs', 'in the wardrobe', 'in the back kitchen' or, for the rich children, 'in the Land Rover'." Mum always got Dad to send a request by telegram for our birthdays, but I loved hearing the requests for other children too, especially those I remembered from when I was at school. But 'Calling South Georgia' was everyone's favourite programme. Broadcast to us by the BBC World Service, it gave us a foothold on the world stage and made us feel especially important. Everybody on The Point listened intently, crowded around the wireless, to hear if any of our relatives had written in to request a song for us. Dad always transmitted a long list of requests to the BBC in England too and everyone waited anxiously to hear 'their' song.

My favourite song on 'Children's Corner' was 'Tubby the Tuba', the story of a plump little tuba who only had 'oompah's' to play. Tubby thought that he would be happy if only he could find a melody to play like all the other instruments in the orchestra. Heading off into the world in search of a song for himself, Tubby had many adventures and eventually ended his journey in Singing City where he found himself a tune. I asked Dad to ask

247

the BBC to play the first part of 'Tubby the Tuba' for me, as the whole story came in two parts. I suppose the producer of 'Calling South Georgia' played my record because it was the only request he received from a child. On the night that the programme was broadcast, I sat beside the wireless and listened intently to part one, thrilled that the story of Tubby was being broadcast from England especially for me. The next morning when I walked around The Point, the men seemed to be unnaturally quiet. I was sure that I wasn't just imagining it. No one seemed to be particularly pleased to see me, while my heart was singing joyfully with the memory of Tubby. I asked Mark, who was new to The Point, if he had enjoyed 'Calling South Georgia' the previous night.

"I would have done if your song hadn't taken up so much time that others didn't get to hear their requests!" he said. My face fell and my heart lay leaden inside my chest. I blinked back involuntary tears. All my pleasure dissipated in one microsecond. Everyone was cross with me! They hadn't liked 'Tubby the Tuba' and I had selfishly spoiled the programme for them because it hadn't occurred to me that I had requested a particularly long record. I was distraught, so full of shame and emotion that I couldn't sit still and walked round and round the table tennis table to calm myself down. I didn't want to say anything to Mum and I hoped that no one would say anything to Dad. I spent the next week playing in the house or on the *Snowgoose* so that I wouldn't have to talk to anyone. I felt deeply, deeply ashamed. The next time Dad asked me if I wanted to request a record on 'Calling South Georgia', I said politely,

"No thank you, Daddy, I hear all the songs I like on 'Children's Corner'. I'll let the grown-ups choose."

"That is thoughtful of you, Beverley." I wanted Dad to say that I could request a song anyway but, as he didn't, I made do with his faint praise. But what I wanted most in the world was to hear the second part of the 'Tubby the Tuba' story being told only for me.

When Mum and I knew that Dad had been hitting the bottle, we stayed very quiet at mealtimes unless we were spoken to first. Gerald knew when to behave too, but he wasn't as tuned in to the nuances of Dad's behaviour as Mum and I were. One dinnertime when we were all sitting together at the kitchen table eating macaroni cheese, Gerald said, "Beb, where's Big Panda?" Before I could answer him, Dad cut in. "Gerald, your sister is not called 'Beb', her name is Beverley and that is the name you will use." We froze and a heavy silence filled the room, cold and chilling. Gerald sat up very straight and still, he looked directly at Dad, his little face a mask of fear and concentration.

"He's just a baby, Peter! Everyone else calls Beverley, 'Bev'; why shouldn't Gerald call her that too?"

"I object to you calling her 'Bev' as you well know and I will not allow my son to call her by that name. Her name is 'Beverley' and that is the name he will use. Actually, if you called her by her proper name, he wouldn't be using the shortened version of her name himself." We cowered in our seats, our limbs stiff, unable to lift a fork to our mouths. On our plates, the macaroni cheese hardened into a solid lump. Gerald sat like a statue in his high chair, knowing that he had done something wrong, waiting for the storm to break over his head. Dad put down his knife and fork with great deliberation. He lifted his head and leaned forwards across the table towards his son.

"Gerald, your sister's name is Beverley and that is the name you will use. Say it! Beverley." Gerald swallowed hard, his little face contorted with the dread of getting it wrong. He was fully aware that being shouted at and dragged from his chair by his arms, followed by a slap, was just moments away.

"Belly." Said very quietly.

"No! Her name is Beverley. Say it again." Silence. Gerald's little mouth formed the whispered word.

"Belly."

"No! Say it after me, Be-VER-ley."

"Be-LL-y."

"Be-VER-ley."

"Be-L-L-y." Silence. Dad leaned even further across the table and stared directly into Gerald's eyes. Gerald's face crumpled in terror and I was afraid that he was going to make Dad even angrier by crying. Mum moved to stand against the corner of the table so that she positioned herself between Dad and Gerald.

"He's too young to speak properly, Peter. He'll get Beverley's name right when he's older." We held our breath and waited for the explosion to come. Then Dad drew back and picked up his cutlery. He had obviously decided that Mum was right and that Gerald wasn't deliberately being provocative. "He had better get it right, p.d.q." he said, and went back to eating his food. Mum put Gerald's spoon into his hand and encouraged him to lift some macaroni cheese to his mouth. She gave me a look which told me to do the same. We ate yet another meal in silence, on our best behaviour as always.

When Dad left the kitchen to go back to the Wireless Room, we breathed easily again as Mum hugged us close to her, free from fear until supper time.

Over the next few days I tried to get Gerald to pronounce my name correctly, but 'ver' was too much for his tongue to cope with. I decided to stop trying as we weren't getting anywhere. I was Belly for several months and as Dad chose to ignore Gerald's mispronunciation, we were left free to ignore it too.

Dad's usual evening pattern was to sit quietly reading his back copies of The Daily Express. A week's newspapers were bound together in a thin, yellow papery binder and Dad read each individual paper from cover to cover, time and again. While he listened to the World Service News, he leant towards the radio, concentrating hard, imbibing each fact and detail through every pore of his body. He read the newspapers to extend his knowledge and understanding of world events further.

"An educated man is a man who has the facts at his fingertips, Beverley. Living on a remote Antarctic island is no excuse for a man to fail to keep abreast of world events."

Unfortunately for us, Dad was still able to keep abreast of world events whilst drinking at the same time. When the newspapers fell to the floor from his hand and his glass swayed unsteadily in his grasp; when his head lolled forwards and he began to swear and complain about the ineptitude of politicians and world leaders, I stopped playing, listened and watched him through the open sitting room door. If Dad was really drunk, his demons crept out from within their hidden crevices inside his brain and raised his old ghosts. His anger doubled then trebled in its intensity and his whole body quivered and exploded in a loud

251

"Fe farn! Fe bloody farn!" Gerald, knowledgeable ahead of his years about the effects of alcohol on a parent, looked up at me and whispered, "Bedwoom Belly?"

"Yes, take Little Panda and Sandy to my bedroom, Ger. I'll bring Big Panda and your lorries later." Legs bandy from the terry-towelling nappy wrapped voluminously between them, Gerald made his ungainly way along the passage, Sandy walking quietly behind him. Even Sandy knew how to behave after the times when Dad's shoes had lifted him off his feet and sent him spinning across the room. I sat back on the rug, watching and listening. I could hear my heart and lungs thumping in unison. Despair filled our house. Wherever I looked, it stretched out before me, restricting, suffocating and blocking out our future. How could Mum and Gerald and me live with a secret which we couldn't even keep from Betty and Uncle Ron? How could we continue to live with Dad's pent-up anger which exploded like shrapnel over our heads whenever he had too much to drink, which was every day? There was no future for us, but we had to live through it anyway.

When the sea elephants came ashore to moult, a large group of cows surrounded the *Snowgoose*. They lay amongst the tussac bogs, snoring and snuffling their days away. One particularly large cow lay just beyond her bow. I didn't take much notice of her at first, but then it dawned on me one day that she didn't seem to move. I left Gerald sitting on the deck and walked the few steps between the seal and the boat and bent over her. She didn't react to my calling her so I stood close beside her head, but still she didn't move. She didn't seem to be alive. I picked up a handful of pebbles and threw them at her with all the force I could muster, but there was still no reaction. She had definitely died. That evening at supper, I told Dad that

252

there was a dead seal near the *Snowgoose* and he said that I should just keep out of her way.

A fortnight later, it was obvious that the body of the elephant seal was decaying. A pungent odour, sickly and acrid, emanated from her flesh where it suffered from open, bloody wounds. I wondered if the rats had been attacking her.

"Smelly, Belly!" was Gerald's comment, and I had to agree with him. I told Dad at suppertime that the elephant seal was smelling and that it made me feel sick, and he offered to walk to the *Snowgoose* with me and see what I was talking about. We walked the short distance together and, before we even reached the hulk, Dad wrinkled his nose and said,
"I see what you mean!"

The following day, Dad went up to see Basil and they decided that the body of the seal was too heavy for them to drag down to the beach and sink. They needed help so they asked Ringdal at Pesca to send round one of the tractors to remove the seal. In the meantime, Dad cautioned me to keep away from the *Snowgoose* as the rotting corpse might well spread disease. Disease was pretty much unheard of on The Point. The only 'disease' prevalent on South Georgia was alcoholism with its attendant hangovers and brutal side effects.

Several days later, Gerald and I stood outside the conservatory, watching the tractor make its slow way around the cove. When it reached The Point, Dad and Basil met it beside the *Snowgoose.* They tied a sturdy rope around the seal's tail and the tractor driver hauled the seal across the shingle path and down to the water's edge. The men pushed the corpse the last few feet into the sea with shovels and it floated for a while, before it sank out of sight. The cause of death for the poor seal then became obvious. She had skewered herself on the sharp edges of the abandoned Try-pot which I had been warned by Dad to stay well away from. She had had her belly cut open in the instant that her huge weight had flopped down on the shards. As she moved to try to get away from the jagged metal, it would have injured her even more. What a horrible death. I shed some tears for her and made a little cross out of tussac leaves to lay where she had died. Gerald and I kept away from the *Snowgoose* for a few weeks until the memory of her agonies disappeared from my mind.

CHAPTER 10

OUR THIRD WINTER

In June, at the end of the season, Mr Matthews left and the new Magistrate, Mr Hooper, arrived. Mr Matthews was a genial, gentle man, widely liked and respected. We were all sorry to be seeing him go. The whole population of The Point, some fourteen or so souls, waited on the jetty for our first sight of the new Magistrate and of his wife.

When they stepped ashore, the first thing that I noticed was that the lady was taller than her husband. I'm not sure why this struck me so forcibly, but it did. I expected men to be taller than women and for that not to be the case, struck me as odd. The second thing that I noticed was the lady's calf-length fur coat. Practical, definitely, for South Georgia was a very cold island. But a fur coat on The Point where we all wore clothes which had seen better days, or purchased them whatever their size and shape from the Slop Chest, appeared incongruous. Mrs Hooper wore a headscarf tied tightly beneath her chin and short sheepskin boots with a zip up the front. As she and her husband followed Mr Matthews up the path to their house, Betty whispered to Jenny, Mum and me,

"She looks like the Queen!" The nickname stuck! Forever afterwards in the privacy of our own homes, 'The Queen' was never known by any other name.

The previous September a dour Geordie, born and bred in North Shields on the River Tyne, came down to fulfill the role of Housekeeper to the Magistrate. Jimmy and Mr Matthews had rubbed along together pretty well. Jimmy cleaned the house, cared for the laundry and cooked Mr Matthew's meals. Finding himself working for a more zealous lady now, Jimmy was outraged. Every afternoon, once his chores were completed to Mrs Hooper's satisfaction, Jimmy stormed down to our house, flew open the kitchen door with an extravagant flourish of his hand, flounced into the room and collapsed into a chair, blowing out his flexible hamster-cheeks in disgust. "Pearl! You won't believe what she had me doing today! I had to clean all the furniture with the small end of the hoover tube. It took me hours to do it all! I told her, I did, that I keep the furniture clean but, would she have it? No! She would not! 'I want to know that the furniture is as clean as possible before I live with it' she says to me. I can't stand it, Pearl, I really cannot! What does she think we've been doing in that room? Inviting bloody seals in for afternoon tea?" Mum made him a strong coffee and fed him Victoria sponge to calm his nerves. Jimmy's heavy accent became ever more difficult to decipher as his consternation grew. His face, mottled at best, suffused into a patchwork of uneven shades of red as adrenaline coursed through every capillary of his body by the bucket full. Mum and I looked across the kitchen at one another and smiled. Jimmy brightened our long winter days with his outbursts, and on such a tiny settlement, the poor man had nowhere else to go to vent his spleen! With Mrs Hooper's arrival, Mum, Betty and Jenny were given plenty to gossip about. It became abundantly clear that Mrs Hooper did not intend to spend more time with the other residents of The Point than she had to, nor was she going to invite us to the Magistrate's House for tea and certainly not for parties. She brought us all together as no one else had – we were exiles in a conspiracy of exclusion, so we relied on each other even more.

When the huge winter snowflakes began to fall like cold, dense and suffocating kisses, I spent most of my time indoors. Once the tussac bogs were lying dormant beneath four or five feet of snow and the world outside was sparkling white and without contours, I expected the snowflakes to stop falling and I looked forward to being released from my internment and getting out on my skis again. But the snowflakes didn't stop falling. Day after day an unending phalanx of white soldiers parachuted down from grey clouds which blotted out the weak sun. When the winds blew, the soldiers still fell, swirling in angry whorls and beating their swords against the windows in a constant tap, tap, tap. Each day Dad and Uncle Ron dug out the chickens at least once. As the snow continued to fall, they had to dig steps down to the henhouse as it was now too deep for them to get down to feed the hens in any other way. Inside, the house grew dark and we lived under constant electric light as the windows were entombed. Dad tried to keep digging out the main door but eventually gave up as the snow became too deep and blizzards and high winds repeatedly blew the snow that he had sweated to move right back to where it had originally lain. Uncle Ron moved in to our house from Discovery so that he could get to the Wireless Room easily. Dad took a stepladder up into the attic and he and Uncle Ron used it to get out through the attic window onto the roof. There was so much snow on the roof that they were able to ski off it and glide over to where their snow steps down to the henhouse were marked by a long pole, which they had intelligently stuck into the snow so that they knew where to start digging on

257

their twice daily mercy missions to keep the hens alive. By the time the snow did stop falling, the buildings on The Point were completely covered. The only way we could get out of our houses was to climb out through the attic windows on to the roof. It was exciting to climb up into the attic then scale the stepladder up towards the apex of the roof and wriggle out through the small window before slipping on my skis and gliding off onto the sticky snow. For Dad, who by now had become very portly from the combined effects of Mum's good cooking, little exercise and lots of alcohol, squeezing his bulk through the attic window was a painful and slow process.

"Fe bloody farn!" was the usual accompaniment to his travails and he tried his best to ensure that everyone other than him completed the outside chores. Ron and I fed and cared for the hens between us, and Uncle Ron took control of clearing the snow from the aerial masts.

Even though the pipes which carried water from the dam to our houses were buried underground, when the temperature fell to minus eleven degrees Celsius, the water froze inside them. For three weeks we were unable to have a bath and then, once the men had managed to unfreeze some of the pipes, we were able to get enough water to share a bath only once a week.

Once outside, The Point was almost unrecognizable. The contours of the moss hills had been erased entirely. The *Snowgoose* was completely hidden and I was able to ski over where I thought she was lying beneath me. Roofs protruded like Saxon barrows around us, their outlines softened and blurred by a thick snow blanket which sparkled like sugar crystals in the sun. Hope Point was outlined as a dome but Shackleton's Cross was completely hidden from view and even the dam on Mount Duse was barely visible. The ice which had formed in the harbour was hidden beneath a thick layer of snow and it looked as if we could ski directly across it to Pesca.

As I spent most of my time in the company of adults, there was a lot that I learned to do that was part of their world rather than mine. I hated to be excluded and it upset me greatly whenever they read something written in joined-up writing and then wrote something themselves in response. This was a club that I was excluded from. I was desperate to learn how to write like them so I copied large tracts from 'The Little Mermaid', but even using a lined exercise book from the Stanley school to help me, my writing was illegible, even to my eye. I tried copying the same passage numerous times, but it didn't seem to get any better. It mattered so much! Joined-up writing was a bridge between the adults and me that I couldn't cross! After another afternoon of abject failure, I ran into the kitchen and showed Mum my book, tears of frustration welling up in my eyes and chasing each other down my cheeks.

"Mum! I can't do joined-up writing!"

"You're just seven years old, Bev. You write very neatly for a girl your age. Leave joined-up writing until you're older."

"Mum, you don't understand! I want to do joined-up writing NOW! It's important. Please show me what to do!"

"I think your Dad is the best person to teach you, but I'll give it a go! Sit down with me and watch what I do." Sitting together at the table, I watched as Mum copied the first line, 'Far out in the wide sea' in large, rounded letters, demonstrating how to make curls to join one letter to the next.

"Now, you copy what I've written underneath." Carefully and slowly I copied each letter and curl. Unsteady and angular as some of my letters were, it was at least legible.

"Good girl! Now, copy this." 'Where the water is blue as the loveliest cornflower', she wrote, extravagant curls forming a blue chain between the individual letters. As the dark days passed with wind howling around the house, throwing snow ghosts high into the air, we sat writing together at the kitchen table. I watched Mum as she wrote passages from Hans Christian Andersen stories and I dutifully copied her lettering as neatly as I could, on the page beneath. I spent hour after hour practising my handwriting. Soon, I was able to copy straight from the text without her help. By the end of the winter I was writing without thinking about how I formed each letter or word and I could read the letters that Mum and Dad had received from Stanley during the summer. I was so proud of myself that I took every opportunity I could to show all our friends my copied stories and I basked in their praise of my grown-up skill.

On the sixth of June, as mid-winter approached, the sun sank beneath the mountains and we succumbed to greyness once more. To keep up our spirits during the long winter it was decided that we should set up a Social Committee. Dad was elected as its Chairman and as the committee had the support of all of the over-winterers on The Point, they felt that they had a chance of putting pressure on Mr Hooper to allow them to spend some of their time painting the Recreation Room and making it a more welcoming and pleasant social area.

On June the twenty-second, we congregated together in the newly decorated Recreation Room, and all our friends came round from Pesca. The party started with Dad making a short speech thanking everyone for their hard work and praising the room which was now bright and welcoming. Mum, Jenny, Betty and I danced ourselves into the ground as we were partnered by each man in turn. It was one of our best parties and Dad enjoyed it so much that he fell into bed smiling and happy, with no demons in sight.

The *Darwin* arrived a few days later on her annual mid-winter visit. Last year's trip to South Georgia had been such a success that this year, The Falkland Island Company opened the trip to paying passengers. When she arrived, to Mum, Betty and Jenny's delight, there were couples amongst the passengers and Mum and Betty coaxed as much gossip as they could from the women who sat around the kitchen table, drinking Mum's coffee and eating their way through mountains of sausage rolls, sandwiches and cakes. Laughter and 'ooohs' and 'aaahhs' punctuated their chatter as juicy pieces of Stanley gossip were embroidered and coloured to such an extent that the original kernel of truth became so deeply hidden within an intricately patterned carpet, that they often lost sight of it altogether.

That night we hosted another party in the newly decorated Recreation Room. For our only time on South Georgia, Mum, Betty, Jenny and I were able to sit out some dances as there were plenty of women to take our place on the dance floor. The party was a riotous success and went on well in to the early hours of the morning. Mum and I watched from the attic as an inebriated Dad tried his best to help equally inebriated friends to clamber up the ladder towards us. It took all of our strength to haul them from the ladder across to the attic window where, with pushes, shoves and uncontrollable laughter, we ejected them out like peas from a pod on to the crisp snow. After the last guest had been unceremoniously dispatched, and before we closed the window, we could hear whoops of laughter as the large party of merry travellers, holding torches in their hands and with their arms wrapped round each other's shoulders, wove an uncertain path across the icy crust of the snow down to the jetty and on to the *Darwin*. Next morning, the *Darwin* slipped out of the harbour very early. Not everyone from The Point made it out of bed in time to join me in waving her off.

On the second of July, Mum began a two day baking marathon in preparation for my eighth birthday party. I was so full of excitement, knowing that everyone was going to make a fuss of me and wondering what presents I would get, that I couldn't stay still. To make the time pass more quickly, I put on my outdoor jacket, hat and mitts, climbed out of the attic window and skied to Mount Duse. For a couple of hours I herringboned up the slope to the base of the dam and skied back down to the bottom. To make it more fun, I skied down from higher up the mountain and felt the thrill of extra speed. The added momentum took me further across the mounds at the foot of the mountain, but with the depth of snowfall we had had, the mounds were now like a level plain and skiing over them required little effort.

It was a grey and dank day and, as I turned at the top of my new piste to ski down the mountainside, horizontal snowflakes flew in from the harbour. By the time I reached the base of the mountain, the snow was so dense that I found myself unable to see ahead. When I came to a stop and looked around me, I couldn't distinguish any part of the landscape at all. Everything looked dismal and white, flat and featureless. I realised that I was caught in a whiteout. I wasn't afraid as I was close to home, but how to get home was a problem. I stood still and reflected on what I should do. My first thought was to veer to my right and ski towards the harbour to find the path. As I thought it through, I rejected that idea as I knew from listening to tales about being in whiteouts that people had been known to walk or ski over cliffs into the sea. I didn't want that to happen to me if for some reason I failed to see where the sea began, as the harbour was frozen over and buried beneath a deep layer of snow. If I skied onto the harbour ice, it could crack and if I fell through, I would drown in minutes, I was sure of that. I decided that my best plan would be to ski straight ahead. That way I would get to the houses on The Point and be safe. I straightened my skis, knowing that they were pointing in the general direction of where the houses were, and I set off slowly. My skis made no sound as I glided slowly over the snow, but the sound of my heartbeats were magnified within the shroud of insulating snow as my pulse raced faster and faster and my level of anxiety rose. When I turned round, I could only see the last few feet of tracks that my skis had made through the snow-fog which enveloped me. I skied on. It was like being in a silent dream where everything concrete disappeared and you were left in limbo with your senses completely cut off from reality. I knew that it was taking much longer to get to The Point than I had expected it to. Usually I was home in less than ten minutes from Mount Duse but I was sure that I'd been going for longer than that and I couldn't understand what was happening. I looked at my watch and saw that it was just after eleven o'clock. I skied on. Then I skied on some more. I looked at my watch again and again but after a quarter of an hour had passed, I still wasn't home. Where had I gone wrong? I was worried now. If I'd gone in the wrong

263

direction, I could be anywhere near the sea and I wouldn't know if it was quietly lying there below me, icy, cold and deep, the abyss waiting for me to fall in to it and sink into its unfathomable depths. I was well and truly lost and I didn't know what to do.

"Think, Bev. Use your brain!" I said out loud to myself. That was one good idea! I shouted until my throat was hoarse, but no reply came. Either I was a long way away from The Point or everyone was inside and wouldn't hear me anyway. I looked at my skis. They were pointing straight ahead.

"Of course they are, you silly!" I said, more for the comfort of hearing my voice than for any sensible reason. "Let's talk this through. You set off for The Point and you weren't going towards the path so you can't be near the harbour. If you'd gone straight, you would be at The Point by now, but you're not. So where are you?" Talking out loud made everything seem clearer and it cut through the eerie silence of the whiteout, boosting my confidence. "If you're not at The Point then you must have gone left towards Hope Point. Now you're in trouble because you could go over the top of Hope Point and into the sea at any minute. What will you do now? Think Bev, think!" And I thought. I had a picture of The Point in my head and if I was off track, I had to make a quarter-turn to get back. I turned through ninety degrees and skied on. This time I went very, very slowly. Before, I had been confident that the houses were going to veer up in front of me at any moment. Now, I was expecting the sea to be at my feet so I could only move ahead a few inches at a time. I peered ahead of my skis into the gloom, looking for any break in the white uniformity of my environment, hoping for something that would give me a clue as to where I was. Every few minutes I stopped and shouted, but I received no reply. Another ten minutes passed and I shouted again. This time, a voice bounced back through the heavy gloom. I shouted,

"Hello! Hello!" and when another "Hello!" echoed back, I turned slightly to my left and skied on cautiously, relief flooding through me like a warm salve.

"Hello! Hello!" and the voice coming back in reply sounded stronger. I was getting nearer home. After a few minutes of our shouts responding to one another, I could hear the voice quite distinctly through the fog and my spirits rose even more.

"Hello! Hello!" and the voice returning through the gloom sounded as if it was right beside me.

"Where are you? I can't see you!"

"Is that you, Bev? It's Nigel. Stay where you are but keep shouting and I'll find you." I stood still and shouted "Hello!" continuously, as if that was the only word in the English language I knew. Out of the mist and uniformity of the landscape, Nigel appeared, his big, dark outline breaking up the persistent light grey gloom that had surrounded me until now. He reached out and touched my arm.

"There you are, Bev, did you lose your way in the whiteout?"

"Only a little bit," I lied. I didn't want him to think that I couldn't be trusted out on my own.

"Well, come into the house and we'll get you a drink, then I'll see you home so that I know that you've got there safely." I skied beside him for a minute then out of the gloom, the door of his bungalow appeared beside us. What a welcoming sight! I slipped my skis off and followed him inside. Jenny was feeding Martin in his high chair. On the record player, Christopher Robin was going down to Buckingham Palace with Alice. The room was warm and flooded with light. My eyes took a few seconds to adjust to the brightness and I shivered, only then realising how cold I had become.

"Have you been out in this weather?" Jenny asked.

"Not for long, I'm on my way home."

"Well, let's make you some hot orange cordial before Nigel takes you to your house. You've done very well not to get lost, you know! Lots of people completely lose their way in a whiteout."

"I know, I suppose I was just very lucky!" I gratefully sipped my hot squash.

The day of my birthday dawned blustery and dark again, bitter winds blew the snow in great swirls across the buried houses and visibility was poor. I played with Gerald indoors, read him stories and chased him and Sandy along the passage, down into the Recreation Room and around the table tennis table. We staged car races on the table tennis table, running to get to the end before the cars so that we could catch them as they flew off onto the floor. We loaded his big metal lorry with sweets and he pushed the lorry slowly and solemnly all the way into the Billiard Room and emptied the contents of the truck into the corner so that we would have 'supplies' for the afternoon. We sat quietly in the Wireless Room and watched Dad call up his daily contacts, but there were no messages for me to deliver. Sometimes the days seemed to be interminably long, especially when we were confined indoors.

I had grown out of my pretty blue net and lace party dress, and for my birthday, Mum had bought me a new red and white striped cotton dress with a scalloped white collar and a long red bow. My other present from Mum and Dad was interesting and totally unexpected. Inside a large box I found several flat green plastic bases with holes into which I could stick metal poles. Red and white bricks slipped down between the poles and, together with green windows I was able to build walls to the top of the poles. The house was topped off with a red roof. It was a new and exciting toy to play with.

Despite the weather, Eskedal brought Uncle Blom, Strand and Uncle Bonski over from Pesca in his motor launch for my birthday party. Uncle Blom carried a large cardboard box which he opened to reveal a large cream gateau with a flat, yellow marzipan duck nestling beneath the words 'Happy Birthday'. Donald Duck had a large orange beak and above his head, little three-dimensional duck nephews sailed serenely on a white cream pond between eight candles. The cake was beautiful and I felt really proud when Mum placed it on the drop-leaf table, lit the candles, and everyone sang 'Happy Birthday' to me as I blew them out.

"Now Bev," Mum said, "I'll take the cake out into the kitchen and cut it into slices which you can pass round to all of your guests." Smiling and happy, I followed Mum into the kitchen where she put my cake onto the kitchen table. She turned to Barry, who was Danny's assistant in the Met office, and asked him politely to move away from the drawer so that she could get out a knife to cut the cake with.

"Sure, Pearl," Barry muttered, as he swayed drunkenly out of her way. As a recipient of Dad's generosity as a host, where his drinks were doubles or trebles and offered unstintingly, Barry's extremities and brain were no longer working with any degree of unison. His uncoordinated feet wound themselves around each other. He lost his balance completely and dived forward, falling headlong into my cake. Mum and Uncle Blom hauled Barry back onto his feet and Mum grabbed a tea towel to wipe the cream, sponge and remnants of Donald Duck from his beard, while trying to hold him upright at the same time. The kitchen filled quickly as everyone left the sitting room and crowded in to laugh at Barry as he leant drunkenly against the sink, licking his lips and laughing loudly in unison with everyone else. Not quite everyone else. My lips trembled as I contemplated my beautiful cake, lying in spongy ruins on the plate. The duck was completely destroyed, its yellow marzipan remains nestling deep within the bristles of Barry's beard like rations waiting to be devoured at a later date. Mum saw my distress and came to put her arms round me.

"Never mind, Bev, there's still enough cake left for you to have a piece and the little ducks are still alright to eat. Don't get upset on your birthday. Remember that if you cry on your birthday, you'll cry all the year round!"

"Beeverley, I will bring you another cake with ducks so you must not be sad," and Uncle Blom hugged me to his side, trying to cheer me up. So I put on a brave face and managed a watery smile, but the fun had gone out of my birthday.

I walked disconsolately into the sitting room and sat on the sofa with Mum to play with the house that I had built earlier from my new kit. Dad, made aware by Mum that I was upset at the sudden demise of my birthday cake, walked uncertainly into the room and squeezed down beside me. Dad leaned towards me, his beard, like a scrubbing brush, rasped against my cheek as he lurched sideways.

My stomach turned a somersault as he pursed his lips and exhaled into my face, blowing stale whisky and tobacco breath into my nostrils even before his wet lips assaulted my cheek. This was Dad at his half-cut, maudlin best, living the fantasy which floated periodically to the surface of his grey matter that he was a loving, caring and doting father, beloved of his children. I struggled to keep my head in the same position despite the nausea and not to pull away as shattering Dad's fantasy would be a serious mistake to make, one which Mum and I would suffer for later. "Don't be upset, Beverley, this is your party and you are supposed to be happy and enjoy it.

I'm going to put on some music and you can get up and dance with everyone like a happy birthday girl should!"

"You're exactly right, Daddy, it is my birthday after all!"   I gave him a big smile and quickly stood up, removing myself from his proximity, ready to dance the night away.

Uncle Ron and I continued our lessons. He moved back into Discovery House as all of the houses on The Point had been dug out and stairways of snow steps led down to each doorway. Two or three times a week, after dinner, I carried my encyclopedia over to his room. Uncle Ron and I discussed tsunamis, deserts, coal and ancient man; zebras and rainbows, oceans and aeroplanes. I still enjoyed listening to Pearl and Ella, but I was enjoying our lessons less and less. During the summer, when I reached Uncle Ron's bedroom door, instead of drumming my usual noisy rap with my knuckles, I tapped as lightly as I could with the tips of my fingers, making virtually no sound at all. I then crept away and sat on the low brick step on the seaward side of the Discovery House chimney and drew up my knees. In this way I was hidden from Mum's view if she chose to look out of our kitchen window. I waited until I was sure that Uncle Ron hadn't come looking for me then tripped back to our house, put my encyclopedia on the kitchen table and announced to Mum in all honesty,

"Uncle Ron didn't answer his door so he must be asleep. I think I'll just walk up to Shackleton's cross and maybe go in and see Jenny."

"Well, if Uncle Ron's asleep then you certainly can't have a lesson today. Go out and get some fresh air, sweetheart. I'll give you a few buns to take up to Jenny. Wait while I find a tin to put them in."

Uncle Ron was a clever man and it didn't take him long to realise what I was up to. Sometimes, from his bedroom window, he kept a watchful eye on the path from our house up to Discovery and stood with his hand on the doorknob so that when he heard my tiptoe approach, he pulled the door open and I was caught in his snare! On other occasions my heart dropped as, through the kitchen window, I espied Uncle Ron's tall figure sway round the side of the Discovery chimney and lollop down the path.

"Hello Pearl! I thought I'd come down for a coffee so that I didn't fall asleep and miss Bev's knock on the door for our lesson today! She can walk back with me later." My opportunities for truancy were being successfully limited by Uncle Ron and now, in the winter, they had disappeared completely. One particular lesson, however, was memorable and it shook me out of my self-satisfied stupor.

On one short ski up to Discovery House, I saw several Martian spacecraft overhead. When I got into Uncle Ron's room I said, by way of making conversation,

"I've just seen a fleet of Martian spacecraft in the sky. Did you see them, Uncle Ron?"

"Ha! Ha! You won't catch me out with that one, Bev! I know that you're very well aware that they are just a particular cloud formation. I know that you wouldn't really fall for that old wives tale about Martian spacecraft. Ha! Ha!" I was completely taken aback but struggled to keep my features under control. I didn't want to look foolish or childish in front of Uncle Ron, but surely he was joking? I couldn't believe that Dad might have told me an untruth. I casually said,

"What particular cloud formation do you mean?" I hoped that he would consider my remark to be a casual enquiry.

"Ah yes, you probably wouldn't know that. They're called Lenticular Clouds. Lenticular describes the way the clouds are stacked in layers, which is what gives them their flying saucer shape. Their shape is caused by the mountains they pass over, which is why you often see them coming in from behind Pesca."

"Oh. Is that why they usually come across the harbour? I often sit on the *Snowgoose* with Gerald and watch them at sunset when they light up in golds and oranges and reds. They do look as if they're being lit up from inside."

"That's it, exactly! While we're on the subject of weather, what about if we talk about fohn winds and williwaws today? We might as well learn about South Georgia weather because we get enough of it!" This was probably one of the most interesting and instructive lessons that Uncle Ron and I shared, but my mind wasn't on the subject matter at all. I couldn't believe that my Dad had told me a fairy story. Worse than that, I'd believed every word he'd said. I felt deeply angry with him for deceiving me and angry with myself for believing him. I had learned a good lesson. My Dad couldn't be trusted to always tell me the truth. It was a lesson that I would always remember.

Crime struck The Point in the depths of that winter! The single men in Discovery House hosted a huge party to which almost all of the over-winterers at Pesca were invited. Even the young mess boys who didn't often come round to The Point were guests. As the evening progressed into night, the party became more and more raucous and the young men especially, for whom alcohol was a luxury, started to sway on their feet and see two of everything. Mr and Mrs Hooper didn't come to the party but dined with Ringdal around at Pesca that night and, on their return, they found that their house had been broken into. Closer inspection showed that someone had lain on the top coverlet of their bed and had inexplicably spilt ink over it. Because whisky had been stolen, it was assumed that the intruder had rested there while they consumed it, but why they had opened a bottle of ink was a mystery. The crime was compounded when Mrs Hooper insisted that her underwear drawer had been rifled through. The first part of the story was believable and it offered a lot of amusement to everyone. Not everyone believed the bit about the underwear drawer though,

"Who would be that hard-up Chay?"

Mr Hooper called upon Basil to investigate the crime and bring the miscreants to justice. This was Basil's first real piece of detective work and he prepared for it methodically. First, Basil skied around the house in order to check the ski trails. Sure enough, he discovered two sets together, one of which was unusual in that it had been made by the specialised skis of a ski jumper. His nose ardently following the scent now, Basil followed the ski tracks around to Pesca, only to find that they stopped beside a pair of very nice skis, obviously designed for jumping, stacked neatly together beside the wall of the New Barracks. He walked inside, asked who the skis belonged to then called on Ringdal. Together they arrested the burglar and his best friend, both of whom admitted immediately to their crime.

Basil arrested the two young men and brought them back to The Point and locked them in the jail. One of the boys, Harry, was not only very handsome, he was the probably the best ski jumper at Pesca. I had watched him fly down the mountainside at the Winter Sports, land gracefully in a kneeling position with his arms outstretched, and ski to a halt just in front of us, his blonde hair dancing in the wind and his cerulean eyes glinting with exhilaration. I was deeply in love with Harry even though I had only seen him on that one day and at the party. Harry was the Prince of my dreams and now Basil had locked him up in the small, dark, unforgiving jail.

Harry and Per were tried by Mr Hooper. Not only was the Magistrate the victim of the crime, he was the sole arbiter of justice on The Point. Judge, jury and, we felt, executioner. He sentenced the two boys to three months in the jail each, a complete over-reaction and there was real anger amongst us and also, understandably, in Pesca. Not only was Pesca now two men short, but Harry and Per would, in all probability, lose three months wages, their bonus and be sent back to Norway as soon as their stint in Basil's jail came to an end.

But the law is the law and Harry and Per spent the next three months working with Basil during the day and sleeping in the jail at night, although Basil never locked them in. They were well fed by Betty and welcomed by everyone else. To us, they were victims of a grievous injustice. On the bright side, I could watch Harry working whenever I wanted to!

It was a surprise to us all when Mum began to feel ill. Over a period of several months, she developed a tingling sensation in her hands and feet, was always feeling tired and complained of weakness and pains in her limbs and felt as if her heart was beating irregularly. Mum was a virago, full of energy, always cooking and cleaning, keeping us all well fed and in good order. To see her sitting for long periods of time, unable to find the energy to move, asking me to look after Gerald, was unnerving and worrying. I tried to hug her and help her, but there was very little that I could practically do. As the symptoms persisted, Dad asked Uncle Bonski to make a request to the Pesca doctor to come round to The Point to see her. Doctor Harkenson, a South African who, like Uncle Ron, had come to South Georgia to flee a broken marriage, examined Mum and came up with the surprising diagnosis that she was suffering from the early stages of beriberi as a result of having too little vitamin B1 in her diet. When the condition was described to her in these terms, Mum said quickly,

"My Uncle Dick is buried at Leith Harbour. They say that he died through lack of cabbage. Does this run in families?"

"There is a congenital form of beriberi, certainly, so it's likely that Bev and Gerald could suffer from it too. I'll give you vitamin tablets to take and that should relieve the symptoms quickly. I'll get the butcher to send you over pigs liver with your meat each week too. When you get off South Georgia,

275

you all need to eat as many green vegetables as you can find! That shouldn't be very difficult to do!"

Dad was drinking heavily again throughout the winter, but unaccountably one night he allowed us to go to bed without any problem. We fell into a deep and grateful sleep then, for some reason, Dad awoke after a few hours. He pulled Mum out of bed by her hair, dragged her into my bedroom, pulled back my sheets and shouted,

"Beverley! Get up NOW!" I scrambled out of bed and followed him into the passage. As he crossed the narrow passage into Gerald's bedroom Mum grabbed his arm and said,

"No. Not Gerald! Please don't get him up, Peter. He's too small!" Throwing Mum off his arm he shouted,

"Don't you dare to tell me what to do, woman! Get him up NOW!" Mum lifted Gerald from his cot, his little hands rubbing the sleep from his eyes. As he looked at us all, I stood behind Dad and put my finger to my lips in a 'sshhh' motion. Intelligent little boy that he was, he fought against sleep to focus his big blue eyes on me and he stayed silent.

"Get into the kitchen!" We did as we were told and lined up by the kitchen table, Gerald still in Mum's arms and me standing in front of her.

"Stand behind the door." Obediently, Mum stood against the wall with me in front of her.

"Put him down." Mum lowered Gerald to the floor and I stood him in front of me, my hands on his shoulders. Dad slowly walked over to the kitchen window and picked up the torch which always stood there in readiness for those times when the electricity might fail. With the room in darkness, he walked back towards us, deliberately and slowly as he switched on the torch. He shone the torch directly into each of our faces in turn.

"Don't do that Peter, it will hurt the children's eyes." Thwack! Dad's left hand swept over my head and landed a back-hander across Mum's face. I heard and then felt the rebound as her head bounced off the wall.

"Shut up, you bitch!" So we all did. Long minutes passed. He turned the torch on each of us in turn, daring us to move or cry. I hugged Gerald against me as hard as I could, trying to give him strength without letting Dad see our fear. Gerald and I stood like little statues, staring directly into the beam of bright light as it shone into our faces from above. No one moved or spoke. I am sure that our ordeal lasted for at least thirty minutes, although time stretches into another dimension when each second is lived through nerves strained and torn. Eventually, Dad moved a little way away from us and shone the torch on us all at once.

"You don't want to be here. Tell the bloody truth! You want to be in bed and you're cursing me, aren't you?" I was terrified that Mum would tell him the truth and say that of course we should be in bed and that this would just make him worse.

"We are really happy to be here with you, Daddy. This is an adventure. It is much better than just being in bed asleep." My shaky voice didn't convince even me. Dad leant his head towards me and shone the light directly into my eyes. I was forced to squint by the incandescence and this probably stopped him from seeing how much of an accomplished liar his eight year old daughter had become. After a searching black look, he drew back his upper body and I shrank into myself, fearing the punch which was coming. Instead,

Dad hesitated, threw the torch onto the kitchen table and bounced off the passage walls towards his bedroom, falling into a stupor across the bed.

Now that the danger had passed, Mum, her hands shaking, made us all a glass of powdered milk as I wrung out a tea-towel under the cold tap for her to hold against her face, which was swelling up rapidly. We clung together around the kitchen table in the dark, shaking and not talking but physically as close to each other as we could get. Mum tucked us up in our beds and gave us shaky kisses then tried to find a corner of her own bed to sleep on. If she slept on the sofa and he woke up to find her not there when he wanted her, we all knew that that would only mean more trouble and we had already had enough for one day.

CHAPTER 11

THE EMPEROR PENGUIN

On the day that the first ship was to arrive for the new season, we were up early and Mum dressed Gerald and me in our best clothes.

"Take Gerald and sit quietly until the Biscoe arrives, Bev. I don't want you getting your clothes dirty or messed up before she even gets here."

"But Mum, I want to go up to Shackleton's Cross and watch for her. Then I can run along the beach as she comes into the harbour, like I always do!"

"Not today, Beverley. I don't want you taking Gerald up there and getting dusty and grubby. Today you will stay near the house." I gave her my best pout but Mum ignored me. I took Gerald by the hand and walked along the passage to the Recreation Room. We walked in silence out through the porch and sat on the low wall outside. Mark walked past with his camera and we posed together for a photograph, but I was feeling angry and fed up with Mum. Why did we have to sit beside the house when we could at least go down to the beach by Discovery House and watch for the Biscoe from there? Gerald wandered off and I reminded him to keep his clothes clean.

"Yes, Belly!"

Minutes later, Gerald came back with white powder spread all over his fingers. He offered his fingers to me to lick but I didn't feel like any icing sugar at that minute so I said,

"No thanks, Ger." He put his fingers into his mouth and gave an immediate strangled scream. His face turned a bright red, tears streamed from his eyes and he began to choke.

"Ger! What is it?" I grabbed him and ran into the house with his choking and squirming little body cradled in my arms.

"Mum! Mum! Something's wrong with Gerald. He's choking!" Mum ran into the passage, grabbed Gerald from me, put his head over the sink and ran cold water into his mouth. Gerald was coughing and spluttering and making the most terrifying sound I had ever heard him make.

"What happened, Bev? What did he put into his mouth?"

"I was sitting outside and he came in and got some icing sugar. I didn't want any but he had some. Then, this happened!"

"Gerald didn't come into the kitchen so he hasn't eaten icing sugar. Run and get your father. I've got to know what Gerald's swallowed." I ran from the kitchen down to The Wireless Room. I ran up to Dad, grabbed his arm and pointed to his earphones, gesturing for him to take them off.

"Daddy, Gerald has swallowed something bad. He's choking and Mum's trying to look after him in the kitchen. She says you've got to come and find out what it is that Gerald's swallowed." Dad jumped up from his chair, sending it reeling backwards onto the floor. Uncle Ron had taken off his earphones too.

"Ron, sign off and then come and help. Gerald's swallowed something and we've got to find out what it was. Beverley, tell me exactly where Gerald was."

"I'll show you, Daddy." I led him into the Recreation Room and out through the porch into the daylight.

"We were sitting here and Gerald went off to get some icing sugar for us to eat. I didn't want any but when he ate it, he got really ill. Mum says he didn't go into the kitchen to get it, so I don't know where he got it from."

"Fe bloody farn! I bet I know where he got it from," and Dad disappeared back inside the porch.

"Just as I thought! The lid has been left off the tub of caustic soda which the men use to clean their overalls with. Gerald must have thought it was icing sugar and eaten it. This could kill him. I need to get to your mother!" With that, Dad ran along the passage into the kitchen, shouting over his shoulder, "Get Ron!" I ran into The Wireless Room just as Uncle Ron was signing off.

"Dad wants you in the kitchen, Uncle Ron. He says that Gerald has swallowed caustic soda and that it could kill him. Do you think he'll die?" I asked, a waterfall of tears coursing down my cheeks. Uncle Ron put his arm round me,

"He'll be alright, Bev, you'll see."

When we walked into the kitchen, Mum and Dad were holding Gerald together in their arms. Gerald was no longer crying, just mewling and moaning gently like a wounded animal, full of fear and apprehension, pain and terror. His tongue was swollen and bright orange, protruding like an angry balloon from his little mouth. I couldn't bear to look. I sat down on the floor and wept more bitter tears into my lap.

"Ron, can you go and watch for the *Biscoe*," Dad asked, "There's a doctor on board. Get him off the ship and ashore as fast as you can. We need him here, p.d.q."

281

"I'm on my way," Uncle Ron replied, "You come with me, Bev, we'll get the doctor for Gerald together." Grateful to have something to do, I slipped my hand into Uncle Ron's and we ran up past Discovery House to the beach. The *Biscoe* wasn't in sight, but after what seemed to be an age, but was probably less than fifteen minutes, we saw the smoke from her funnel curling above Hope Point then she appeared in all her red and white glory. I have never been so happy to see a ship in all my life! Uncle Ron ran along the beach and yelled to the men lining the deck.

"There's been a bad accident! We need the Doctor fast! Get him ready to come ashore as soon as you get to the jetty!"

"We'll get him, don't you worry!" We watched as some of the men sprinted down below then, as the *Biscoe* rounded the shingle spit towards the jetty a voice shouted,

"I'm the Doctor!" and we ran to the end of the jetty to join the other men there. Before the ship docked or had even come to a stop, crewmen helped the Doctor to climb up onto the rail and eager hands leaned forward to grab his and pull him safely on to the jetty. He ran with Uncle Ron up to our house and I followed closely behind. I could hear Uncle Ron telling him what had happened, then we were all inside the house and the Doctor took Gerald from Mum and examined him.

"He'll be alright. Keep rinsing his mouth out with water and watch him all the time, but he will be fine once the swelling goes down. He didn't swallow any of the caustic soda which is a blessing because, if he had, he wouldn't survive. As it is, he'll be in real pain and discomfort for a few weeks, but he should recover completely. Poor little chap, but he's had a lucky escape."

That was the end of our celebrations of the **Biscoe's** arrival. Mum and I stayed with Gerald. Friends from Stanley popped their heads round the door and said hello to Mum, but she and I didn't move or offer them any hospitality. We cradled Gerald between us, doing what we could to bring him comfort. I felt that it was all my fault. I had been in a mood so I hadn't watched my little brother closely enough and look what had happened to him as a result. I tried to share his pain and I promised God that, if he let Gerald live and took his pain away soon, I would swear to always look after my little brother very carefully in the future so that nothing like this would ever happen to him again. Watching Gerald, gently whimpering, cuddled up with Mum, me and his two pandas, my heart broke into little pieces. Life seemed to be too much to bear.

Gerald was very poorly for a week then the swelling began to go down. Mum stayed with him day and night, afraid to leave him unattended in case he choked again. Two new Noddy books had come down on the **Biscoe** and I read these to him over and over again. Snuggled up against Big Panda, with Little Panda clutched in his arms, I read Gerald my Hans Christian Anderson tales, even though they were a bit old for him, and I told him stories about the wonders of the word that I had gleaned from my encyclopedias. We passed the days and evenings together until he was well enough to play with his toys then to come outside with me again. The men made a new lid for the caustic soda bin and locked it securely in place. No little fingers would get in there again.

Over at Pesca, Ringdal was overseeing the building of a meat extract plant. The plan was to purify and dehydrate the liquors which were extracted from lightly cooked fresh whale meat in the meat plant. This was to be

283

treated and concentrated to produce a low fat, high protein base for stock, soups and meat cubes. Now that the number of whales caught each season was falling, Pesca needed to find new ways to increase its earning potential. Ringdal had set up a contract to sell all of the meat extract that Pesca could produce so it was important that the new plant should be completed as early as possible.

The *Calpean Star* returned to Pesca, bringing the Norwegians back for another whaling season. She had suffered from engine failure several times on her voyage back to Liverpool at the end of the previous season. Her British officers lost their patience with Ryan and staged a sit down strike, refusing to sail her to Norway. In order to improve her seaworthiness, her exterior was to be refurbished at Pesca and her engines were to be reconditioned. She lay in the harbour off Pesca and day by day throughout the summer I watched as her outward appearance was transformed and she looked once again like a true ship of the line.

Several weeks later, after Gerald's recovery was complete, Dad came in after the morning sched and announced that an emperor penguin was standing on the path beside Discovery House. I was very excited! Emperors lived exclusively on the Antarctic Peninsula so for one to stray as far north as South Georgia was unusual. There were always some king penguins, nestling in the tussac outside our back door or stretching themselves on the beaches in the weak sunshine and round at Hestesletten, which was one of their main breeding beaches. An emperor was something entirely new and it was a penguin I had never expected to see.

"How has it come to be here, Daddy? Has it been brought up from Antarctica by one of the boats?"

"No, emperor's aren't taken by scientists, even for zoos in other parts of the world as they can't recreate Antarctic conditions and keep them alive. This one must have lost its bearings for some reason, probably while it was foraging for food in the Southern Ocean. Perhaps it's ill or was carried off course by the tides. It could have been attacked by leopard seals and separated from the rest of the colony. Whatever the reason, it's a rare visitor to South Georgia so I suggest you go and have a look at it once you have finished your dinner."

As soon as our meal had been eaten and everyone had cleared their plate, I asked Dad,

"Please may I leave the table and go and look at the emperor penguin?"

"Yes, you may," so I ran to the back door, slipped on my wellies, and ran the short distance up to Discovery House. The emperor penguin was actually coming to meet me! He was waddling slowly past Discovery, down towards our house. He stopped when he saw me, stretched his head and watched me closely through clear, beady brown eyes.

"Hello emperor," I said, "it's nice of you to come and visit us." He looked straight at me and pulled himself up to his full height, which nearly matched mine. He was a very large bird, much taller and broader than the kings. His plumage was similar to that of the king penguins, though his ear patches were a deeper and brighter gold. He cut an imposing figure. As we were looking at one another, Little Ron who was working in the Wireless Room with Dad and Uncle Ron for the summer season, walked round the side of Discovery House with his camera slung around his neck on a thin leather strap.

"Hello, Bev. Lovely feller isn't he? Thought I'd take a few shots while he's here." Little Ron took several photographs of the emperor from various angles while I watched them from a short distance away. The penguin showed no fear of us and seemed to be slightly bored by the whole thing.

"I've got an idea, Bev. As you're both about the same size, why don't you get up close to him and I'll take a photo of you both?"

"Alright, Ron," and I walked slowly towards the emperor. He didn't seem to mind at all and we stood together in companionable silence, smiling at Little Ron while he clicked away.

"Bev, try to get a bit closer. In fact, see if he'll let you hold his flipper. It'd make a fantastic shot!" I moved imperceptibly closer to the emperor penguin until my arm was almost touching his flipper. He didn't seem to mind and stood very still, looking towards Little Ron and not at me. I put out my right hand and closed it around the emperor's flipper. His body didn't move at all, but with a super-fast twist of his neck, he reached up and his razor sharp beak gave me a deep peck on the corner of my right eye.

"Ouch!" I cried, dropping his flipper and moving sharply away, clutching both hands to my eye.

"What's wrong, Bev, did he bite you?"

"Yes he did!" I was crying now. The emperor held his position and his poise, retaining his neck in its relaxed position, but fixing me with his deep, cold, piercing eyes, daring me to move towards him again.

"Don't worry," I said to him, "I won't be holding your flipper again!" and I turned and ran back into the house.

"Mum! I've been bitten by the emperor penguin!" I yelled through my tears.

"Here, sweetheart, let me look at it. Oh dear, he has given you a deep nip hasn't he? Why did you get so close to him, surely you know better than that?"

"Little Ron wanted me to hold his flipper so that he could take a photo of us, but the penguin didn't like it and he bit me!"

"Well, you're lucky. It isn't bleeding very much and he didn't peck you in the eye which would have been much worse. There now, I'll put on a plaster and it'll all be better!" After a kiss and a big hug I felt brave enough to take Mum and Gerald up to see the emperor. He was still standing in the same place, seemingly docile and perfectly happy to let us approach him. However, when he and I looked directly at each other, we exchanged knowing glances of recognition and mutual distaste.

The following morning when I went outside, the emperor penguin was standing on the crest of the rise beside the Discovery House chimney. From his vantage point, the emperor could look down to his right and watch our house and the harbour beyond; he could look straight ahead down to the jetty and across the harbour to Pesca, and he could look to his left and out across Cumberland Bay. As I walked up the path towards him, he turned his head slightly in my direction and fixed me with his customary cold, hard stare. I stopped in my tracks and returned his gaze. He drew himself up to his full height, stretched his neck towards me and opened his beak, obviously as a warning after yesterday. He was the victor and I was the one who needed to be careful about how I behaved and where I stood. He was master of this environment now and I was the interloper, even though in actuality he was the visitor and The Point was my home. Instead of walking up the path and passing him, I walked down to the jetty then turned up the second path to Discovery House, looking steadfastly ahead and without having to go near the emperor who watched my every step without seeming to move his head at all. He might have been beautiful to look at, but I wanted him to go. He was

287

intruding on my patch and I was aware of his malevolent presence whenever I went outside. Every day it was the same, he stood and watched my every move as I deliberately kept out of his way. He was a seriously mean and supercilious penguin.

On the fifth morning, the emperor was no longer at his post. I ran up the path, peeped carefully around the corner at the end of Discovery House, but he was nowhere to be seen. I looked along the beach and amongst the tussac bogs, but I couldn't see him anywhere and an emperor penguin isn't easy to lose.

"He's gone! Great!" I said to myself. I had The Point back once more as my own domain and felt very happy about it.

I often met Mrs Hooper taking the air in her trademark fur coat and headscarf. I noticed that she was spending a lot of time standing still in one place on the path near to the Magistrate's House. Dad noticed her too through the Wireless Room window and remarked on it at dinner time.

"What is she doing just standing there? Sometimes she stands in one spot for half an hour or more at a time. It's very odd."

After dinner I took Gerald and together we climbed on to the *Snowgoose* and sat in the bow looking back towards the houses on The Point. Sure enough, Mrs Hooper came out of her house, walked a few yards then stopped. We slipped down from the *Snowgoose* and I nonchalantly led Gerald by the hand as we walked up the path towards her.

"Hello Mrs Hooper. Isn't it a lovely afternoon?" She turned round, gave a look of recognition and said,

"Oh, hello you two! Yes, it is a nice day isn't it? I've just come out to have a talk to my two girls."

"Which two girls are those, Mrs Hooper?" I asked, looking around me and not seeing anyone else at all.

"My two girls there, Gertrude and Prudence. They know me and always look forward to me coming down to have a little chat with them." She motioned with her hand towards two large female sea elephants lying in the tussac, having come ashore to moult.

"Oh, I see," I said, completely lost for words.

"Yes, we pass the time of day whenever the weather allows me to come out and talk to them. They are always sad when it's time for me to go back indoors."

"Yes, well… we must be getting back home now for tea, Mrs Hooper, Mum doesn't like us to be late."

"Indeed. Goodbye then!" and she turned back to her pet seals and resumed her conversation with them.

At supper time when I recounted my tale to Dad, he shook his head and laughed.

"Pet elephant seals which know you and respond to a nice little chat! That's a new one on me! A pet penguin is one thing, but not two elephant seals. Not in a month of Sundays!"

Before Christmas, Betty and Basil's three children came down to The Point to spend their summer holiday with their parents. I was very excited to meet them and waited keenly on the jetty with Mum and Gerald to watch them arrive. Janet was the eldest, then there was Coleen. Both girls were blonde like Betty and shared her Nordic features. The youngest was Peter who was a few days younger than me.

The second day that they were on The Point, Betty brought the children down to our house for smoko and I met them all. Janet was obviously the leader and in the days that followed, I joined their happy band and we explored The Point together. We played on the tennis court; we climbed the mountain; we made dens amongst a pile of wooden beams behind the jail and decorated them with long strips of brown seaweed and twists of tussac grass. In their house we played pretend games, everyone contributing ideas and scenarios. Betty was oblivious to our noise. If her house was filled with pirates or cowboys and Indians, she didn't raise an eyebrow. If doctors and nurses were littering her sitting room with ill patients, her equanimity was unruffled. I was very happy and loved being with the other children. I woke each morning, gobbled down some breakfast and rushed along the path to Betty's house. I usually went home for dinner, but returned directly afterwards and stayed until supper time.

Betty was the representative on South Georgia for several of the shops in Stanley. Mr Ross had sent down a beautiful bride doll set from his shop, the Speedwell Store, for Betty to sell. There was a bride, a groom, a bridesmaid and a best man, all dressed in stylish finery and I fell in love with them all, the bride doll especially. That night I told Mum about the dolls and, after some persuasion, she told me that I could ask Betty to sell it to her for my Christmas present.

The next day, I asked Betty if I could please talk to her alone. We went out into the kitchen and I whispered to her that Mummy wanted to buy the bride doll set for my Christmas present. Betty looked at me and said, "I'm sorry, Bev, but the dolls have been sold." My heart sank and I'm sure that the disappointment showed in my face. I muttered,

"Oh, that's alright, it's not important." and walked back into the sitting room to join the others.

That evening when Basil came in from taking down the Union Jack, he looked directly at me and said,

"Beverley, I'll walk you home." I was surprised as he had never walked me home before. The Point was a safe place for children to be and it wasn't dark, but I replied politely.

"Thank you very much," said my goodbyes and left the house with Basil walking at my side. We walked in silence past the tennis court, what had been Jackie's house, the Magistrate's House and down the path towards the Wireless House. As we approached the entrance to the Recreation Room, Basil turned to me with a glowering look and said in a tight voice,

"Every time I go into my house, you're there. Haven't you got a home of your own to go to?" I didn't know what to say. It was true of course. I spent each day playing at Betty's house. Betty didn't mind at all, but Basil obviously minded a lot. I felt embarrassed and ashamed. I found a little voice enough to say,

"I'm very sorry if I come to your house too often. I won't do it again." I wanted to rush into our house but I remembered my manners. With my head held low, I muttered,

"Thank you very much for walking me home. Goodbye." Basil said nothing so I ran down the slope into the house. I was mortified! I had outstayed my welcome; Basil was cross with me; and I had lost the bride doll too. I burst into tears and fled into the Billiard Room and hid beneath the table. The heavy green cloth afforded me some privacy and I cried out all my unhappiness and desolation. When I had no more tears left to shed, I crept

291

outside again and walked through the tussac behind the Wireless House so that my face would lose its blotchiness and my shame would remain hidden amongst the tall tussac bogs.

When I went in for supper, I told Mum that the doll had been sold. "Never mind, Bev. I'm sure Father Christmas has something nice to bring you anyway." I gave a wan smile and said,

"Yes, I'm sure he has," and escaped to my bedroom as soon as I was able to without drawing attention to myself. I cuddled Sandy close, finding comfort in his nuzzlings and warm body. The following morning I said to Mum, "I don't think I'll go up to Betty's to play today. I'll take Gerald onto the Snowgoose instead."

"That's nice of you, Bev. Gerald will like that!" For that day and each day thereafter, I stayed at home and played with Gerald. On the fourth day, Betty came down at smoko time and I heard her asking Mum why I hadn't been up to play with the children.

"I don't know," Mum replied, "she just says she'll stay home and play with Gerald. Did she fall out with anyone that you know of?"

"I asked but there doesn't seem to have been a falling-out. My three don't know why she hasn't come up to play. Have you asked her?" Mum came into the passage.

"Bev, why haven't you been up to Betty's to play? Did something happen?"

"No, nothing happened, Mum. I just thought that I was being horrible to Ger, leaving him on his own all the time, that's all." This explanation seemed to be acceptable to Mum and Betty. When Betty left she said,

"Bev, why don't you come up and play this afternoon?"

"Yes, go on," Mum agreed, "I'll take Gerald out for a walk after dinner so he won't be lonely." This was a fait accompli. I couldn't refuse to go up to Betty's as that would lead to more questions. I had to agree.

Once dinner was over, I walked up to Betty's but did so cautiously, waiting until I saw Basil working in the jail so that I knew that he had left the house. I ran in and had a wonderful afternoon playing with Janet, Coleen and Peter, but I kept an eye on my watch and made my excuses and left before five o'clock when Basil usually came home. This became my new pattern. I went up to play but only in the afternoon, and ensured that I never once ran into Basil in his house, or around The Point.

On the nineteenth of December, Dad came in from the Wireless Room with the news that a whaler had been killed on the R5 and that they were sailing straight back into port. Considering how dangerous an occupation whaling was, there were few serious accidents amongst the men and a death was very uncommon. We learned that the man who had died was someone we didn't know personally, his name was Gunnar Langaas. Apparently Gunnar had been leaning over the side of the catcher winching a whale alongside by its tail fluke. While he was injecting gas into the whale's body to make it float, the catcher had dipped downwards in a trough while, at the same instant, the whale had been raised up on a wave and its fluke hit Gunnar on the side of the head, its force killing him instantly. This death came as a shock to everyone. Work came to a halt both in Pesca and on The Point on the twenty-second of December, when all of the adults attended the funeral service in the little church. I wasn't allowed to attend the funeral service so well before the service was due to begin, I ran round to Pesca and hid behind a rock on the mountain above the church. I watched as Gunnar's coffin, draped in the Norwegian flag, was carried to the church in the trailer behind the newest tractor. After the service, all of the men from the whaling station followed the tractor in silent tribute through Pesca to the cemetery where he was laid to rest, facing east to west and not looking towards Antarctica as Shackleton does.

On Christmas Eve we all walked round to the church together to attend the Carol Service before the usual round of parties. Janet, Peter and I joined in with the adults. Coleen, very pretty, very quiet and a little bit removed, watched everyone's antics from her vantage point in the corner of the room, keenly observing the behaviours of each individual and deciding that the behaviour of the grown-ups was much worse than that of the children. As the alcohol flowed freely and everyone except for Mum and Jenny got particularly merry, Coleen was absolutely correct in her conclusions.

On Christmas morning I opened my presents and found a beautiful doll. She was clearly an expensive doll with an unglazed bisque ceramic head. Her face was beautifully painted, giving her an ethereal quality, quite unlike the plastic, monochrome pinkness of my other dolls. Her features were delicate and lifelike. A wig of dark brown wavy hair was topped with a small blue hat, tied with a pretty ribbon beneath her slender neck. Her body was plastic and her dress matched the hat perfectly. Small white shoes fastened with a button at the ankle, completed her attire. On any other Christmas Day I would have been thrilled with this doll, but I was disappointed that she wasn't the bride doll that I wanted so badly. She was beautiful though and I called her Daisy after the tiny flowers which decorated her hat.

After dinner, Mum, Dad, Gerald and I walked up to Betty's for some tea or, for the men, a wee snifter. At Mum's suggestion, I took my doll with me. We walked into Betty's sitting room and I had to fight to hold back my tears. Sitting on the floor, Coleen was playing with the bride doll. The bride was proudly holding on to her new husband and Janet was assisting the best man and the bridesmaid to follow them down the aisle. Between Christmas and the end of the season when the children left South Georgia and returned to school in Stanley, Coleen often let me play with the bridesmaid or the best man, but never with the bride doll herself. It was only fair that Coleen should play with her as she was the rightful owner of the bride doll, but my heart was forever heavy with envy and longing for the doll who was so nearly mine.

Walking around The Point one afternoon, the four of us met Mrs Hooper standing in her customary position on the path below her house and looking towards Prudence and Gertrude. As we drew nearer, she looked up at us and said,

"Hello, children! I'm just having a conversation with Prudence and Gertrude who are my special friends. Do you know, the two girls really do know me? They always look up whenever I walk down the path." Nobody said anything and I felt that the resulting stunned silence was too deep for comfort so I replied,

"I'm sure they do, Mrs Hooper."

"Indeed, yes, Beverley. We are becoming boon companions, don't you know?"

"Well, goodbye Mrs Hooper, we're walking up to the dam so need to be going." The others followed my lead and said their farewells and we walked off along the path. Once out of earshot, we broke into a run and burst into uncontrollable laughter.

"Sea elephants don't know you!" Janet giggled.

"She's been talking to them all summer," I said, "she started it when they first came ashore and she talks to them every day." Coleen, thoughtful and precise as ever, announced quietly

"She's mad!" I was shocked to hear Coleen say such a thing about an adult, but when I thought it over, I conceded that she might be right. There were only a small number of adults on The Point, but all life was represented there in one form or another.

The refit of the *Calpean Star* was progressing well and we were invited on board for lunch. Up on deck they erected a swing for us children and we took turns in swinging high up over the deck, laughing and enjoying the fun. The meal we were served was excellent and I luxuriated again in the elegance of the dining room and the saloon. I imagined what it must be like to be rich and well travelled like American and English people seemed to be from the films that we saw at the Kino. I wanted to see the world so much, I dreamed every day about our forthcoming trip to England. I couldn't contain my excitement at the prospect of experiencing the wider world and how different sophisticated people who travelled on trains and buses and on liners rather than on small cargo ships must be to us.

Janet, Coleen and Peter returned to Stanley to resume their education and I found myself alone again with just Gerald and Martin for company. Jenny was very patient with me and I visited her regularly in her snug bungalow. She had brought a good selection of books with her for Martin and she read stories to him frequently. She sat on the sofa with Martin in her lap and read to both of us. I particularly liked the books by Beatrix Potter which humanised animals in much the same way as one of my new books did. I had been sent two of Alison Uttley's 'Little Grey Rabbit' books for my birthday and given another two for Christmas. One of these, 'Little Grey Rabbit's Christmas', was a favourite book now, but not in preference to Hans Christian Andersen. I recited the little poem from the book to Gerald every night when he was lying in his cot and on the verge of sleep:

"Holly red and mistletoe white,
The stars are shining with golden light,
Burning like candles this Holy Night,
Holly red and mistletoe white.

Mistletoe white and holly red,
The doors are shut and the children a-bed,
Fairies at foot and angels at head,
Mistletoe white and holly red. Goodnight Ger!"

Then I gave him a kiss and tiptoed out of his room.

Apart from Nigel, other naturalists came to South Georgia to study the flora and fauna and some, to collect penguins and seals for European zoos. A German collector, called Eric, came to The Point and sailed around the island collecting a large number of king penguins and fur and elephant seals. He also captured a leopard seal. Earlier in the season, unusually, some albatross had been taken back to another zoo. As he prepared the animals for their journey to Montevideo on the *Calpean Star*, he kept each species on board in its own quarters with a pond. He left some cages crafted from wood and chicken wire on the jetty at The Point and along the shore beside the boat sheds. My favourite penguins had always been chinstraps. These small penguins, named for the black strap beneath their chins, looked sweet, cuddly and friendly. It hadn't ever occurred to me to catch a chinstrap myself and keep it as a pet but now, as I followed Eric around, I found the courage to ask him if I could please have one of the cages as I wanted to keep a chinstrap as a pet.

"Of course you can," he beamed, "I will find for you a cage and you can choose your penguin. But you must care for him carefully and feed him fresh fish every day, not too big. If he does not feed, you must let him go free so he does not die."

"I'll take good care of him, I promise, and I won't let him die. That would be terrible!" I chose my penguin and one of Eric's helpers caught him and put him into a small cage for me. Lacking imagination, I named my penguin Percy. Once I saw him happily settled, I bade Percy a very fond goodnight and went home for supper.

The following morning I sat with my fishing line dangling over the end of the jetty and hooked fish after fish, taking them off the hook with some difficulty and feeling disgusted by their slipperiness and sliminess in my hands. I plopped them into a bucket at my side and threw back the big ones and the crocodile fish, because Percy was only a small penguin after all. Armed with my catch, I went to Percy, opened the cage warily, held up a fish, and was thrilled when he swallowed it in one gulp. Percy ate the smallest fish and seemed to be quite happy to be close to me and fed by me, but I realised very quickly that the slightly larger fish were much too big for him to swallow, so I emptied the contents of my bucket over the side of the jetty and returned to fishing. This was harder than I thought it would be. The bigger fish darted for the bait on my hook, forcing the tiny ones out of the way. I baited my hook with smaller and smaller pieces of bait which helped a bit as some of the bigger fish thought that it was beneath their dignity to take, but catching enough really small fish for Percy became a long and difficult daily task and I often spent two hours or more fishing for Percy's dinner.

With memories of the emperor penguin still fresh in my mind, I thought very carefully about how I was going to handle Percy. I gently put both hands around his feathery body and, making sure that his tail pointed towards me and his beak was pointing away, lifted him from the cage and on to my lap.

"There you are, Percy. Isn't it nice to be out of your cage and sitting with me?" I stroked his feathers as best I could, but Percy was not in a cuddly mood. He struggled and his neck flailed from side to side in constant motion, trying to find some exposed part of my body to bite.

"Percy, stay still!" I told him, but he took very little notice of me and I thought that I'd better put him back into his cage before he did me some permanent damage.

As I lifted Percy into the air in preparation for slipping him back into his cage, a large, liquid spurt of white, fishy-smelling excreta, squirted backwards from beneath his tail, and dribbled down the skirt of my cotton dress.

"Percy! That is horrible!" I said, "Why did you do it?" I dropped Percy into his cage and he turned quickly as I secured the door with wire, giving me an angry stare. I gave him an angry stare straight back.

"If you think you're going to beat me by messing up my clothes, young penguin, you've got another think coming!" I said, as I turned on my heel and walked back to our house.

When I walked in through the kitchen door, Mum took one look at me and said,

"Bev, what have you been up to? Look at the mess you've made of your dress."

"I didn't make a mess of my dress, Mum, Percy did!"

"Well take if off right now before you come any further into the house, and I'll put it in to soak. If this is how you're going to come home from playing with that penguin, you're going to have to let him go, and that's that!"

When I fed Percy again that afternoon, I took the precaution of tying an old apron around my waist to protect my clean dress from his bottom. He ate well but was still very difficult to hold. I spoke soothingly to him and held him firmly but gently, to little avail. He squirmed and tried to peck me at every opportunity. This was clearly going to be a clash of wills and I was determined that it was my will which was going to succeed. Percy was equally determined not to be stroked and loved and, at the very moment when the wind blew my apron up, he fired a dart of smelly white excreta back at me which neatly caught the hem of my dress and ran stickily down my leg.

"You dirty penguin! Now you've got me into trouble again! Why can't you behave and be a nice penguin?" I put Percy back into his cage and walked home, wondering how to get into the house without Mum seeing the mess I was in. I crept into the house through the Recreation Room door, sneaked along the passage into the bathroom, carefully pulled the door to, and washed my leg and dress as best I could. I then sneaked out again and ran around The Point, waving my skirt in the air until it had dried enough for me to dare to face Mum again.

The next day was a repeat of the first. Percy fed from me, but he resisted everything I did to make friends. I talked consolingly, tried to smooth his feathers, cuddled him, gave him extra fish, but he resisted my kindness and love with a ferocity surprising in such a small penguin. Each time I reached into the cage to stroke or catch him, Percy bit at my arms and hands. When I held him, Percy defecated all over me, sometimes more than once. Where he got all that excreta from was an imponderable, it seemed as if he was producing amounts that an emperor would have been proud of. I found an old sack which I used to protect my clothes, but this soon became so soiled and disgustingly smelly that I didn't want to wrap it around myself anymore. When Percy and I looked at each other, the power in our relationship was moving from me to him. I had control of his captivity and I brought him food, but that mattered little to Percy. I was his jailer and he wasn't going to give an inch. Instead of growing to love me as I thought he would, Percy hated me with a vengeance and took every opportunity to demonstrate his feelings towards me. I went home each evening knowing that Sandy and Gerald would greet me with a wagging tail, smiles and hugs. They wanted me but, from Percy, love was never going to flow.

301

I kept Percy for ten days then I decided that I could see penguins whenever I liked so I didn't need to keep one as a pet. Catching fish for him every day was becoming an unpleasant chore and when the winds blew and whipped the harbor up into a maelstrom and threatened to carry me off the jetty into their turbulent depths, I worried for Percy because I couldn't feed him at all and I didn't want him to ever go hungry. I carried Percy's cage to the edge of the beach, opened the door and offered him his freedom. "I'm letting you go Percy, take care. I'll never forget you!" Percy scuttled from the cage, threw himself off the stony bank into the sea, and swam furiously out into the harbour. I ran along the jetty, watching his torpedo-shaped little body dart through the water. I waved and shouted, "Take care Percy! Take care!" but Percy ignored me and just swam on. I thought that he might at least turn round and give some semblance of farewell, some indication that he was grateful for the care and love I had showered on him, but no, he couldn't wait to get out to sea, away from me! I shook my head and walked back to the cage, stacking it neatly beside the boat shed before walking slowly home, my heart heavy in defeat.

CHAPTER 12

THE BLUE WHALE

By late February the long re-fit of the *Calpean Star* was
completed, her exterior had been refurbished and her engines
had been overhauled. We were invited on board for a meal by her Norwegian
Master. Up on deck I swung through the air again on the swing. Two days
later, we all gathered on the jetty at The Point and watched as she swung
round from her anchorage and slowly made her way out of the harbour
towards Husvik where she was going to load a cargo of frozen whale meat.
When she slipped her moorings at Husvik, the *Calpean Star* was so
overloaded that she was too heavy to sail away from the jetty so quantities of
the frozen whale meat had to be taken ashore again. As she sailed back
round to Pesca, the fog came down and she went aground on a submerged
rock in Stromness Bay. Dad listened in to the messages which flew between
the *Calpean Star* and Pesca. Her rudder had apparently been folded up 'like
a ball' and she had been extensively damaged. We all lined the beach a few
days later and watched as she limped back into port.

"The Master was apparently ill when she ran aground, they say."

"He's often ill after a couple of bottles!"

I was playing with Gerald in the conservatory after dinner the
following day when Dad burst into the house from the recreation room.

"I've just heard that they're bringing a blue whale into Pesca. Actually, I've never seen one myself, so I thought that we'd all go round and have a look."

"I've seen whales being cut up once and I'm not keen on seeing any more," Mum replied, "why don't you take Bev and leave Gerald here with me?"

"Very well! Beverley, get your coat!" and within minutes, my hand was in Dad's and we were on our way to Pesca.

"Blue whales are the largest whales, Beverley. Actually, they are the biggest creatures on earth. They have been over hunted and are now nearing extinction. Seeing one today will be a part of history. You must never forget it." Then, as an afterthought, "What do I mean by extinction?"

"That the blue whales are like the dinosaurs and that they will disappear from the world completely."

"Exactly so, yes!"

"Why will they disappear, Daddy? Can't anyone save them?"

"Let me ask you a question. Imagine that I have got four bars of chocolate in my hand. I have got one very large bar, a smaller bar, an even smaller bar and a tiny bar. If I say that you can choose a bar of chocolate but that you can't have any more chocolate again until next year, which bar will you choose?"

"The biggest bar."

"Exactly! Even a child knows that! After the war the United Nations set up an International Whaling Commission to safeguard stocks of whales across the world. This Commission set a quota for the maximum number of whales which can be caught every year. What they failed to do, however, was to give quotas for each species of whale. So you can guess what happened. Whalers did what you would do, they took the largest whales because they were more profitable, with the obvious result that the blue whales were over hunted. Even today there is no limit on the number of blue whales which can be caught. The only reason that so few come into Pesca is because, as a species, they are now very few in number."

"I think that's sad. Why can't the men in charge just tell everyone to leave the blue whales alone?"

"You would think that the United Nations had some of the world's cleverest men working for it, wouldn't you? Men who would have enough common sense to realise that the International Whaling Commission has done its job very badly indeed and who would change the system to name particular species of whale. Actually, I sometimes wonder if those people even realised that there were different species of whale in the first place." We walked on in silence as I digested this information. I hadn't ever thought about the whales as being living, breathing creatures, really. They were talked about on The Point and especially in Pesca as commodities. All the whalers were excited at the prospect of big bonuses at the end of every season. Now, Dad had made me think about individual whales and what was being done to them. If blue whales were becoming extinct, I couldn't see why we were going to Pesca to see one if it was dead. It seemed wrong. I didn't understand.

"Daddy, why do we want to see a dead blue whale if it's wrong to harpoon them?"

"We are going to witness history, Beverley. History is not always good and that is something that you are old enough to learn. Actually, it is bad more often than not. We are going to see a blue whale while there is still one blue whale to be seen on this planet. We have to hope to God that there are many

305

more which are swimming safely in the ocean and which will not be caught. If not, then you and I will be witnessing the end of a species which must be one of the saddest sights on earth."

We got to Pesca and took our place once again by the blubber cookery. The air was heavy with the pungent and sickly smell of old ropes, oil driven winches and cooking blubber and meat. Seabirds screamed as they wheeled and dived for the detritus in the bloody harbour. The Plan foreman left the carcass which he had been supervising and came over to chat to Dad. "I hear there's a blue whale coming in," said Dad.

"Yes, it is here. We will bring it up on to the plan after this sei which is being winched up now. I will let you look close at it when it is up." Smiling, he walked back to his work. A very long baleen whale slid onto the plan in front of us.

"Beverley, how do you know that this is a sei whale and not a fin?"

"It hasn't got a two-coloured face and I think that it looks darker than the fin whale did."

"There is some colour difference, yes. You can see the two blowholes on the top of the head very clearly on this one. Actually, do you know what the grooves along the lower side of the jaw are for?"

"No, Daddy." He entered into a long explanation about the process by which baleen whales filter krill through their flukes. On any other occasion I would have listened very carefully to anything Dad told me, but today I felt uneasy and not happy to be there. I was thinking about this whale and how frightened it must have been when it was being chased by an R boat and how it must have hurt when it was harpooned.

When they hauled the blue whale on to The Plan, it was obvious that this whale was enormous. It was over eighty feet long and it seemed to take up the full length of The Plan. It had a broad, flat head but its body tapered elegantly towards triangular flukes. I had expected it to be a pretty blue but it was more of a soft, mottled grey with a yellowish underbelly. The Plan foreman measured the whale then came over to us. By now it was obvious that word had got round and many of the men who didn't work on The Plan came over to see this rare sight. Uncle Bonski was one of them.

"You have come to see a blue whale, Beeverley. It is bigger than you thought, yes?"

"Yes, Uncle Bonski." The Plan foreman led Dad and I towards the whale. The other men followed.

"It's a female, they are bigger than the males and this one is eighty-three feet long. Look at the baleen plates, there are more than three hundred and twenty pairs of plates and you can see the hairs at the end of each plate." The plates were huge, towering above me like a giant's hair comb. I was interested in all that I saw, thinking that this might be the last blue whale on the planet and I needed to store everything in my memory. We walked around the whale for a minute or two then The Plan foreman shouted something in Norwegian and everyone cleared the plan and the flensing began. Her blubber was very deep, about fourteen inches. As it was torn away from the front of her carcass, Dad said quietly in my ear,

"You can see why these whales were taken first. There will be a lot of profit from this one." I nodded, unable to speak. Dad was standing behind me with his hands on my shoulders. I leaned back against his legs for comfort. I hated all the men on the whale catchers, especially the gunners who I had

307

looked up to before because of their high status within the whaling community. I especially hated The Plan foreman and the flensers and now the lemmers who were beginning to do their job with precision and efficiency. I hated the men up in the lofts and most of all I hated the United Nations who were so useless. This was very bad history. Tears filled my eyes and flowed freely down my face for the poor female blue whale which was fast becoming just another slab of meat and bone in front of my eyes. When it was over we walked back towards the Slop Chest with Uncle Bonski.

"Would you like chocolate, Beeverley?" Chocolate! Into my mind flashed Dad's story and I had chosen the largest slab, just like the whalers at Pesca. I felt ashamed of my greed. Dad said our goodbyes and we walked past the Bakery towards home. Neither of us felt like a pastry today.

When we got back to the house, Dad poured himself a large whisky and downed it in one.

"This has been a bad day, Pearl, a very bad day." As if to emphasise the point, Dad poured a second large whisky and carried the glass through to the Wireless Room with him to ease him through the evening sched.

That night, Basil and Betty threw a party to celebrate Basil's birthday. Dressed in my best blue frock and with a matching blue ribbon in my hair, we walked up to their house in the glowing light of a calm evening, Dad carrying a sleeping Gerald in his arms. Everyone from The Point was there and Uncle Bonski, Strand, Tor, and Ras had come round from Pesca. As soon as everyone had their drinks, Basil said,

"Let's get this party going!" and he put on his favourite record, Elvis singing 'Hound Dog'. With a broad grin across his face, Basil started jiving and we all joined in. All through the night we partied. As always, Mum, Betty and I were asked to dance every dance and no one was left out.

Dad refused to dance, sitting on the sofa drinking steadily and arguing more and more loudly with anyone who would hold a conversation with him. Even Uncle Ron and Uncle Bonski who normally humoured Dad, kept away from him as the night wore on and he became increasingly aggressive in his speech, hitting the arm of the sofa to emphasise each point as he made it. It was well after midnight when the party broke up. Dad was reluctant to leave and became very aggrieved when Mum told him that everyone else was going home and that we should too.

"Fe farn woman! I'll go when I'm ready and not before."

"Come on, Peter" said Uncle Ron, "we're all going now. Let's stroll back together." Reluctantly, Dad pulled himself up and staggered out the door into the night. Mum was carrying Gerald and I walked beside her. Dad and Uncle Ron weaved their unsteady way in front of us in silence. Uncle Ron called a cheery

"Goodnight!" as he went left to Discovery House and we went in the Recreation Room door. I ran ahead and opened the internal doors for Dad to fall through and he staggered along the passage and fell into his room and onto the bed.

"Woman! Get in here NOW!" he shouted.

"I'm putting Gerald to bed and I'm going to see to Bev as well," Mum replied.

"You bloody well get in here NOW!" Dad shouted. Mum was settling Gerald into his cot.

"I can get myself into bed, Mum. You go to Dad before he gets even crosser." With a kiss on my forehead, Mum went into her bedroom.

"You bloody well showed me up tonight telling me when to come home. Don't you ever talk like that to me in front of my friends again."

"Everyone was leaving, Peter. The party was over and Betty wanted to get to bed."

"I decide when I go or stay, not you!" I heard the first slap followed by Mum's body falling against the bedroom wall.

"Peter! Stop that! You're hurting me!"

"Get back onto the bed woman or I'll hurt you some more." Crouched in the passage outside their room I listened to every sound, terrified at what he might do next. I didn't have long to wait, I heard another slap, then another and Mum started to cry.

"Shut up, woman! You think that when you start bloody crying I'll stop, well I bloody well won't!" After a few moments, everything went silent. Slaps, crying, yelling, swearing, I had listened to so much of that during these long nights, but this deep silence was something new. A minute passed and fear grew inside me, chilling my bones and causing sweat to break out on my brow at the same time. If Mum was making a noise, however fearful it sounded, she was at least 'alive and kicking' as she always said. Now she was completely silent. I knew I would only make things worse if Dad knew I was out of bed and spying on them, but I couldn't stay motionless where I was. Their bedroom door was ajar and I gently pushed it open a little more. Moonlight streamed in through the window and I stealthily pushed my head around the door. Mum was sprawled across the bed and Dad was sitting astride her, holding her down. He was completely oblivious to me, his whole

310

energy and concentration focused on the recumbent woman beneath him. I
couldn't see what he was doing to her, so I stood up and walked into their
bedroom. In the grey light, I saw Mum's head had fallen backwards over the
far side of the bed, her tongue swollen and sticking out, her eyes lolling
backwards in their sockets, and Dad's hands were gripping tightly around her
throat. I screamed.

"Daddy! Daddy! What are you doing? Let Mum go!" But he was too deeply
immersed in his own world to even register that I was there. I climbed onto
the bed behind him, pushed my two hands deep into his hair and I pulled
back with all my strength and weight. Springing back to life, Dad let out a
deep roar of anguish as he swung his left fist round, hitting me in the stomach
with such force that I flew backwards off the bed, across the floor and my
back crashed into the hard metal flanges of the radiator. I slid to the floor in
a crumpled heap, fighting for breath. Dad looked at me as if he didn't realise
who or what I was. Without a glance at Mum he climbed drunkenly off the
bed and took a step towards me, his fists clenched. Then his eyes seemed to
clear a little and he changed his mind. He grabbed the door and used it to
lever himself into the passage. I heard him crashing his way towards the
kitchen.

I was winded and breathing was difficult and painful. Holding my
stomach I crawled to the bed and pushed up Mum's head so that it wasn't
hanging down over the side anymore.

"Mum! Mum! Are you alright?" I whispered through my tears.

"Mum! Mum! Please be alright." I pulled myself up onto the bed and lifted
her head into a supported position on the pillow. She opened her eyes and
they slowly focused on me. She put one hand to her throat and we sat

311

together, me holding her other hand as we both gasped for breath. Mum tried to say something but I couldn't catch what she was trying to say. Leaning close to her I heard her rasping whisper.

"Gerald?" Gerald! I hadn't given him a thought! What if Dad had got him? Breathing more normally now, I slipped off the bed and cautiously made my way across the passage into Gerald's bedroom. He was sleeping peacefully in his cot. I needed to know where Dad was so that we could all get out of the house if he was still in a dangerous mood. I crept along the passage and peeped into the kitchen but he wasn't there, so I assumed he must be in the sitting room. Sure enough, Dad had fallen in a heap onto the sofa. I listened to his sonorous breathing until it descended into nasal snoring. We were safe! He wouldn't wake up before the morning now.

I went back to Mum and told her that we were safe and so was Gerald.

"Water, please." She rasped. I crept back to the kitchen, brought her a glass of water and held her head, feeding her small sips when she felt strong enough to take them. When Mum was settled with her head as comfortable as I could make it, she asked me to bring Gerald in to her. I lifted him from his cot with some difficulty as he was getting heavy for me to lift now, but I got him into the bed next to Mum then I lay down myself. If Dad did wake up again, at least we would be all together this time.

I slept fitfully that night. My stomach was painful and my back even more so. I tried to sleep on my side, but with my ears constantly straining for the sounds which would tell me that Dad had woken up, I mostly lay awake. Mum, Gerald and I rose early the next morning and Mum and I gingerly crawled out of bed to inspect our injuries. Mum had a wide blue bruise across each cheek from the slaps and a splitting headache. Her neck was very swollen and the imprints from Dad's fingers resembled a purple garland of flowers around it. My stomach looked like a dartboard, with a deep blue inner and concentric circles of shades of lighter blue towards the outside. My back had swollen welts of bruised flesh running down it in parallel stripes from where I had hit the radiator flanges. It made me cry when I looked at myself in the mirror. Obviously my tears were silent as I didn't dare to wake Dad, but they flowed as if they would never stop.

Mum, Gerald and I sat silently around the kitchen table, Mum and I being unable to swallow anything more than coffee laced with generous quantities of condensed milk. We heard Dad get up from the sofa, walk to the toilet then go into the bathroom to wash. Mum went to the bedroom and laid out his clothes for the day, then came back to the kitchen to make toast for his breakfast. When he was ready for work, Dad came in and Mum put his breakfast in front of him. For the first time I could ever remember, she stayed silent. She usually upbraided him for his behaviour the night before if he had been bad and had hit her, or spoke lovingly to him if he had been good. This morning she said nothing and I expected Dad to get cross with her. Perhaps the sight of her swollen neck and purple necklace gave him pause for thought.

During the day Gerald and I played quietly in my room. I was in real discomfort and bending caused a searing pain to tear through my stomach. Dad came in for his lunch but didn't stay long. We stayed in my room out of the way. I asked Mum if he had said anything and she said that they hadn't even exchanged two words. I looked at Mum with a newfound wonder. I had never known her to treat Dad in this way before. She loved him so much

313

that whatever he did to her, she forgave him. But today she was different.
Something had changed, but I couldn't work out what it was.

At about six o'clock Mum ran a bath for us and while we were in it,
Dad came in from the Wireless Room. The bathroom door was open and I
heard Dad say to Mum,
"I don't remember last night, but I can see that I have hurt you and I'm
sorry." Usually Mum would have a little moan and say how violent he had
been, then forgive him and they would hug each other, but today she didn't.
She just said
"Go into the bathroom and wash your daughter." Dad had never washed me
since I was a baby and I didn't want him to do it now, especially as I was
hurting all over. Surprisingly, he walked meekly into the bathroom and said,
"Hello, children." And Gerald answered,
"Hello, Daddy!" I stayed silent and bent forwards so that he couldn't see the
bruises on my stomach.
 "I'm going to give you a wash, then you can get out of the bath." Dad
picked up the flannel, rubbed soap on to it and walked towards me.
"Sit up straight, Beverley, I can't wash you if you are hunched up like that."
I sat up straight and looked directly into his eyes. He saw my bruised
stomach and I half-turned so that he could see the welts on my back as well.
My eyes never left his face. He took in my injuries and blanched. He
dropped the flannel into the bath, turned on his heel and left the room. Mum
was standing outside in the passage.
"That is what you did to your daughter, never mind that you nearly throttled
me. You would have strangled me too, if Bev hadn't stopped you." Dad said
nothing and walked into the sitting room. Mum got us out of the bath, gave

us some sops and put us both to bed early. As usual I listened to what was going on between Mum and Dad but this night it seemed as if it was going to be safe to go straight to sleep. They were only talking quietly.

The next day Mum and Dad were all lovey-dovey at breakfast time. I replied politely to Dad's
"Good morning, Beverley," but I stayed silent otherwise. I wasn't sure what was going on between them, but he had obviously got round Mum again and I felt deeply angry with her. I had really thought that this time was different, Mum had seemed cold and in control yesterday, but now it was as if nothing had happened. That definitely wasn't how I saw it.

After Dad had gone through to the Wireless Room, I said to Mum in my coldest voice,
"You've forgiven him again, haven't you?"
"Yes I have, Bev. Your Dad can't remember anything and he is very, very sorry for what he did to us both. He has promised never to do it again."
"He has promised that plenty of times before and look what he's done to us this time! He just gets worse and worse!"
"You know that Dad gets angry when he's the worse for drink, and he knows that this time he has gone too far. He has promised me that he will go on the wagon and he didn't have one drink at all yesterday."
"You believe that old story, do you?"
"Yes I do, Bev. Daddy has made a promise to me and he knows that if he ever does anything like that to you, me or Gerald again, I will take you kids and leave him. He knows that I mean it. Things will be different from now on, you'll see." I couldn't believe that Mum had been strong enough to threaten to leave Dad. I turned the possible ramifications of it over and over

315

in my mind. Where would we live if she left Dad? How would we cope for money? Could she really keep to her word if he did do it again? I admired the new strength that Mum had found, but it scared me too. Without Dad what would our life be? Even with his drinking, perhaps it was better to be with him than without him.

It took until April for the divers and engineers at Pesca to repair the damage which had been done to the *Calpean Star* when she ran aground in February in Stromness Bay. The Master had been relieved of his duties as he was found to have been suffering from 'ill health' and Harald was appointed as her new Master, charged with getting her safely back to the United Kingdom. During the war years, Harald had studied for his full Master's Ticket but the other captains of the R boats held only limited Maritime Tickets and were restricted to sailing ships of lower tonnage than the *Calpean Star*. This meant that Harald had no choice but to take command of the embattled ship and nurse her across the South Atlantic Ocean as best he could. He held a heavy responsibility and when we walked round to Pesca to see him to say goodbye, Harald didn't have the lightness of step and confident bearing that he had always had when he was simply the Captain and gunner of the *R2*. Instead of his huge grin and jovial exclamations whenever he saw me, Harald seemed distracted and even careworn. He shook hands with us all and we made our farewells in a subdued vein. This wasn't the Harald we all knew and had so much fun with.

Early the following morning all the residents of The Point met at Discovery House to wave the *Calpean Star* away. Dad told everyone about saying farewell to Harald the previous day and that it wasn't a surprise to him that Harald had seemed so preoccupied.

"I feel really sorry for him. The poor bugger is taking six thousand tons of cargo, over two hundred crew and whalers, not to mention live seals and penguins back to the UK on a ship which Lloyds of London are wary about insuring. I wouldn't like to be in his shoes for all the tea in China." There was a general assent amongst all of us watching from the safety of the beach as we waved her out of the harbour.

"Well, that's the *Calpean Star* gone. Nothing left for it now but to batten down the hatches for another winter!" and the men went their separate ways.

Dad didn't come into the kitchen for smoko, so Mum sent me into the Wireless Room to see if he wanted her to take his coffee through to him. Dad lifted one earphone away from his ear and said,

"The *Calpean Star* is in trouble. Harald has sent to Grytviken for the *Petrel* to go out and tow her back. Tell your mother that I'm going to man the Wireless Room continuously until she's back safely just in case they need assistance from further afield. It's the least I can do for Harald."

Harald had radioed back that the *Calpean Star* was unmanageable and he asked for further assistance from the *Sabra* at Leith Harbour, as well as from the *Petrel*. Dad monitored all of the traffic between the three ships and Pesca. As the day wore on, the attempts by the *Petrel* and the *Sabra* to tow the liner back proved to be much more difficult to achieve than everyone had previously thought. Then, to everyone's horror, a typical South Georgia gale blew up and the *Calpean Star* became almost completely unmanageable. The two smaller ships couldn't get in close enough to stabilise her in the high seas. The aim of the rescue had to be changed. Now the expedient was to tow the *Calpean Star* into the comparative shelter of Jason Harbour to protect

317

her from the high winds and raging seas. There was no chance at all of bringing her back to Pesca now.

By five o'clock in the afternoon, everyone from The Point had brought a chair and we all sat with Dad in the Wireless Room, hanging on to his every word as a life and death drama was being played out at sea. We were all terrified that the *Calpean Star* would be lost with the two hundred and twenty five crew and men who had spent the summer season at Pesca, many of whom were our friends. Mum made endless cups of coffee and cooked batches of Falkland Island biscuits to keep everyone's spirits up. It was nearly midnight before the three ships crept into the shelter and relative safety of Jason Harbour and we climbed into bed.

Nearly two weeks later, we stood on the beach again to watch as the *Calpean Star* limped back into Pesca. After another delay, she put to sea again with one of the *R* catchers chained on either side of her to help the stricken vessel with her steering. I ran along the beach to Hope Point to wave her farewell and I sat with my back against Shackleton's Cross, watching as the liner and her entourage crept further and further out into Cumberland Bay. I was about to leave my vantage point and go home when the *Calpean Star* appeared to come to a stop. I watched carefully, not trusting my eyes. Surely nothing was going to go wrong this time? The whalers were already well past their due dates for leaving Pesca and returning home to the UK and Norway. There would be very real anger amongst the men if they had to come back to Pesca, yet again.

As I stared into the distance, unmistakably the *R* catchers were turning the liner around. Slowly the view of her stern was replaced by the view of her bow, and the *Calpean Star* was obviously being nursed back towards Pesca once more. I ran down from Hope Point to go back to the house to tell Dad what I had seen. I passed Basil by the jail and shouted, "Basil, she's coming back! The *Calpean Star* is coming back into port again!"

"What? I can't bloody believe it. Not again surely!" and Basil walked towards his house to tell Betty. Back in the Wireless Room, Dad had picked up the message from Harald, he had told Pesca that the *Calpean Star* was too unsafe to cross the Atlantic and he was bringing her home.

It was a silent group which stood together outside Discovery House to watch the poor old *Calpean Star* limp back into the harbour, weary and wounded. Her decks were lined with dismayed whalers who must have wondered if they were ever going to get away from South Georgia. The only positive thought that they could have had, was that their contracts stated that they had to be paid for every day between leaving Norway or the UK and arriving back. Ryan's risk in buying an old, cheap boat to work the southern oceans hadn't paid off and these delays for the *Calpean Star* were going to cost him dear.

"Poetic justice for the miserly old bugger," was Dad's considered opinion on the matter.

Even though the attic, cellars and the storeroom were bursting to the seams once more with every sort of alcohol, Dad stayed on the wagon. Three months of a glorious summer had sped by with Dad taking Gerald and I out for walks around The Point and playing hide and seek with us among the tussac bogs. One day, as a family, we took a picnic and walked round to Pesca, calling in to the Bakery to beg for a pastry each. We walked through the station, along the shore and on up to Gull Lake. This was still one of my favourite places on South Georgia, its mossy, green valley with its backdrop of majestic mountains made me think of Alpine scenes written about by Hans Christian Andersen and I was able to imagine how it would look if it was covered in Alpine flowers which shook their heads gently in the summer breeze. We spent a whole day together, Dad chasing Gerald and me around the shores of the lake, laughing and throwing us up into the air when he caught us.

I suppose all good things must come to an end. On one windy and damp afternoon Dad called to us to get ready to go for a walk with him. When Gerald and I joined him in the kitchen, I could see from his narrowed eyes, silly grin and unsteady gait that he had fallen off the wagon. We made our unsteady way along the track, past the houses towards Shackleton's Cross. Instead of walking up to the cross as I had expected, Dad said,

"I know, let's go round Hope Point!" I had been around Hope Point enough times by myself to know that you couldn't get far before the rocks became too jagged and spaced out for anyone to jump between them, and that the sea was deep and swirled in between the rocks with force, even at low tide. I was sure that Dad would soon turn around and come back so it seemed to be sensible to go along with his plan and not upset him.

Once we got to the rocks, Dad swung Gerald up over his head so that he was sitting on his shoulders. Gerald screamed with delight.
"Hold on to my collar, Gerald, we're going to jump!" and with that, Dad took a run along the last few feet of shingle beach and leapt onto a rock several feet away. He struggled to find his balance as the sea swirled around them both. Gerald was whooping and cheering and Dad shouted,
"Again?" With that, he jumped onto the next rock, a bit further out from the beach. The waves broke out to sea then rushed back in to the shore, brown sea kelp in concentric circles breaking its pattern as the waves threw it against the uneven rocks. I was terrified. I knew with certainty that it was only a matter of time before Dad lost his balance and he and Gerald would fall into the sea. I wasn't worried about Dad, he was big and he could swim, he could take care of himself. But what if Gerald was thrown forward out into the sea, away from the shore? The undertow here was so strong that Gerald would be swept out into the bay in seconds. I could never get to him through the deep sea and the kelp. Dad would be no use, he was half-cut anyway and if he did try to save Gerald rather than himself, they would probably both drown.
"I think this is too dangerous, Daddy," I said," shouldn't we go back now?"

321

"Nonsense, Beverley, we've just started!" Dad leapt across to a third, then to a fourth rock. Gerald swayed crazily backwards and forwards on Dad's neck and Dad's hands flailed in the air as he strained to hold his balance. I followed behind. He was right, really, we could go a bit further. If he hadn't been three sheets to the wind, it could have been an adventure. As it was, his balance on flat land was uneven. On wet, jagged rocks with the weight of Gerald's body on his shoulders, it was negligently dangerous. Asking him to stop and come back hadn't worked so I stood my ground on the third rock and pretended to cry loudly. After half a minute or so, imagining my baby brother's little body being dropped into the swirling waters, pulled under by the tree kelp and washed out to sea in front of my eyes, real tears were pouring down my cheeks. Dad looked at me impatiently.

"What are you crying for, Beverley?"

"I'm frightened, Daddy. My legs aren't as long as yours and the sea is so deep around the rocks it really scares me. Please take me home!" I knew Dad's moods and he was not in a good one now. I had spoiled his fun and he wasn't pleased at all. Still, he jumped back across the rocks, Gerald swinging like a pendulum across his shoulders as Dad used his arms for balance and left Gerald to hang on alone, without support. When we were back on the beach I slipped my hand into Dad's big one, wiped my tears away dramatically and said,

"Thank you for coming back, Daddy. I'm sorry I got so scared but I've never been around Hope Point before and the big rocks and the deep sea really frightened me."

"It is right that you shouldn't have been around Hope Point alone, Beverley. I understand that it can be frightening for a little girl, but you were with your father." He clearly wasn't appeased by my apology. I tried again.

"Yes, Daddy, I know that you were with me, but you had to look after Gerald and I'm not brave enough to go round Hope Point unless you're holding my hand when I jump between those big rocks. I need to have you with me on my own."

"Actually, you're right to want to have me with you without Gerald to look after too. We'll go round together another day. Now, let's go home and see if your mother has made us some cakes for our tea." He was mollified at last. Perhaps his mood tonight would be a good one, even if he was going to keep on drinking.

In 'The Canterbury Tales', Chaucer wrote:

" At other times she used to sit and think
With eyes cast downward to the water's brink
And then her heart endured a thousand shocks
To see such jagged, black and grisly rocks,
So that she scarce could stand upon her feet."

Dorigen's 'reisly rokkes blake' may have been in Brittany, but the description is a perfect one of the horrors I remember from that day on the shore beneath Hope Point.

Ryan sent down a German ocean-going salvage tug from Gibraltar called the *Atlantic* to tow the *Calpean Star* to Montevideo, but the first

323

attempt to tow her out of the harbour failed when the towing gear broke in a heavy storm. Eventually, we waved goodbye to her for the last time at the end of April and twenty days later, she docked successfully in Montevideo. That wasn't the end of the saga of the poor old *Calpean Star* though. In June as she left Montevideo bound for Liverpool, only two miles out into the River Plate, an explosion occurred onboard and she was crippled once again. The crew and the Norwegian whalers were flown to Norway and England in specially chartered aeroplanes and the seals and penguins were rescued from her decks. Ryan later sold her for salvage but this came to nothing and eventually the Uruguayan authorities took responsibility for her. Over the years the *Calpean Star* sank, stern first, into the mud of the River Plate until only her masts could be seen above the water.

CHAPTER 13

TO ENGLAND!

Dad had now completed his three year contract on South Georgia. He signed on for three more years but first, as one of the conditions of his contract, the whole family were given free passage to England where we would stay for three months during their summer, leaving the Antarctic winter far behind.

Mum found that we had very few clothes to pack to take with us. When we sat down together to look through the fashion catalogues Betty had ordered from England, Mum and I realised that our old, well-worn clothes would look completely out of place. Ladies there didn't buy men's clothes from the Slop Chest which were numerous sizes too big for them! Even worse, I was wearing a skirt and top which Mum had fashioned from the flared skirt of her old party frock. She had no paper patterns to guide her so she took her scissors and a tape measure and created her own design. The flowery cotton skirt was alright, it fitted around the waist but the poppers which fastened it together sprang apart whenever I bent over or ran and breathed heavily. The top was too tight beneath the arms so I walked like a penguin, my arms pinned to my sides. Riding my bike was impossible as my arms couldn't reach forwards far enough for me to be able to grab hold of the handlebars.

"When we get to the UK, we're going to go shopping and buy a couple of new outfits for ourselves. I'm not going to walk around the streets of England with everyone looking at us and asking where those old-fashioned people come from!"

We were booked to sail with Salvesen on the *Southern Garden*, a modified oil tanker which brought down fuel oil and whalers from England to Leith Harbour and returned with the same men and her tanks filled with whale oil at the end of the season.

The *Garden* didn't have lovely saloons and dining rooms as the *Calpean Star* had. She was built for work so everything was basic and this was also going to be her last voyage as she was scheduled to be scrapped as soon as she got back to England. Our cabin was on the officers' deck, it was quite roomy with a top bunk big enough for Gerald and I to share and a nice bottom one for Mum. The daybed made up into a very comfortable bunk for Dad.

"As long as it doesn't get too rough, then I'll be thrown out of bed and on to the deck in no time!" he observed.

We stood on deck and watched as South Georgia slipped beneath the horizon behind us, then went below to unpack and settle into our cabin. Dad had just left to go and see what was happening on the bridge, when we heard a knock at our cabin door. I answered it to find a smiling man we didn't know standing in the companionway, holding an unsteady, straggly red geranium which looked as if it was trying to make good its escape from its grimy terracotta pot.

"Hello! I've brought this flower as a gift for your mother. Would you like to invite me in?"

"Yes, please come in," I invited, and he introduced himself to Mum as Dave, a Geordie who had worked at Leith Harbour for two seasons.

"I thought this flower would brighten up your cabin," he said and Mum took the plant, expressing her thanks for his kindness. For a few minutes Dave and Mum exchanged pleasantries, then he asked,

"Why don't I take your daughter down and show her around the ship? I bet she hasn't been shown round yet, has she?" Mum seemed a bit taken aback and said that she thought I should stay with her. Dave became quite insistent.

"But I bet she would like to see down below." He stepped closer towards me and smiled down at me.

"You would like to come with me to see around the ship, wouldn't you?"

"That would be very nice, thank you."

"I'm sure we could find some nice things to do together, just you and me!"

" I don't think so", said Mum, "I do think that Bev should just stay here with me."

"She will be perfectly safe with me and we will both enjoy each other's company. I'm sure she's bored here. I've got two more red geraniums in my cabin and you are very welcome to have them too. She can bring them both back for you."

"You would like some more flowers, wouldn't you, Mum? I don't mind going down to Dave's cabin and getting them for you."

"Beverley, you will sit there on the bunk and do as you're told. And, don't speak unless you're spoken to!" I sat down in bewilderment. Dad talked to me like that all the time, but Mum never told me to speak only when I was spoken to, and she only ever called me 'Beverley' when she was really angry. I wasn't sure what I had done to get myself into so much trouble.

The atmosphere in the cabin became somewhat strained as Mum stood directly in front of me, chatting politely to Dave, but always resolutely refusing his suggestions that I would enjoy going down to his cabin with him and that she should let me go. She seemed to be completely uninterested in his lovely geraniums. After a while, Dad came back into the cabin and Mum introduced him to Dave and told him what Dave had suggested. Dad said, "Well, old man, it's too late for Beverley to go anywhere today. How about if we go up on deck and see what's going on up there." With that, Dad put his arm around Dave's shoulders and manoeuvred him out through the cabin door. I stayed on the bunk, sulking in silence as Mum unpacked our suitcases, deep in her own thoughts. It was only a short time before Dad came back.

"I've spoken to the Captain. He's going to make it a rule that the only men allowed up on to the officers' deck are the officers and those members of the crew who will look after us, like the cabin boys and the stewards. I'm afraid you and the children are going to have to spend the whole of the voyage up on this deck too. It's for everyone's safety, as we both realise," looking directly at Mum.

"Good," said Mum, "and you can get rid of that disgusting geranium too. I don't want it anywhere near us!" Dad took the geranium out onto the deck and threw it overboard.

We hit some rough patches of weather in the southern Atlantic, and I wanted to be out of the cabin as much as possible as Dad was very seasick. Sometimes he lay in Mum's bunk, at other times he wandered the decks trying to pretend that he was as hale and hearty as the next man, while looking like a green Martian from one of the spaceships who had to keep rushing to the rail to hang over the side and look at the view. The view was of unremitting sea and sky, both universally grey. Wandering and sooty albatrosses flew above, behind or beside the ship, never coming too close, majestic and controlled in flight. Wrapped in Dad's coat against the cold, thin rain, I sat on the deck for hours at a time, watching these magnificent birds, the huge white wandering albatrosses in particular, with dark wings, soaring effortlessly upwards, riding the thermals, then gliding back down towards the surface of the ocean. Sometimes they rode just above the crests of the waves, swooping to procure a hapless fish which had swum too close to the surface, or to gorge themselves when the mess boys threw the remains of our meals overboard.

My only place to play indoors, apart from our cabin, was in the bathroom which had been set aside for our use exclusively. There were two hand basins along the outer wall and two toilets at the far end with a bath beside them, hidden inside a cubicle of its own. The walls and floor were tiled in black and white, the tiles imitating the pattern of a draughtboard. I brought in my one doll and a collection of my clothes and used them as draughtsmen. Instead of playing the game properly, I laid out my draughtsmen on the black squares so that I could be the counter which literally jumped over all the other hapless pieces until it reached the far end of the board. There, I took a crown which I had made from a linen napkin, stolen from the dining saloon, and crowned myself 'queen'. Then I jumped over the pieces again on the return journey to the other end of the board and crowned myself queen all over again. Having left South Georgia behind where I was free to roam as far as I wanted to, I found the confinement of the officers' deck and the bathroom unbearable. Apart from playing draughts in the bathroom and running round and round the small officers' deck, I had no physical activity. I followed the stewards into the dining saloon each day and helped them to lay the tables for dinner and supper, but there was little else for me to do. The days were very long and unbearably tedious.

I imagined that the English children I was going to meet would be very sophisticated and would laugh at me because I was so foreign and knew so little about their world. When I thought about myself honestly, I realised that I knew very little about anything, really. I had recurring nightmares in full colour where girls in bright dresses pointed their fingers at me and laughed until tears rolled down their cheeks. I awoke with sweat standing out on my forehead like droplets of fine rain, and tears flooding my eyes. Mum only allowed me to bring one doll on the ship with me so I had chosen Daisy. She was my most expensive doll and I thought that I should take her as she would be more in keeping with the expensive and beautiful toys that English children had. One day, I decided to give Daisy a bath. I ran nice warm water into the bathroom sink, took off her clothes and popped her in. She seemed to enjoy the water as I washed her plastic body. When I pushed her head under the water to wash her hair and face, Daisy's beautiful features crumbled. They became misshapen in my hands and her face caved inwards. As I stared at Daisy in horror, I realised that I no longer had a beautiful doll, instead I held in my hands a plastic doll's body with a huge lump of grey knobbly clay attached to it at one end. I pulled Daisy out of the water and ran back with her into the cabin.

"Mum! Mum! I gave Daisy a bath and look what's happened to her!" Mum looked at Daisy's remains and said,

"Bev, you shouldn't have got her wet! You can't wash a doll with a clay face. Whatever were you thinking of?"

"I didn't know that I couldn't wash her, nobody told me not to."

"I don't remember hearing you ask," Mum replied. I thought that was unfair. It was her job to tell me which dolls I could wash and which I couldn't. It was all her fault! With tears of anger and remorse streaming down my face, I ran to the rails of the ship, held Daisy over the side and watched as she plunged, heavy lumpen head first, into the ocean. I wept and wept. Now I was completely alone without even a doll to play with.

The long days stretched on into an abyss of boredom and the month it was going to take us to get to England appeared to be never-ending. The weather improved as we entered the tropics. In warm sunshine I walked desultorily around the deck, watching the crewmen working on the main deck below me, and the whalers who came up on deck to sunbathe. Often just in their underpants, tattooed and muscular men lined up like rows of sardines on the hot, metal deck. Pasty, sun-starved bodies which had been kept warm by thick shirts and jumpers at Leith Harbour, now luxuriated in the heat of the sun and turned pink, then red, then puce. The sun grew hotter and hotter and ever more fierce. At the end of one day, Dad came into the cabin and told us that one of the whalers had sunstroke. The following day the ship was subdued, we heard the news that the Captain thought that sunstroke victim might die. Everyone's thoughts were with the sick man and very few whalers came up on to the main deck to sunbathe. At breakfast the following morning, the Captain told us quietly that the whaler had, indeed, passed away during the night. I thought about what it meant having a body on board and asked Dad what would happen to the dead man; would we have a service and bury him at sea?

"No! No! Beverley. The poor man's family will want to bury him in England. The Captain will take his body home to them for burial in the UK."

"Won't his body be smelly by then?" In the tropics, flying fish, which had been a cause of wonderment when I first spotted them gliding over the surface of the sea beside the ship, were now becoming a nuisance as they glided onto the main deck in huge numbers and died there, frying on the hot metal deck and quickly becoming smelly and foul in the searing heat of the sun.

"They will keep his body in the meat freezer until we arrive at Tilbury. He will be perfectly preserved for his family to see. I am sure that will bring them some comfort." It might bring his family some comfort, but I wasn't going to eat meat which had been stored in the same freezer as a dead body! At supper that night, I said a polite

"No, thank you," when I was offered a rissole, "I think I'll just have vegetables today, thank you!" From that point onwards, I became a vegetarian. Dad noticed my change in diet and remarked on it to Mum, but she said it wouldn't do me any harm and that,

"It's just one of Bev's fads. She'll grow out of it." I was determined that I wasn't going to grow out of it until we walked ashore at Tilbury.

Mum kept Gerald close beside her, afraid that he would slip through the rails into the sea, so I had no one to play with unless I stayed in the cabin. I spent hour after hour on my own, sitting on deck beneath an old canvas tarpaulin with my back resting against the bulkhead of the bridge, watching the bow as it rhythmically dipped up and down, pushing on inexorably through the flat, calm sea towards England. A gentle breeze from our forward motion wafted over me, the sparkling sun reflected back into my face as a million golden sparkles from the surface of an azure sea, held safely in the hollow of a circular horizon which knew no limits. The superstructure of the *Garden* gently massaged my body and the movement of the ship comforted me as we journeyed together through the interminable days, each day seeming to last hours longer than its predecessor. Surrounded by several hundred people, but essentially alone, my mind strayed into the surreal and I began to believe that I was the only living being on the earth. I watched the sailors moving around the deck below me, the steaming bodies of the whalers as they soaked up the sun's rays, and it seemed to me that they were simply players within the wider sphere of my existence. When they came near me or stepped into the range of my vision, they burst into life and played out their role, until they disappeared from my view and ceased to exist again. This hypothesis gave meaning to my days. When I went to the officers' mess to help to lay the tables, I hid round corners then jumped out on the stewards and cabin boys to try to catch them in the dormant state they would occupy when I wasn't physically there in the room with them. I deliberately closed my eyes and opened them in a flash to see if the people around me were moving, or whether I could surprise them, standing like statues, waiting until the instant when my eyes focused on them and they sprang into life. I knew that there would be only a split second in which I could catch them out, but no matter how hard I tried or what tactics I employed, I was unable to prove my theory. It made little difference, however. Inside my head everyone else was a bit player, a supporting act for the main play of my life. I knew for certain that I was the only person who truly existed. It all made perfect sense.

Our estimated arrival date at Tilbury was the fourth of May. Princess Margaret was marrying Anthony Armstrong Jones at Westminster Abbey in London during the morning of the sixth. Mum was a great fan of Princess Margaret. Mum felt deeply that the Princess should have been free to marry Group Captain Peter Townsend and was thrilled that she had now found happiness with another man. Dad promised Mum that he would take us straight up to London from Tilbury, so that we could stand on The Mall and watch the Royal Family drive past. Dad had no interest at all in Princess Margaret, but he was a committed royalist and was eager to get a glimpse of the Queen himself.

The *Southern Garden* was a very old lady on her last voyage. As we entered the Bay of Biscay, her engines failed. One day later, as we wallowed in calm waters, enjoying the silence which surrounded us now that the engines were completely idle, Dad told Mum not to fret because we would still get up to London in time for the Royal wedding.

" Tilbury stands on the Thames estuary. It's only a short ride away from London by train, so we're almost in London itself when we arrive." The next day the engines were still idle. A major part within the engine had sheared through and the engineers were trying to weld together pieces of metal from other parts of the ship to fashion a temporary replacement. The day after, they were still working on the repairs, and it wasn't until the fourth day that we all stood on deck, crossing our fingers and listening as the engineers down below started the engines. When we began to move forwards through the ocean once more, everyone on board gave an enormous cheer, but Mum was desolate. Her dream of seeing a royal wedding had been completely dashed and we were now due to arrive in England two days after the wedding, instead of two days before it. She and I sat together on the bridge on the sixth of May and listened to the BBC World Service. The reception was so poor that we lost chunks of commentary from time to time, but we heard enough for Mum to feel that she had been a part of the Royal wedding day in some small way. I felt deeply for her in her disappointment. It was Dad who was eager to sample life 'in the mother country'. Mum had only wanted to be at one special event and the *Garden* had robbed her of that pleasure. I felt that life treated my Mum very unfairly.

We sailed slowly up the River Thames into Tilbury on a clear but chilly morning. Our first views of England were not of green, rolling hills as I imagined from Uncle Ron's lessons about UK geography, but of flat marshes and brown, muddy riverbanks. Tilbury seemed to consist of a crowded dockside with large warehouses and bustling jetties stretching as far as the eye could see. Once we docked, customs and immigration officials came on board. Dad had been dreading this moment as we didn't have any passports. When Dad left Stanley for South Georgia, he hadn't thought ahead about the offer of a free passage to and from England at the end of his three year contract, so he hadn't arranged to have a proper passport issued to him by the Falkland Island authorities. In order for him to gain entry to the United Kingdom and for us to accompany him as his dependents, Mr Hooper, in his role as Magistrate of The Point, wrote Dad a certificate on official paper from the 'Magistrate's Office, King Edward Cove, South Georgia', to enable him

'…to reach the British Consul at the first port at which he may call.' The certificate carried a description of Dad as,

'Colour of hair… black

Colour of eyes... light green

Height... five feet nine and a half inches', and a small photograph of Dad standing in front of our sitting room curtains. The flower pattern of the curtains was in full focus but Dad's face was blurred, with only his tartan tie standing out clearly as his main feature.

Armed with this certificate only, we were allowed to enter England as a family and it was with genuine relief that we swept down the gangway, Dad manoeuvring our two suitcases with difficulty and Mum clutching Gerald and me so tightly by the hand that we squirmed in her strong grasp. Thirty days at sea with a few extra days added on had worn us down and we were deliriously happy to be back on dry land at last. As we walked along the dockside to the road where we had been told we would find waiting taxis for hire, Dad said,

336

"We should turn around and have a last look at the Garden as she is going on from here to the scrap yard, so we will never see her again."

"Good riddance, I say!" Mum exclaimed, still smarting from her disappointment at missing Princess Margaret's wedding. I felt sad for the Garden but not for long, we were in England, the home of the Queen and Shackleton, of Scott of the Antarctic and Uncle Ron. I turned my face towards the road, overwhelmed by the number of cars and huge lorries which sped past us, determination stamped on the faces of the drivers as they hunched forwards over their steering wheels, hurtling determinedly on their way. Dad bundled us into a taxi and the driver said to him,

"Where to guv?"

"I don't know exactly," Dad replied, "we want to get a train to London but it's getting late. Do you know of a hotel which isn't too expensive and which is near to the railway station for London?"

"Sure, guv, I know one which is so close to the station that you will be able to walk there tomorrow with no bother at all."

The hotel was a bleak, grey building with green flaking paint on the windowsills. Inside, we were greeted by a tiny man whose hair was so slaked in Brylcream that it mirrored the contours of his scalp with such exactitude that a phrenologist could have read his character without ever getting his hands sticky. We were shown to a dank family room with a small double bed, two tiny singles and an apology for a chest of drawers. Unused to anything better, we were perfectly satisfied with our first experience of a hotel and we washed our faces and hands in the sink in the communal bathroom.

"The sink is quite clean, but we are NOT having a bath in that filthy tub," Mum propounded, "we all had a bath last night and that'll do us until we can find one that will get us cleaner, not dirtier like that one will!"

With hands clean and faces shining, we went downstairs into the dining room of the hotel. We were the only guests eating in there in the early evening. The waiter came to our table and handed Dad and Mum a menu each. Before she had glanced at the menu, Mum leant across the table towards the waiter and said,

"What we really want is four glasses of cow's milk, please."

"Of course Madam", and he walked away to get them for us.

"That was a stupid thing to say, Pearl! What will he think of us? Of course it would be cow's milk! Do you think they milk goats or sheep or something in England?"

"I don't care! It doesn't matter what he thinks! It's cow's milk that we want and that's what I asked for!" Mum and Dad sat in angry silence studying their menus until the waiter returned with four glasses of unctuous, white liquid. We held the precious liquid in our hands, twirling the glasses to look at it. With smiles on our lips, simultaneously we lifted the glasses to our mouths and drank. After a few deep quaffs, our glasses were empty. We looked at each other, united within a mutual cocoon of happiness and pleasure.

"By God, that was good!" Dad said, "Let's have another one!" As he ordered our food, cottage pie and vegetables of the day, Mum said to the waiter,

"Is there cabbage with the vegetables? We need to have cabbage, please."

"I can make sure that you have cabbage, Madam", he replied courteously and Mum rewarded him with a huge, grateful smile. When the waiter had gone, Dad got very annoyed with Mum again.

"Are you going to make a habit of showing me up every time we go somewhere? He must think that you are completely stupid! You get what you are given in a restaurant, you don't ask for bloody cabbage!"

"I need cabbage to keep my attacks at bay, and the children probably do too. I don't see why I can't ask for what I want. We are paying for it after all."

"You can ask for what you want without sounding as if you've come from somewhere out of the ark!"

"I asked him politely. Why do you always have to go on so much about each simple thing?" Gerald and I sat in silence, our hands neatly folded in our laps, looking down at our shoes as if they were the most interesting shoes ever created by a cobbler. The waiter returned, bearing a large tray loaded with four plates of steaming cottage pie nestling beside four mountains of limp cabbage, the whole floating in a sea of thick, dark brown gravy. We tucked into our food with relish, swallowing vitamin free, overcooked cabbage as if it was caviar enriched with the elixir of life. As I ate the cottage pie, Mum said,

"Bev! You're eating the meat! What's come over you?"

"I just didn't like the meat on the *Garden* Mum, that's all. This is fresh and delicious!" I consigned my vegetarian days to the past now that I knew that the meat I was eating hadn't been kept in close proximity to a human body. Washing down our supper with another glass of milk, Dad and Mum's disagreement was forgotten. We left the table in complete harmony and accord. With milk to drink and overcooked food like that, living in England for three months was going to be an idyll.

CHAPTER 14

OUR FINAL SUMMER

After a happy holiday in England visiting friends and family and seeing 'the sights', we took the train to Falmouth and found a small bed and breakfast for the night. The following morning, in bright sunshine, we carried our now heavy and bulging suitcases along the length of a vast jetty to where the *Southern Opal* lay. A more modern version of the *Garden*, the *Southern Opal* lay heavy in the water, a full load of fuel oil and five hundred whalers weighing her down. We watched as two tugs pulled her away from the quay and we set sail, past some of England's green rolling hills so beloved of Uncle Ron, and out into the open sea.

Ryan, now firmly based in Britain, transferred the activities of the Compania Argentina de Pesca to his new company, Albion Star (South Georgia) Limited. He had placed the *R* catchers under the Panamanian flag in 1957 and now all of his links with Argentina, in as much as they pertained to South Georgia, were severed. Dad said to anyone who would listen that Pesca had, to all intents and purposes, ceased to exist. We should now call Pesca by its proper name of Grytviken as our pet name for the whaling station had been based on its parent company. He suggested that a good name for Pesca might be 'Albion' after the new parent company and because it was a good, solid English name, being the earliest name that the islands of

Great Britain had been known by. Dad was in full flight about this proposed name change for Pesca and his strongly held patriotism for Britain and everything British came to the fore, especially when he had had a bit to drink. However, nobody took any notice of his often repeated remarks and Pesca was how it remained to us all. Eventually Dad gave up trying to change everyone else's habits, but to him, Pesca now became Grytviken. He liked everything to be accurate and correct.

When the new whaling season began, the meat extract plant which had been completed during the winter we were in England, came into full production. Only fresh whales, within twenty four hours of death, could be processed for meat extract and the levels of hygiene required in the plant were very high. A new group of skilled men were brought down to Pesca and, with a continuous supply of whales, they were able to produce up to three tons of meat extract each day. The meat extract was shipped to England in large sheet metal containers and proved to be very profitable for Pesca that season. We talked about it amongst ourselves as 'Bovril'.

Although I was now nine years old and able to read a lot of joined-up writing, especially Mum's large, round, clear letters, Dad's writing baffled me. It was small and neat, but the individual letters were difficult to decipher. In the Wireless Room, Dad wrote messages in a different hand. He used capital letters, but joined each letter to its neighbour as Mum had taught me to do with lower case letters. When I asked him why he wrote like that, Dad said,

"For accuracy, Beverley. A person's handwriting is very individual and when someone is writing at speed, their writing can become illegible. Actually, that is more often than not the case so, because my job requires me to copy and send messages with complete accuracy, I write in capital letters. Then there is no doubt whatever about the nature of the message." This explanation made me see my Dad in a heroic light again. He was an intelligent and thoughtful man who always knew how to do things better than anyone else did. My Dad was the cleverest Dad in the world and I was determined to be as good as he was. I surreptitiously collected notes and messages from his waste-paper basket as Dad threw them away. Safely seated at my desk, I unscrewed the paper balls and copied the writing from them. I wasn't only going to be able to write in joined-up lower case letters like all the grown-ups on The Point, I was going to be able to write in joined-up upper case letters too, like my Dad. Wasn't everyone going to be amazed when they could see what I could do?

For the first month back on The Point, Dad drank but not heavily. We lived in peace and were a happy family together, sharing memories of England and looking forward to the South Georgia summer. One morning when Dad came in from completing the sched, he appeared to be out of sorts. He drank his coffee without talking to us and refused any cake. He even refused a newly baked sausage roll when it was proffered by Mum. Then he rose from the table, pushed back his chair and turned to me and said, "Beverley, you can come with me for a walk." Uncertain as I was about why he should be asking me to accompany him, I nevertheless got up from the table and collected my coat from the hall.

We walked in silence along the main path between the houses and on around the beach until we reached Hope Point. Dad climbed the bank to the top of the bluff and I scrambled up behind him. When we reached Shackleton's Cross, Dad walked a few steps beyond it and stood with his hands on his hips, legs wide apart, looking out across Cumberland Bay to the mountains beyond. When it became clear to me that he wasn't particularly desirous of my presence, I sat down on the moss and rested my back against the cairn. For about twenty minutes we stayed there, motionless and not addressing each other in any way. The sea washed the stones on the shore gently, as if it too was afraid to make too much noise. If Dad was aware of my presence behind him, he didn't give any indication at all.

My bottom was cold and damp from the moss and my back was uncomfortable against the hard, uneven rocks of the cairn. I was plucking up the courage to move, afraid of disturbing Dad but almost ready to take the risk when, with no warning whatsoever, he held up his fists to the sky and his voice boomed out,

"Alone, alone, all, all alone,
Alone on a wide wide sea!
And never a saint took pity on
My soul in agony."

His voice was hoarse and forced, as if it had been drudged up from the deepest depths of the earth beneath us. He didn't move, didn't look round, but stood in the same position, fists clenched to either side of his skull, staring out to sea. I froze, forgetting my discomfort, not daring to break the silence. Dad's mind was somewhere other than with me. I had to stay hidden in full sight.

For another ten minutes we remained as statues then, abruptly, Dad turned and walked back down the hill towards home. I followed at his heel, half running to keep pace with his long, determined strides. I sensed, rather than saw, a heavy, black pall covering his head, just like the black handkerchief Uncle Ron had told me about when he described the sentence of death being delivered by a judge. My mind was racing as I tried to make sense of what had just happened. Several times I tried to open my mouth to speak, but I couldn't find the confidence I needed to get the words out. As we drew level with Discovery House and were only a few yards from home, I knew somehow that I had to speak now or I would never be able to refer to this day again. I forced myself to find a thin, uncertain voice and I asked, "Daddy, what was the poem you recited at Shackleton's Cross?" He stopped and swung on his heel towards me, as if he had become aware of my presence for the first time. He looked through me with sunken black eyes from beneath the pall around his head. His brow was deeply furrowed and, as if he was speaking in a voice stolen from the grave, he tolled, "The Rime of the Ancient Mariner." He turned rapidly away from me, entered the house through the Recreation Room door at the side of the house, walked rapidly along the corridor to the sitting room and poured himself a large whisky.

All afternoon, Dad drank whisky steadily. When the time came for the late afternoon sched, Mum told me to go up and ask Uncle Ron to do it because we both felt too afraid to go into the sitting room and tell Dad the time. I ran up to Discovery House and knocked on Uncle Ron's bedroom window. When he opened it, he asked,

"Do you need me, Bev?"

"Yes, please, Uncle Ron. Mum and I need you to do the afternoon sched. We don't think that we should ask Dad to do it." Without asking for clarification, Uncle Ron lolloped around the side of Discovery and went directly into the Wireless Room through the side door. Once the sched was completed, Uncle Ron crept into our part of the house and asked Mum if she needed him to stay with us.

"Bev, creep into the hall and see what your father is doing." I crept into the hall, carefully peeked around the door and saw that Dad was asleep in the armchair. I tiptoed back into the kitchen and reported on what I had seen.

"Thank you, Ron," Mum said to him, "but I think we'll be alright if Peter's asleep."

"No problem, Pearl. You know where I am if you need me." Uncle Ron left us and Mum and I sat together in the kitchen and Gerald lay on the floor, his head resting against Big Panda. I had told Mum about what had happened on Hope Point and she was baffled too as to what it might mean.

" Anyway, Bev, as he's sleeping it off, whatever it was, at least he's not taking it out on us."

The *Biscoe* arrived with Uncle Ernest, Mum's youngest brother, on-board. They had called in to Leith Harbour before coming to The Point and

Uncle Ernest asked Mum if she had visited Uncle Dick's grave as he had done? Mum said that we visited his grave whenever we went round to Leith. "Do you know that I got a form of beriberi last year which is what Uncle Dick died of? The Doctor said that it could run in families so I keep a close eye on Bev and Gerald while we're down here."

"He didn't die of beriberi!" Ernie replied, "He was working at Leith hooking whale meat into the cooking pots. Some meat got stuck on the hook and it pulled Dick into the pot with it. They got him out eventually, but he was dead. They stopped work for half an hour, but then they got back down to work and that was that!"

"That's rubbish! I was always told that he died through lack of cabbage so I know he died from beriberi and that it runs in our family."

"It's you who's talking rubbish, Pearl! I was told the story when I went to Leith myself only the day before yesterday. He drowned in a cooking pot!"

"I do know for certain that he came down south to earn enough money to get married, and that the poor man never made it back home again. You ask Dad how he died when you get back to Stanley and see if I'm not right!" They left the disagreement floating like a cumulonimbus in the air and moved on to a less contentious topic of conversation.

In Leith Harbour, as in Pesca, when the whale catchers were in port, they tied up alongside one another forming a chain which stretched out into the harbour from the mooring jetty. On the afternoon of Christmas Eve, the Leith whale catchers came in and tied up alongside each other. Sverre Akseth, the lovely Manager who had hosted us all at inter-station sports and who had joked with us during the shooting contests on The Point, went from one catcher to another to wish the men 'God jul'. Jumping across from one

348

catcher to the next on his way ashore, Sverre lost his footing and plunged headlong into the sea between the two ships. The story which came back to The Point was that the swell brought the hulls of the two ships together, and though he was crushed, he didn't die instantly. Men on the catchers called out to him and rushed to rescue him, but he begged them not to and he died as the ships moved against each other again in the swell.

This was the second Christmas funeral in two years and everyone felt the shock very keenly. Celebrations were subdued and far less extravagant than in previous years, both in Pesca and on The Point.

We hosted the Inter-Station Shoot again. Dressed in a blue cotton dress with a large red sash and my open-toed sandals, still damp from a thick covering of Blanco, I joined Dad, Basil and John who were the backbone of our team again for that year. A fohn wind began to blow as the motorboat arrived from Pesca with Ringdal and their team. The Leith and Husvik teams were already on The Point and practising up at the firing range. As the wind was quite light, but very warm, the temperature rose to a mighty twenty degrees Centigrade giving us a rare hot day. Dad's social committee had decided that we would have a barbecue beside Discovery House if the weather was good, so they built a makeshift brazier and in the heat of a friendly fohn wind, they cooked pork steaks and sausages. With jacket potatoes to accompany the meat, we feasted in the sunshine.

In February, the Royal Navy Patrol Vessel, *HMS Protector* brought down the Colonial Secretary, Denton Thompson, from Stanley. Mr Hooper didn't want any of us to meet Mr Thompson. Jimmy came down to our house, full of angry indignation, cheeks puffed out and an even brighter shade of red than usual, and told us what had been going on. Mr Hooper instructed Jimmy to tell Mr Thompson that, when he had come to our houses to invite us to the Magistrate's House for the party which Mr Hooper was giving for the Captain and senior officers of the *Protector*, he was to say that we were all out when he called. The Whaling Inspector at Pesca was the father of one of the junior officers on the *Protector* and neither of them were invited to the party either. Everyone on The Point was angry and scandalised that Mr Hooper should behave so rudely and in such an underhand way so the following evening, Jenny and Nigel hosted a party for all of the people who had not been invited to The Magistrate's house! It was a brilliant party. The junior officers from the Protector were young, handsome and very lively. They told us tall stories which kept everyone laughing for the whole evening and we had a much better time than we would have done had we been on our best behaviour in the Magistrate's House.

The following day, there was a knock on the door of Nigel's lab and Mr Thompson walked in. He was very polite and didn't criticise Mr Hooper in any way but, when Nigel extended an invitation for him to eat with him and Jenny that evening, Mr Thompson accepted the invitation with alacrity. They had a very enjoyable meal together, much to the annoyance of Mr Hooper who was beside himself with anger. That only made it even more fun for the rest of us!

In March, Nigel found an abandoned fur seal pup on Bird Island. She had obviously been separated from her mother for a long time but, as she had been weaned and had shed her puppy fur, he thought that he might be able to feed her up so he brought her back to The Point. As a Sealing Inspector, Nigel never interfered in the lives of the animals, but in this case, he made an exception. He built a small compound for her near the henhouse to keep her safe and to prevent her from wandering back to the beach. Jenny mixed together a broth of whale oil, milk and sometimes, pureed fish. As she was so light and docile, Nigel carried the pup into their back porch several times a day and fed her through a rubber tube. Nigel called her Gazella, from her scientific name Arctocephalus gazella. Each day I walked up to Nigel and Jenny's bungalow to see Gazella. She was very undersized, emaciated really, but seemed to be perfectly happy to be carried and fed by Nigel. She didn't mind being patted and talked to, her little nose muzzling into my hand just like Sandy's did. There was never a thought in my mind that she might try to bite me, even though she definitely had enough teeth to do some serious damage. Gazella became like my second pet and I tried not to think ahead to the day when she would be well enough for Nigel to release her back into the wild.

The rats on the island were increasing in number and they were also becoming increasingly bold. They attempted to gnaw their way into the henhouse and sometimes when Mum went out to collect the eggs, she found only licked-clean shells lying on the floor and the hens distraught after a night of being worried by rats. Dad decided that he had the solution and took out his rifle. He stationed himself at my bedroom window and waited patiently for the rats to come out from amongst the tussac bogs as evening fell. At first only one brown, twitching nose appeared, followed by a long, sleek body, but soon a dozen or more rats circled the henhouse. With precision, Dad fired and each bullet found a target. Unfortunately, the other rats quickly dived for cover so his tally of corpses was never very great. Evening after evening Dad shot at the rats, killing many of them and we waited and watched as they crept back later and dragged their fallen comrades into the safety of the tussac.

"What do they do to the dead rats, daddy? Do they try to bury them?"

"I imagine they eat them. Their meat will make up for the eggs which they are no longer able to steal."

"That would make them cannibals! I can't believe that rats would do that, however horrible they are."

"The rules which animals live by are different to our rules, Beverley. Never assume that animals share your feelings. Especially rats."

There had been few icebergs but, late in the summer, a particularly huge one broke off from one of the glaciers in Cumberland Bay and began its slow progress towards us. Clearly it was a monstrous ice-block, much taller than was usual and not very wide. I first recognized her when she was still very distant, floating deep in Cumberland Bay. From my vantage point at Shackleton's Cross, there was no doubt that it was an old lady, sitting upright with her hands folded on her lap. Day by day she floated closer to The Point. Day by day I sat beside Shackleton's Cross or stood on the beach behind Discovery House to gaze at her. As she floated nearer I began to make out her features, a long, hooked nose and full fleshy lips. She held something in her hands, it looked like her knitting. She wore a long pleated skirt down to her ankles.

As the sun shone on my old lady her features glistened and sparkled, but in the kind warmth of the golden sun, she gradually became thinner and thinner. She drifted into the mouth of King Edward Cove and Dad said that she could become a threat to the whale catchers and, if so, the men at Pesca might have to try to move her. I was terrified that they might damage her in

352

some way. I began to keep a very close watch on my old lady, feeling that my careful concern for her might protect her from being harmed by the whalers. Gerald and I played on the beach or walked up to Shackleton's Cross carrying his lorries and cars, letting them run down the slopes with us running and whooping behind them. The old lady was becoming ever thinner, her nose longer and more pointed.

One morning when I walked up to Nigel and Jenny's bungalow to see Gazella, Nigel met me at the door.

"It's bad news I'm afraid, Bev, Gazella died last night. I've just returned from taking her body down to the sea."

"That is so sad! I thought we were doing so well with her. I thought that she was putting on weight and getting better."

"She was so undernourished that we were probably always fighting a losing battle. Still, we did our best for her so we can be pleased about that. Are you going to come in and see Jenny and Martin?"

"No, thank you. I'm just on my way for a walk. Goodbye!"

"Goodbye, Bev. Enjoy your walk." I could feel Nigel's eyes trained on my back as I climbed the slope up to Hope Point. He probably knew that I wanted to go up to Shackleton's Cross on my own and have a good cry for poor, dead Gazella, but he was too gentlemanly and kind to say so.

After dinner I took Gerald out for a walk and, as we stood on the beach below Discovery House watching the maturing elephant seals play-fighting, my old lady iceberg began a slow, controlled forward roll. Fascinated, we watched as her pointed nose moved slowly through a great arc towards the sea. She executed a forward-somersault faultlessly, her head hitting the surface of the sea with a mighty 'crack'! Her head and torso split apart and small ice floes littered the sea around her. As she tumbled beneath the water, the base of the iceberg broke through the surface and a cratered, rounded hill emerged. Around the remains of the old lady a tidal wave was building, it spread out from the iceberg and rushed across the narrow expanse of water between it and us, gathering in height as it came.

"Quick, Ger, we've got to run!" I grabbed Gerald and with him in my arms, turned and ran up the slope of the beach, through the tussac, across the path beside Discovery House and in through the open door. We watched from the safety of the doorway as the small tsunami crashed onto the beach and swept up over the shingle and into the tussac. We would have been washed into the sea had we stayed where we were. So much for my kind old lady!

The season was drawing to a close. I was nearing ten years of age and both Dad and Mum were insistent that I should return to Stanley and attend the Senior school there. Uncle Ron and I hardly ever met for lessons now and apart from reading Dad's newspapers, my encyclopedia and Mum's Mills and Boon love stories, my education had come to a grinding halt. My bedroom still contained all of my belongings, though my clothes had been folded neatly into suitcases or lay on the floor in neat piles, awaiting their turn to be packed. Gerald's and my toys were lying in a large cardboard box and we were under strict instructions to leave them there so Sandy, Gerald and I took every opportunity to get out of the house to play. I had only a few last days on South Georgia before Mum, Gerald and I were due to leave on the Shackleton to return to Stanley, so I went to every part of the island to look for one last time at the play places and views that I had come to love so much.

On a particularly warm afternoon, I lifted Gerald on to the seat of my bike and with one arm around his waist and the other steering it, we walked round to Pesca. Sandy ran in circles around us, sniffing at the base of tussac bogs for rats and getting more and more excited as we neared Pesca and he discovered the scent of other dogs. I knew that I was going to have to leave Sandy behind at The Point with Dad because Granny McLeod had sent a telegram to him saying that under no circumstances would she have a dog in her house. I was upset at having to leave Sandy and kept him close to me. Sandy, unperturbed by thoughts of parting, enjoyed all of the extra attention that I was giving him and became ever more playful and coltish, even going so far as to be daring enough to sleep on the foot of my bed instead of on the mat.

When we reached Pesca, I walked on through the whaling station without meeting anyone we knew. We passed the hydroelectric power station and stopped beside the cemetery. I thought that I should say a polite goodbye to Sir Ernest and Gerald and I had each chosen a small toy to leave with him as a farewell gift. I rested my bike against the white cemetery fence and, taking Gerald by the hand, walked across to Shackleton's granite gravestone. As we stood before the nine-pointed star, I touched the gravestone and said,

"We've come to say goodbye Sir Ernest Shackleton, because we're going back to Stanley in a few days time. We can't say goodbye to Great Uncle Dick because he's buried at Leith, but Gerald and I have brought you a present each so you will have something to remember us by." I bent down and put my gift of a small, soft penguin against the headstone.

355

"Give him your present now, Ger." Gerald knelt down and placed a small, red plastic lorry beside my penguin. We stood in silence, thinking about what we had done. Being of a practical turn of mind, a sudden thought struck me and I said,

"It's silly to leave our gifts here like this. In the first storm that comes, they'll be blown away and he'll lose them. We'll get some stones and make a nice shelter for the toys, then they'll be safe." I took Gerald by the hand and together, with Sandy at our heels, we walked the short distance down to the beach.

"Choose some nice stones, Ger, as many as you can carry." With our arms full of stones, Gerald and I walked back to the grave. We knelt on the ground and carefully built a stone corral around the penguin and lorry to protect them on all four sides from the wind. When we had finished, we stood back to admire our handiwork.

"That looks good, doesn't it, Ger? I bet he'll be pleased with that!"

"Yes, Bev. Can we go and get a bun now?"

"Alright, let's go!" and we turned away from Shackleton, leaving him to his rest, as I pushed Gerald on my bike back through Pesca to the Bakery. Holding Gerald's hand, I knocked politely on the door and walked in. As ever, the Norwegian baker greeted us with a huge smile, and handed us each a pastry before he came outside with us to fill my saddlebag with bread and pastries for Mum.

"Tusen takk!" I smiled, as I thanked him in my best Norwegian.

"Mmmmmmm" Gerald said, his mouth full of warm, crumbly pastry. This was my last visit to Pesca and I shed a few small tears as we crossed over the mooring rope and left the busy whalers toiling behind us. The R catchers were still bringing home their catches, but soon the crews would leave South Georgia for Norway. For the first time, the end of the season felt depressing and sad because it was coming to an end for me too. Dad said that I would be back next Christmas for a visit, but it seemed to be a very long way away.

Three days later, in full sunshine, Dad and Uncle Ron carried our suitcases down to the *Shackleton*. Jenny and Martin came down to the jetty to wave us goodbye, as did everyone else on The Point. Dad gave me a big hug and a bristly, bearded kiss and exhorted me to
"Be good for your mother and grandmother."
"I will, Daddy, I promise. Goodbye!" I sniffled. I bent down to hug Sandy who returned my affection by licking my tear-stained face, leaving it even wetter. Mum, holding Gerald in her arms, stood beside me on the deck and

357

we waved as the *Shackleton* slipped out into the middle of the harbour, turned around then sailed past The Point, out into Cumberland Bay. I strained my neck to get my last glimpse of Shackleton's Cross but all too soon, it slipped behind the cliffs from my sight. I walked to thestarboardt side to watch as we glided past the Nordensjold Glacier and The Snow Queen's palace. I stood on deck until the island dipped beneath the horizon and the open sea enveloped us in its grey mistiness.

CHAPTER 15

LIVING IN STANLEY

How do you measure time? Prosaically in hours and minutes, days and years, decades, centuries and millennia? As a child, from birthday to Christmas and back again? For me, during those next two years in Stanley, I measured time as the period between Dad's sackings. That period of a little over a year when we could pay our rent and food bills, sandwiched between the months of fear, distress and hunger when the future was bleak and the present bleaker still.

S tanley, Falkland Islands; six parallel streets of brightly roofed houses, clinging on to a steep, peaty hillside on the southern shore of the harbour by their toenails to keep themselves from slipping inexorably down into the sea. Protected from the west by Mounts Longdon, Kent and the Two Sisters and from the east by the Narrows which guard the entrance to the harbour, two thousand souls dwelt there in imperfect harmony.

As we sailed in through the Narrows from Port William where the wreck of the *Great Britain*, Isambard Kingdom Brunel's great iron ship, lay beached in Sparrow Cove, the town opened out before us, bathed in sunshine. The roofs shone red, blue and green; rocky outcrops and stone runs on the bare mountains glistened and on the surface of the clear blue water of the harbour, a million golden stars danced and sparkled in welcome. On Ross Road, the four brick Jubillee Villas, built to celebrate Queen Victoria's Golden Jubillee, stood at the end of the public jetty where we tied up. Christ Church Cathedral, the southernmost Anglican cathedral in the world, thrust its brick and stone tower towards heaven above the jawbones from two blue whales, linked to form Whalebone Arch. The green grass of Victory Green reached westwards towards the cream town hall, King Edward the Seventh Hospital and the Battle Memorial or 'Monument', commemorating the battle of the Falkland Islands in 1914.

Stanley has a quiet, simple and individual beauty, a multi-faceted jewel set on a golden mount floating in an ice-blue South Atlantic Ocean. Within Stanley itself lay the flawless diamond of Drury Street. Here Mum, Gerald and I were to live with Granny McLeod in her beautiful colonial style house at number 7, until Mum and Gerald returned to South Georgia at the end of the winter.

Number 7 was a large, seven-bedroomed boarding house with two full stories and an imposing conservatory at the front. Covered with sheets of white painted tin to protect it against the weather, it was a proud structure with a roof of red-painted galvanized tin and timberwork of dark green. It stood raised behind a green fence constructed roughly from pointed batons, topped with a diamond-patterned trellis through which pushed a high boxwood hedge. In the summer the hedge burst into a profusion of light blue inflorescences, an uncommon sight in Stanley. To the right of the house stood a large garage, neatly painted to match the house. Largely unused and totally out of bounds to us, we could sneak over to peer in through the window at Doctor Slessor's Rolls Royce, safely ensconced there while he was away on his holidays in Scotland. Behind the garage and running the depth of the property was a vegetable garden which made the house largely self-sufficient. Neat row after neat row of potatoes, turnips, swede, carrots and cabbages were planted each spring to sustain us throughout the year.

Horses and sheep belonging to boarders who came into Stanley from farms in The Camp, could graze in safety in the paddock to the left. The fence which divided the paddock from the road was some ten feet long and it wasn't firmly attached to posts at either end, but was tied on by rope. In high winds the fence wiggled and buckled and bent in a vain attempt to get free.

361

In my bedroom at the front of the house the noise of the fence heaving and groaning made stormy nights exciting and wild. Like every other Stanley house, number 7 had its own peat bog and at carting time, when the peat was brought home, the large fence was removed so that lorries could reverse up the paddock to the rickety peat shed at the top to disgorge their loads.

In front of the conservatory there was a forbidden front garden where no one but Granny was allowed to go. From within that front garden, a small wooden door led beneath the house. Terrified of discovery and afraid that my friends might tell, I forced open the small door alone and crawled through into a large void, deep at the point of entry but narrowing steeply towards the back where the foundations had been cut into the side of the hill. The space was littered with wooden planks, standing inches deep in black stagnant water seeping continually from the peat. As I got braver and explored more thoroughly, I noticed a faint strip of light above me. Pushing upwards with all my might, a trapdoor opened and I peeked into the conservatory! Using wood to secure the trapdoor and an old box to stand on, I was able to pull myself up inside. Sheltering from the wind and basking in the heat from the sun, I could hide amongst the lilies, cacti and nasturtiums which Granny grew in empty biscuit tins. It was my secret garden, my hidey-hole, the originator and repository of my dreams.

Three semis stood to the left of number 7, their individuality and unity in cream and green created a congenial wholeness. Some of the oldest houses in Stanley, the Chelsea pensioner's cottages inhabited the street to the right; simple, unique and true to their origins. The Green where we played swept up towards the houses, the bank growing deeper and steeper as it rolled away from our play corner where double steel bars became the meeting point for us children at the end of each day.

Being back in Stanley, Mum was transformed. The careworn woman from South Georgia was replaced by a happy, smiling, energetic and ebullient lady. All her friends came round to Granny's to gossip and we sat around the huge kitchen table with its motley assortment of wooden chairs and shiny, worn velveteen tablecloth, eating home made biscuits and drinking coffee. Some friends brought their children with them and we were exhorted to go outside and play on the Green. The other children were only too happy to go outside and play but I stayed indoors and listened to all of the latest Stanley gossip with Mum.

"Bev, why don't you ever go outside and play with the other children?"

"I think that they're childish and I prefer to stay in and talk with your friends and you."

"Your trouble is that you've been on South Georgia on your own for far too long. You've got so used to being with adults that you've forgotten how to play with other children." Later that day when school ended and children assembled on the Green to play, Mum took me by the arm, pushed me unceremoniously out through the back door and said,

"Now you go down to the Green and play with the other children until it begins to get dark. Don't you dare to come back before then! And to make sure you go, I'm going to watch you from the conservatory window!" I dawdled down the path and across the road. I looked back at the house. Sure enough, Mum was standing in the conservatory and she made a 'shoo, shoo' motion with her hand to urge me on. I shuffled my way down the incline of the bank and walked as slowly as I could across the grass towards the steel bars where two girls of about my age were swinging. I walked up to them and waited, hands clasped in front of me, head down, hoping that they would talk to me, but they were too happy chatting together and turning upside down on the bars to notice me at all. I agreed with myself that I would stand there for as long as it took me to count up to a hundred in my head then I would go back home and tell Mum, in all honesty, that no one would talk to me. By the time I had counted up to eighty, my nerve failed completely and I turned on my heel to run back to the house to beg Mum to let me in.

"Hello. Have you just come in from the camp, Chay?" a voice from behind me asked. I turned back to make sure that it was me she was talking to.

"Me? No, I've just come up from South Georgia."

"Are you going to go to school or are you going straight back?"

"No I'm staying here to go to school. I'm going to go to the Senior school."

"We're there so you can play with us if you like!" What beautiful words! They shuffled along the bars so that I could just squeeze on too. I had made two upside-down friends. I was claiming my childhood back.

Claiming my childhood back was one thing. Learning Stanley social etiquette was quite another.

"Beverley, Mrs Smith has just told me that you walked right past her this morning without saying hello!" She thought you were very rude."

"But I don't know Mrs Smith Mum, so how could I say hello to her?"

"She is your third cousin on the Clifton side of the family and you don't treat family in that way."

"But Mum, everybody knows me but I don't know them, I've been in South Georgia remember! And everyone seems to be related to us one way or another, I can't keep up!"

"You'll be called a stuck up snob if you ignore people in the street so you need to mind your manners more."

"I will Mum, I promise." There was nothing worse in Stanley than being called a 'snob'! I definitely didn't want to be called one. Whenever I walked down the street from that day on, I called out a bright and cheery "Hello!" to everyone I met and gained a reputation for being a polite and well-mannered girl. Easy peasy!

Mr Draycott, our tall, elegant, fair but feared Headmaster, led me into Class 8 in the Senior school and left me in the care of Miss Gleadell. We found that my time in South Georgia hadn't been totally wasted as I was ahead of the class in arithmetic and reading and I found that I could write compositions too. My general knowledge from years of reading my encyclopedia was good. But I was behind in everything else. Nobody seemed to mind very much, least of all me. I picked up Falkland Island history, British history and geography as we went along, but handicrafts proved to be my downfall. Whatever I attempted to knit had to be cast off and given to Granny as a dishcloth. I did manage to knit one square which was close enough to a square in shape and tension to be called a kettle holder. When the other girls graduated on to knitting a pair of mittens, the task was beyond me, however hard I concentrated. Either the wool wound itself so tightly around the needle that it was impossible to insert the second knitting needle into the stitches, or the stitches were so loose that my mitts resembled Gruyere cheese. Like the mice in the 'Tailor of Gloucester', Miss Gleadell worked on my mitts in the dead of night, unpicking my failure and reworking it. At each new handicraft lesson I unearthed my mitts from the box and found to my surprise that they looked just like everyone else's. We never discussed it but I always shot a smile of deep gratitude at Miss Gleadell and redoubled my efforts, though to little avail. The mitts turned out well but I never wore them. They were orange, a colour I hated. If the wool had been red or blue, or even green, my prowess in handicrafts might have been greater.

Mum was due to go back to South Georgia at the end of the winter but, by then, Dad had been sacked. Without Mum to keep him under some sort of control, Dad drank away the winter and completely neglected his duties in the Wireless Room. On a bright October morning when the *Biscoe* sailed back into Stanley from her first journey south of the season, Dad was standing on deck bearded, hands on hips, legs akimbo, like a dark version of Henry the Eighth. Sandy, tied by a rope to the mast, ran round in circles chasing his tail in excitement. When Dad sauntered ashore, I could see from the narrow slits of his eyes and the simpleton smile on his face that he was three sheets to the wind already.

We eked out Dad's money but there was very little of it left. He had ordered huge quantities of alcohol to tide him over the winter and it had swallowed up his money before being swallowed itself in great gulps. We were unable to pay Granny any rent for the bedroom which we shared as a family, nor for the food we ate. Mum cleaned and cooked, gardened, fed the chickens, washed and ironed to help Granny and to pay in kind for our keep. Dad sat in a chair in the kitchen, morose and moody.

During his first weeks back in Stanley, the FIDS and shepherds who were staying with Granny too, invited him to join them at night when they went out to the pub for a drink. Soon though they learned that not only was Dad unable to pay for a round of drinks in return, but when he had a few too many, he became argumentative, loud and aggressive. On one occasion when some FIDS, newly arrived in Stanley on the Shackleton, took him out to the Victory bar and got him drunk, Dad argued with one of them and hit him so hard on the side of the jaw that the poor man lost consciousness for a few seconds. So much for gratitude! From then on, Dad's invitations to go

367

out ended. He was forced to sit at Granny's fireside and dry out. His moods were even more unpredictable than usual. He shook from head to toe uncontrollably on occasion, vomited and clutched at his abdomen when sudden pains struck. He criticized everything that Mum and Granny did around the house and became anxious if Mum went out to the shops and stayed away for too long. Mum did everything she could to comfort him and cooked his favourite meals to entice him to eat.

At night Dad's behaviour became worse. I lay in my narrow single bed on the opposite side of the room to their double bed. For several weeks Mum, Gerald and I were woken nightly by Dad shouting in his sleep. His strong, clenched fists hit out, trying to attack and destroy his ever present demons. Mum frequently had to jump out of the bed for her own safety.

After two months, by which time he was living soberly and much more calmly, Dad found a job with The Falkland Islands Company in their accounts department. Fired up with enthusiasm at finding himself earning forty pounds a month and able to hold his head up high again in Stanley society, Dad put himself on the 'Blacklist' with the police for six months. This meant that no shopkeeper or pub owner could sell him alcohol. He was determined to stay sober and to do his job to the best of his ability. By the end of the six months we were able to move away from our one bedroom in Drury Street and rent one of the Jubillee Villas, the one proudly bearing '1887', the year of its construction.

Mum's Great Aunt Vi and Great Uncle Chris Andreasen were our next door neighbours. Aunt Vi was a true Victorian, born to live in a Jubillee Villa. Mum said that Uncle Chris was 'a Love, gentle and kind', but I only ever met him briefly on a few occasions when we were invited round for a cup of tea. No stray cups without a secure family history or pedigree, such as lived in our house, inhabited Aunt Vi's Villa. Her cups matched perfectly and she served our tea at a round table covered with a white lace tablecloth. Gerald and I were always on our best behavior when Aunt Vi walked into her back garden to hang out the washing or to bring in the peat and never made any noise which could annoy her across the garden fence. This was especially true throughout Uncle Chris's gradual decline into death.

Uncle Chris was famous in our household for two reasons, one that he was Danish by birth and Mum said that some of our earliest ancestors on her side of the family had come from Denmark. The second reason was that he had been knighted by the King of Denmark in recognition of the credit he had brought to his country during the Battle of the Falklands in the First World War.

As a lookout on Sappers Hill behind Stanley on the eighth of December, 1914, Uncle Chris was the first person to sight the approaching German squadron commanded by Admiral Graf von Spee. Because he had maritime experience, Uncle Chris was able to give Vice Admiral Sturdee accurate information about the five German cruisers, their distance, speed and bearing towards Stanley. The British Vice Admiral had brought his squadron into Stanley harbour only the previous day to take on food and coal and he was taken completely by surprise by the arrival of the German battle cruisers. Uncle Chris's information gave him time to plan and by nine o'clock in the morning, the *Canopus* was ready to fire on the German ships from her hiding place behind the hill to the east of the Narrows. The German ships, realising rather late that the British were better equipped than they were, turned tail and headed back out to sea. An hour later, the British squadron had got up steam and left Stanley in hot pursuit. By ten o'clock that evening the German ships had all been sunk, with the exception of the light cruiser *Dresden*. The British squadron suffered very little damage. On his return to Stanley, Vice Admiral Sturdee invited Uncle Chris onboard the *Invincible* and thanked him personally for his presence of mind and Governor Allardyce held a special parade in Stanley to commend him.

Because he was famous in the Falklands and because he was very well liked, Uncle Chris's funeral was going to be very well attended. Before she left for the funeral service, Mum and I stood in the bay window of her bedroom and looked down as four men solemnly carried Uncle Chris's coffin

370

out through the front door of their house. This was the closest I had ever come to death, his body was barely six feet below me. I shivered and said a prayer inside my head.

"Dear God, please keep Uncle Chris safe and make sure that I don't die soon as well. Thank you! Amen."

When storms raged and the winds were 'blowing a gale again, Chay!', the Jubillee Villas took a battering. At high tide with a northerly wind behind it, waves broke over the sea wall and spray curtained across Ross Road into our front garden. On one such day, because it was payday and Dad had brought home two crisp twenty pond notes at dinnertime, Mum gave me one of them and asked me to buy some groceries for her from the West Store. Because I was going to fill two large shopping bags, I put one on each handlebar of my bike and pushed it out through the gate onto the road. I hadn't even gone as far as the Cathedral, less than half way to the West Store, when a gust of wind, like a williwaw, lifted me and my bike off our feet and wheels into the air. We were dropped like sacks of lead into the road and I landed heavily across my bike. In spreading my hands wide to save myself, I let go of the twenty pound note and the wind, laughing with glee, whipped it away from me and threw it into the sea. I ran to the sea wall, ignoring the seawater lapping at my feet, and bent down to try to reach out and grab the note. Now the waves joined in with the wind and with each lap and slurp of the high tide against the sea wall, the twenty pound note sailed further and further out into the harbour. It was no use, I had lost half of our money for the next month. What was Mum going to say? More to the point, what was Dad going to say?

Wet, shivering from fear more than from the cold, I pushed my bike forlornly back to the house, crept along the dark passage and into the kitchen.

"You're back quickly. What happened? You look soaked through!"

"Mum, I can't bear it!" I said as a torrent of tears burst through the open sluice gates of my eyes. "The wind blew me over and the twenty pound note blew into the harbour and I can't get it back!" Mum opened her arms and welcomed me into them as I sobbed so hard and so deeply that my diaphragm knotted and choked my cries.

"It can't be helped sweetheart! Stop crying now. It wasn't your fault. I shouldn't have sent you out in this weather but if we didn't go out in the wind and rain, we'd never be able to leave the house would we! I'll come with you this time and we'll do the shopping together."

"Mum, what will we tell Dad? He'll be so angry with me for losing so much money."

"I've thought of that already, Bev. We'll give Dad and Gerald the same amount of food as they always have for supper but you and I will go on a diet and eat smaller amounts ourselves. I'll feed you kids before Dad gets in for his dinner and I'll say that I ate with you. We'll stick to bread and jam for as many of our meals as we can. At least it's only for a month. We'll have some nice treats next month to make up for it! Thank goodness your Dad is still not drinking, if he was buying booze we'd be in a right mess!"

On Saturday mornings I sat Gerald on the seat of my bike and wheeled him to Granny McLeod's house. Our return trip was to the West Store where we filled four battered, worn, cavernous bags with her groceries for the week ahead. Then Gerald walked beside me as I wheeled the bike, now heavily laden, back up to Drury Street. In return for this errand, I was

372

allowed to buy myself a pound of sweets worth three shillings and sixpence and charge them to Granny's account. Herein lay untold riches! I shared my good fortune with Gerald and we chose half a pound of sweets each. Dolly Mixtures and alphabet sweets were his favourites and he got an enormous bag of them because they weighed so little. My sweet bag was of a more modest size because my chewing nuts and aniseed balls were heavier, but at least they lasted for a long time.

Every Sunday morning Dad insisted that Gerald and I went to Sunday school at the Church of Scotland Tabernacle. Doctor McWhan, a broadly accented Scot who came to the Falklands in 1934 as an independent missionary and who led the church, had the incredible knack of inhabiting and portraying two completely different personas at the same time. He was always the dour, hellfire and brimstone, morally upright, spear bearing leader of the God squad, out to save souls and drive your sins out of your mind and body whether you wanted him to or not. If in the same second though, a smile broke out, it lightened and illuminated his still stern face and welcomed you unreservedly into his life, warming your heart and soul.

In Sunday school, we sat in the front two rows of the pews, looking at the carved, dark wooden choir stall to the left and towards Doctor McWhan's pulpit and simple communion rail to our right. The man himself stood in front of us, telling Bible stories and leading us as we sang choruses from a small, light blue book. Soon we all knew the choruses by heart and belted out 'Jesus Bids Us Shine', 'A Little Ship Was On The Sea', 'Jesus Wants Me For A Sunbeam' and a dozen others week by week.

373

During the month following the loss of Mum's twenty pound note, I didn't buy sweets for myself on Saturdays, only for Gerald. Instead I used my one shilling and ninepence to buy spreads like jam or meat paste to flavour our meals of bread only. When Doctor McWhan told us in Sunday school that bread was indeed the 'staff of life', I knew exactly what he meant.

By the time my eleventh birthday arrived, I had found my feet in Stanley. School was fun every day, interesting but not particularly challenging. I played with girls and boys from my class on the Green as well as with other children of all ages. We went from a birthday party in the schoolroom behind the Tabernacle to one in the hall of St Mary's Roman Catholic Church, to another in the Cathedral hall. Dressed in full-skirted nylon frocks held out by petticoats washed in sugar water so that when they were ironed they stiffened, and wearing white open-toed canvas shoes cleaned with Blanco, we played 'Sardines', 'Oranges and Lemons' and 'The Farmer's In His Den'.

One Sunday as I left our house with Gerald on our way to Sunday school I met Edward, probably the naughtiest boy in our class, with his brother.

"Hello, Chay! Where are you going?"

"We're off to Sunday school at the Tab. Where are you going?"

"We're going fishing at the top of the public jetty, off the sea wall just there, behind the Philomel Store."

"Do you catch many fish there?"

"Yes Chay! Usually a couple each time we fish. Why don't you come and have a go? I've got a spare line you can borrow."

"Can we go fishing, Bev? I don't want to go to Sunday school!" I looked down at Gerald's upturned face, shining with excitement at the thought of sitting on the sea wall in the sun, fishing. I thought about the alternative, being stuck in the Tabernacle singing the same old choruses and singing the same old hymns. Fishing would be a sin and I would have to be careful that we didn't get caught out. But no one could see us if we were hidden behind the Philomel Store and I had a watch, so as long as we got back home on time, who would know? When Mum asked what we had done in Sunday school, it would be easy to name a few hymns that we might have sung to make it sound as if we really had been there. All Gerald would have to do is keep silent.

Every Sunday, unless it was pouring with rain, Gerald and I met Eddie behind the Philomel Store. He lent us a fishing line, wound around an old piece of driftwood, with a home made hook on the end of it and an improvised weight. He gained by keeping the mullet that we caught and we gained twofold. We had fun and also got to keep the two sixpences which Mum gave us to put into the church collection. After school on a Monday and Tuesday, I took Gerald into the Philomel Store to spend threepence each on sweets or on a tangerine whenever the *Darwin* brought some down from Uruguay. When the tangerines came to the end of their lifespan and were too old to sell, Des the shop owner tipped "The not too bad ones, Chay!" into a bag and we smuggled them into the house and had a secret feast in my bedroom.

In Class 9 the girls behaved impeccably and the boys got away with behaving badly whenever they could, which wasn't very often. In the playground one day I caught the boys ball and Don ran over to take it from me. Apropos of nothing in particular, and probably by way of general conversation, Don shouted across to me as he bounced the ball back to his mates,

"It's good having you in the class, Bev. When no one knows the answer to a question, we can just sit back and relax because Miss Armitage asks you sooner or later and when you give the answer, it lets us off the hook!" When we moved up into Class 10, Don took the desk at the back of the room and draped himself round the radiator. I sat directly in front of Mr Lellman like the class swot and answered as many questions as he wanted to fire at me. Between us, we had devised a system which worked well for everyone in the class.

  Mr Lellman was a physically strong man who stood for no nonsense. I worried about moving up into his class because I had grown up with the apocryphal story of what had happened to Dad when Mr Lellman taught him in his final year in school, before he left to become an apprentice wireless operator at the age of fourteen. I was afraid that Mr Lellman might do the same to me.

Dad was eleven years old when the family moved to Stanley from the farm at Goose Green and he was enrolled straightaway into the Senior school. Interested in anything other than schoolwork and inherently lazy, dad was astute enough to realise that the boy who came out of school with the top exam results could expect to get a good job. In such a small community, the really good jobs were few in number. Dad was determined to be that top boy.

When Mr Lellman read out the final exam results for that year's school leavers, Peter McLeod had come top in every subject. Dad had confidently expected this outcome and knew that praise and rewards were certain to follow. He swung backwards on two legs of his chair, smiled around at his classmates and basked in his own glory. Mr Lellman threw down his mark book in anger, strode across the classroom, dragged Dad from his desk by the scruff of his neck and belted him so hard across the side of the head that he flew backwards into the radiator and knocked himself out. When Dad came round, Mr Lellman was standing over him, jabbing his finger at him, shouting that the slap was because he had been a lazy and self-indulgent boy for the whole of the short time he had been in the school and had done no work at all. A bit dazed, Dad walked home and told granny what Mr Lellman had done.

"You ARE bone lazy Peter! Let that be a lesson to you!" Later that evening, grandad agreed with his wife's sentiments, only more colourfully. This was one of Dad's favourite stories. The joke was against him but not completely, just how he liked his jokes to be!

About eight weeks after our first fishing adventure with the boys, Mum and Dad were busily painting the cupboards in the back kitchen while Gerald and I played quietly in our playroom in the cupboard under the stairs. Mum wanted to modernise the house so she bought a tin of deep red gloss paint to brighten the old wooden cupboard doors in the back kitchen. While she and Dad were painting, a loud knock rattled the back door.

"Who the bloody hell is that!" Dad said loudly, a dripping paintbrush held aloft in his right hand.

"It's only me!" and Doctor McWhan's head peered through the chink in the door which he was gently pushing open.

"Oh! Doctor McWhan! Come in!" Dad said shamefacedly, "We're painting so it's all a bit of a mess. Sorry about that!"

"Not at all, Peter, I will only keep you a minute. Hello Pearl!" Dad hurriedly pushed paint tins aside and ushered the Minister through into the kitchen. Mum ripped the scarf from her head, hastily tried to rearrange her tumbled locks, and followed them.

"Can I offer you a cup of coffee?"

"No, thank you Pearl, I won't stay very long as I can see you're busy. I just popped in to see why Beverley and Gerald haven't been to Sunday school for the past month or more. Is anything wrong? They usually attend so regularly."

"I've been sending them every Sunday as usual," Mum replied, "are you sure that you haven't seen them?"

"No Pearl, they haven't been there when I've taken the register."

"Well, that's a surprise! I'll have to ask Bev what's been going on. I don't understand it at all."

"Whatever has happened, Doctor McWhan, they will be at Sunday school next week. I can assure you of that!" Dad's tone of voice was unequivocal. Nobody was going to question his resolve.

"Thank you, Peter. We mustn't let their religious education lapse, must we? We want them to grow up as obedient children in the sight of God."

Doctor McWhan took his leave. I pushed Gerald across the passage into my bedroom so that he would be safe from Dad's anger when the storm burst over our heads, as it surely would.

378

A loud, peremptory voice shouted,

"Beverley! Get in here! Now!" I left Gerald sitting on my bed and walked slowly into the kitchen. I knew that I was in serious trouble and that I was in for a hiding. I'd be lucky if I could sit down for a week after it was over. Shaking with fear, I walked into the kitchen, my hands folded before me and my head bent low.

"Where the hell have you been going every Sunday? You sure as hell haven't been going to Sunday school as you have been telling your mother and I you have!"

"When it isn't raining, I have been taking Gerald fishing from the sea wall with some of the boys from my class. I am very, very sorry, Daddy, I know it was wrong and that I shouldn't have lied to you and Mummy."

"And what, may I ask, have you been doing with your collection money?"

"I've been buying sixpence worth of sweets for us to share on my way home from school each Monday and Tuesday afternoon." Behind Dad, Mum was standing with a mixed look of anger at my duplicity and fear at what was going to happen to me, written as clearly as a text across her face. I waited for the lightning to strike. Dad looked at me for long seconds, as if he was trying to read my mind. As the seconds grew even longer, hairs on the back of my neck stood to attention, goose pimples covered my arms like a cobbled street and I unclasped my clammy hands, surreptitiously wiping the sweat from the palms on the back of my skirt.

"For this once only Beverley, I will accept your apology. But you and Gerald will attend Sunday school religiously every week from now on." A tiny twitch creased the corners of Dad's mouth as he acknowledged and appreciated his own wordplay.

"Thank you for accepting my apology, Daddy. We will go to Sunday school every week from now on, I promise."

"I hope so. You may go to your room." I was dismissed. I was astounded! Nothing more? No shouts or the sting of his hand across the back of my legs? Before he could change his mind, I scuttled from the room and prepared to close the kitchen door behind me. Then a thought struck me. Why wasn't he more angry? Why hadn't he hit me? I stood behind the almost closed door and listened. Mum spoke first.

"I'm pleased you didn't hit her, Peter. I was afraid that you'd be so cross with her that you might give her a good hammering."

"Good God, no! Ha! Ha!" he was laughing loudly and I couldn't believe my ears! After a few minutes his guffaws subsided.

"I've never heard anything so funny! I can't believe that Beverley had the gumption to truant from Sunday school to go fishing! And to spend the collection money on sweets! I never thought that she had it in her! It's just what I would have done myself, only I would have done it at a much younger age than her! Ha! Ha!" I crept back to the bedroom, knowing that I had got away with it this once, but that trying something similar again might not be my brightest move.

In Class 10 in the early months of 1963, we were only a few years away from leaving school at fourteen. You could stay on at school for two more years in the Continuation class, as the brightest girls did, to take commercial courses. If I had thought about my future at all, I would probably have said that I would stay on at school too. There was a Scholarship sponsored by the Falkland Island Government whereby each year they sent the two most able children, usually a boy and a girl, to be educated in boarding schools in England. Mr Draycott suggested to Mum and Dad that it would be good for me to have a go at the examinations. "She won't win it at her first try of course, but it will be good practise for her in case she wants to sit the exams properly next year."

For a week we sat two exams a day, and were allowed to leave school and go home at the end of each to give us time to prepare for the next exam. I sauntered out of school half way through each morning, waved up at Don sitting in Class 10 hugging his radiator, laughing at how thoroughly annoyed he was that I could get out of school and he couldn't! I sat on Whalebone Arch or dangled my feet over the sea wall and indulged myself in my favourite daydreams.

The exam which I enjoyed most was one which was like playing a new game. The 'fun' exam began with Mr Draycott standing in front of us, the lid and base of a Sellotape tin in either hand. He explained that if there was a rubber band running around the circumference of both tins, when they turned, both would turn in the same direction. If the band was removed and the tins moved in contact with each other, they would move in opposite directions. The exam paper was full of diagrams of increasingly complex machines where wheels moved in juxtaposition or within a band. All we had to do was draw an arrow to indicate the direction in which the last wheel in the machine would move.

I really enjoyed doing the exam and finished well before the time was up. Mr Draycott walked over to my desk and with a look of genuine concern, told me that perhaps it might be an idea if I spent the remaining time checking my answers for the difficult questions at the end of the paper.

Obedient as always, I worked backwards through the machines until he told us to put down our pencils and go home.

"What was that exam about, it was so easy?" I asked the older girls as we left the classroom.

"I think it's called an 'Intelligence Test'. It's supposed to measure how clever you are."

"Oh no! I didn't know there were such things! Anyway, I must have messed that one up because I finished early then didn't change any of my answers when Mr Draycott told me to check them. Oh well, it's only a practice, I'll be more careful next year!"

Class 10 was an interesting place to be. Mr Lellman introduced us to poetry, which I loved. I waited in vain for him to let us study the 'Ancient Mariner' as Dad had done in his class so many years before. Instead we read 'The Inchcape Rock' by Robert Southey and 'My Heart's in the Highlands' by Robert Burns. We studied Scottish history and I fell in love with Bonnie Prince Charlie. We studied the geography of Scotland, especially the Highlands and Islands like Lewis, where my Scottish great grandfather, Sandy McLeod emigrated from.

Not everything in Class 10 smelt of roses however. The plague of handicrafts came back to haunt me. In the small classroom squashed behind the boys' cloakroom, for one afternoon a week I was subjected to sewing class. I was given a long, rectangular piece of white cotton with a transfer at one end of flowers garlanded together by a profusion of leaves which sprouted forth riotously from a central, curving stem. Embroidering pretty flowers on a pillowcase and giving it to Mum was an exciting prospect and I set to my task with enthusiasm. I chose a bright pink silk and threaded my needle ready to begin to 'fill in' a pretty flower.

"What do you think you're doing Beverley? That is not where you start. Take brown thread and start on the stem. When you finish the stem you can start on the leaves. Only after they're done, can you go on to the flowers."

The curse of colours struck again! I hated brown and the dark brown silk would not behave itself in my hands. At the end of the first lesson Mrs Grade examined my work, told me that my stitches were uneven and often outside the transfer pattern. I had to unpick it all before I could go home. My best friend Amy could sew, unlike me. However Amy and I could both talk rather effectively too and as we grew to hate sewing more and more, we chatted instead. As her voice, even when we were trying to whisper, was louder than mine, Mrs Grade inevitably scolded Amy for talking. As we grew ever more disillusioned with the class, Amy spent most of her Thursday afternoons standing outside the classroom door in disgrace while I developed a 'freeform' embroidery style which was untidy but fun and could be unpicked easily at the end of each lesson. I vowed to myself that not one single brown stitch would remain behind on that pillowcase at the end of the school year.

"This afternoon we will have a display of your handicrafts so that the girls can see what the boys have been making and vice versa." My heart sank. Mr Lellman wanted us to display our sewing and I had nothing at all to show. That afternoon, we sat at our desks and displayed our work in front of us. I folded my pillowcase neatly so that the now crumpled, grey, holed fabric which should have been my embroidered border, was hidden from sight. When Mr Lellman walked in front of my desk and raised a quizzical eyebrow at me, I said quickly,

"I haven't had time to do any embroidery yet, Sir, so I've got nothing to show you." After just enough hesitation to make me think that I hadn't fooled him at all, Mr Lellman walked away from my desk and on to the next pupil.

When Mr Lellman had completed his inspection, we wandered around the classroom to see what others had done. I was completely astounded to find that Mike Pole-Evans had made a horsewhip and a full set of reins and headgear from raw cowhide. The workmanship was not only perfect but the gear was truly beautiful to look at.

"Can I hold them please, Mike?"

"Sure you can!" In my hands the reins and headgear felt light and smooth. The whip cracked satisfyingly when I drew it through the air.

"I think that this is exceptional, I really do! You must be really proud of yourself for making these. I can't even embroider a pillowcase!"

"Not really, Bev. It's not that difficult you know." Modesty. I was overwhelmed by his skill which threw my pathetic and childish lack of achievement into stark contrast.

In the winter playground, the boys slid down the snow-covered slope sideways, their feet together, arms outstretched to balance and created an ice slide. After a few days when the ice was shiny and almost frictionless from use, the boys in our class invited Amy and I to "Come and have a go!" Mike positioned himself at the end of the slide, his back pressed up against the pointed fence posts of the Cathedral hall, ready and prepared to catch us. I stood at the top of the slide, nervous not just because of how long and steep the slide was, but because if I fell over, my dress would fly up in the air and everyone would see my pants. If that happened, I'd be the laughing stock of the school. I instantly regretted my impulsive acceptance of the boys offer and tried to think quickly of a way to get out of it without looking like a scaredy cat. But everyone was watching to see how a girl would cope with the slide, so very gingerly I stood sideways at the top with my feet together as I had seen the boys do. Before I could think, my feet began to slip. Struggling to stay upright, wiggling all over the place and with my arms flailing in the air, I flew down the slide and smashed into Mike with a thump. Laughing, he held me upright and helped me off the slide onto the snow.

"That was brilliant!" I shouted. "Come on Amy, it's fun!" Braver than me, Amy stepped on to the slide and plummeted down with much more grace than I could muster. Again, Mike the gentleman caught her and deposited her on the snow beside me.

"Are you going again?"

"You bet, Mike!" we answered and ran back to the top of the slide for another go.

At the end of playtime as we walked back towards the girl's entrance into school, Amy said,

"He's good looking isn't he? Mike, I mean?" As I walked into Class 10, I glanced across at Mike on the opposite side of the classroom. He was taller than any of the other boys, definitely stronger and Amy was right, he was handsome. He was also sensible and mature and could make riding gear any adult would have been proud to make. As I watched, he and Amy flashed a secret smile across the room to one another. With a jolt I recognised the beginning of an attraction between a boy and one of my girlfriends. This had never happened before! We were growing up! Or at least, Amy and Mike were. My brain and body were still very definitely mired in the depths of childhood.

At home, life had not been good for a very long time. Dad came off the Blacklist soon after we moved to Jubillee Villas. To celebrate, he went out to the pub. Then he went back to celebrate again… and again… and again. Soon he was hiding bottles of whisky in the peat shed and Gerald and I turned over the sods of peat every day to find the hidden bottles and take them to Mum. Dad became increasingly ingenious and hid his bottles in the highest parts of the peat stack, but Gerald and I were nimble enough to take up the challenge and we became experts at 'seek and find the bottle'. By the time I moved up into Class 10, Dad was arriving late at work. After his dinner which always involved a trip or two to the peat shed, he rolled back into the office with the staggering gait, slit eyes and seraphic smile of the McLeod inebriate splitting his face. In the evenings Gerald and I sat and played quietly in the sitting room, looking out on the harbour, keeping out of Dad's way. Mum attempted to keep Dad from drinking too much by interesting him in radio programmes which she hoped would entice him to stay home. Her plans hardly ever produced a positive outcome and Dad drank away our money in the pubs and ran up huge bills for alcohol in the West Store and the Globe Store. Once again Mum and I went on a diet as money for food became a problem. Inevitably, before Easter, Dad was given a month to work out his notice.

We lived in a house of broken dreams and broken promises where we walked on broken glass. We pretended to the world that all was well, but our frequent bruises and skinny arms and legs indicated to anyone who wished to

386

see beyond our assurances that our income was being spent on alcohol instead of food, and that we were more accident prone than was the norm for even the most active of human beings.

Being given the sack from work is never a good experience. In a small community where everyone knows everyone else, it is the kiss of death. Peter McLeod, sacked from two good jobs in as many years because he can't keep off the booze. Who would want to employ a man like that, even if he has got a good brain? Without any income to support us except for the money Mum earned cleaning for the more wealthy Stanley citizens who lived beyond the Monument on Ross Road West, or as it was colloquially known, 'Monkey Island', we crept unwillingly with our tails between our legs back to Granny's protection in Drury Street. Once more, Mum worked for Granny to pay for our keep. Once more we shared one family room. Once more Dad sat in the chair beside the Stanley range, morose and angry, flailing at his misfortunes and physically hitting out at us should we be foolish enough to stray within an arms length of him.

Living back near the Green again, I played there every afternoon after school. Once the evenings drew in, my friends wandered off in ones and twos, back to their homes. As I lived just across the road and also because I didn't want to inhabit any space where Dad was, I sat on the double bars and watched the sun set over Drury Street as often as I could.

Falkland Island sunsets, like those in South Georgia, are pageants of breathtaking beauty. On some evenings the sky was serene, touched by gold on the horizon with a blue backdrop framing fluffy clouds, bright pink and delicate like the lace of a mantilla. Seeing its own perfect beauty reflected in the roof and front of Granny's glass conservatory, the sky blushed ever more pink until it exploded in an exuberant flash of pure gold light, forming a halo around the yellow sun as it slipped into another world.

On certain days, as if to match my fervid mood, the sun set in crimson heat. Clouds, hovering orange above the horizon, burnt fiery red against the canopy of a darkening dome above. Orange, gold and red rays struck the roof of Granny's conservatory with devastating effect, melting the glass in a cauldron of searing fire. Hanging upside down on the bars, I watched as flames of light danced a furious tango together on the roof before soaring back up into the sky to reinflame the clouds with their brightness and energy.

Week after week at Sunday school, Doctor McWhan warmed to his theme of finding salvation. Salvation for us came in the form of Osmond Smith, the Manager of one of the sheep farms in the Camp. In the north-eastern corner of the island of East Falkland, Johnson's Harbour is known mainly for its colony of king penguins at Volunteer Point, but to the McLeod family it was going to provide a home and a means of feeding themselves once more. Dad was offered employment as a general farmworker and Mum was going to cook for the single men who lived in the Cookhouse. With free accomodation and a double income, the McLeod's were going to live in the Beach House overlooking the harbour and Berkeley Sound. The McLeods minus their daughter, that is. She was going to have to search for her salvation elsewhere.

CHAPTER 16

SCHOLARSHIP GIRL

The 'rrrrring' of the ancient telephone reverberated along the dark Victorian passage in the Jubilee Villa at 39 Ross Road. Pearl walked quickly towards the phone, wiping flour from her hands on to a thin cotton tea towel which had seen better days.

"Hello."

"Can you say that again, please?"

"If you're sure, I'll tell Peter. Thank you, Mr Draycott. Goodbye!"

Back in the kitchen, squeezed around three sides of a small table pushed hard up against the window, Dad, Gerald and I looked up at Mum expectantly.

"That was Mr Draycott! You know he told us to put Bev in to sit the Scholarship exams this year just as a practice, well… she's won it! She leaves for school in England on her twelfth birthday! On the fourth of July!"

Habitually, I fixed my eyes on Dad's face, searching, unsure about how he would react to this unexpected piece of information, mind racing in anticipation of finding a quick and apposite response to appease whatever mood it engendered in him.

"I can't believe it! That'll be one in the eye for the snobs with money who expected their children to win it! Now they will have to congratulate me and stop looking down their noses! My daughter won the Scholarship and beat theirs into nothingness! You did well, Beverley." He was smiling and happy!

Breathe. Allow straight back to slump a very little. Add discrete smile to visage. Keep eyes lidded and modest. Keep hands neatly folded in lap. Relax, but still remain on guard. Don't think about your own feelings at all.

"Thank you Daddy, I'm glad that you are pleased with me."

"We're going to lose her, Peter! We'll only see her every two years when she comes home on holiday. I'm going to miss her so much!" Mum's arms enfolded me and drew me so tightly to her that the tears from her left eye gathered in a little pool in the trough where our cheeks pressed together.

"Don't be silly, Pearl! This is a great opportunity for Beverley to get a good education and we'll be the parents of a Scholarship child. That'll be something to crow over I can tell you!"

In school I was congratulated by everyone, with the exception of two sisters I had beaten in the exams.

In Hardy's shop, old Mrs Hardy came out from behind the counter and presented me with a writing case.

"We're so pleased that an ordinary Falkland Island girl has won the Scholarship, Beverley!"

At the end of my last sewing lesson in school, I unpicked the afternoon's freeform brown stitching and held out the unloved and unembroidered fabric towards Mrs Grade.

"You can keep the pillowcase, if you want to take it home to your mother."

"I think not, thank you!"

At my last Girl's Life Brigade meeting, Velma Malcolm, the statuesque cousin who terrified me into perfect behaviour and precision marching with a single glance, smiled and softened and presented me with a fountain pen.

Uncle Gug gave Auntie Doreen the money to take me to the West Store and buy me two petticoats, two vests and four pairs of plain white pants to ensure that I arrived in England suitably and modestly garbed 'underneath'.

Mum bought me two new dresses and a pair of red shoes to wear to school in England. We hadn't heard about school uniform.

During my last week in Stanley, a kind FID who was living like us at Granny McLeod's, took photographs of us all so that we would have more than unreliable memories to keep us together while we were apart.

I sat on the green leather chaise longue in Granny's kitchen and gave all my toys away to my friends. Once they had gone, I wept for the loss of my toys but not for the loss of my childhood. I didn't realise at the time that it had slipped out through the back door too.

AKNOWLEDGEMENTS

Pearl and Gerald McLeod for their strength and love in remembering good times and some difficult ones.

Adrian Verwoert C.B.E. for his warmth, encouragement and support; his proof-reading and editing skills and for being brave enough to point out the boring bits!

Jenny Williams for her generous encouragement and invaluable advice, especially when the book was in its infancy.

Jenny Bonner whose attention to detail is amazing, and who has generously allowed me to use her and Nigel's photographs.

Henry McLeod for his encouragement and for his memories of Dad, South Georgia and the Wireless Room.

Carl Thorsen for his kind memories of processes and social occasions at Grytviken.

Torgeir Eskedal, my Viking, who shared his photographs with me before we lost him.

Odd Rasmussen for his photographs and warm support.

John Mo for his photographs of South Georgia.

Jackie Davies (Goodwin) for the original 'Mondongo' recipe and fond recollections.

John Quigley for Blaze and happy memories shared.

Janet Cheek and Coleen Biggs for allowing me to use their story and for sharing Betty's photographs with me.

Jimmy Smith whose detailed knowledge of South Georgia is legendary.

Sarah Lurcock for reading extracts, from her perspective as a King Edward Point resident at the present time.

Amy and Mike Pole Evans for 'going back to school'!

Neil Porter for his patience and for sharing his photography skills with me.

'The South Georgia Association' members for their invaluable support.

(Norwegian) Friends of the island of South Georgia:
'Øyas venner', The South Georgia Times.

Debbie Knox, my Editor.

Jenny Bonner for giving us permission to use her and Nigel's photographs which have been included in, Chapters 2 ,3 ,4 ,6, 7, 9, 10, 13, 14; The title page and the cover images

My Publisher, Ian Farnell, for his wisdom and guidance.

BIBLIOGRAPHY

"Antarctic Housewife"
Nan Brown
Pub: Hutchinson & Co (Publishers) Ltd

"Pesca"
Ian B Hart
Pub: Aidan Ellis

"The Island of South Georgia"
Robert Headland
Pub: Cambridge University Press

"The Dictionary of Falklands Biography (including South Georgia)"
Editor: David Tatham
Privately published.